CW00419026

TRAVELS WITH MY

MOTHER-IN-LAW

THE TRAVEL DIARIES OF
LINDA MCKELLAR HALL

EDITED BY PAT BURNETT

Extracts from the diaries appear in bold type.

Designed by Liz Croll.

Copyright © 1994 Pat Burnett.

ISBN 0 646 21275 3.

This book is dedicated to
Linny and Pop
with happy memories

CONTENTS

LIST OF ILLUSTRATIONS

INTRODUCTION

FAMILY GROUP SHOWING LINDA (CENTRE FRONT) WITH PAT BURNETT (TOP LEFT)

L inda McKellar Hall was my mother-in-law, and a better one it would be hard to imagine. She was born Linda Winifred Anderson at Middle Park in the state of Victoria on 11th. June, 1903. Her father, James Anderson, was a merchant who conducted a chain of family furniture emporiums in Melbourne and her mother, Jessie Ballantyne Anderson (née Gray) died of cancer when she was 16. She first travelled abroad in 1922 at the age of 18 and the earliest diary in the series on which this book is based was started at this time. Thereafter she kept diaries on each of her numerous journeys.

She had left school when her mother died, as her two older sisters Elsie (Mrs. H.C. Tudehope) and Ritza (Mrs. P. Carney) were already married and she saw it as her duty to look after her father. She had been a good scholar and was widely read, qualities which are amply displayed in the diaries. They also reveal her romantic and sympathetic nature, her curiosity and interest in her fellow human beings, and her love of nature and outdoor activities. They are in fact a unique testimonial to a person whose zest for life and powers of observation and understanding were remarkable.

I first met Linny in Perth, Western Australia at Christmas, 1949. A year before I had met her elder daughter Jennifer travelling from Perth to Sydney in S.S. Strathaird and we had fallen in love. I was then a sub-lieutenant in the Royal Australian Navy and my duties and sea service kept us apart after our first short period together until the end of 1949. I then travelled to Perth to meet her parents and spend my Christmas leave with them, and was shown the most generous hospitality and treated like one of the family.

In 1928 Linda had married Reginald Dalton McKellar Hall, the younger son of Anthony James Alexander Hall of Broken Hill and Florence Mary Hall (née McKellar). He was then 31 and clinical assistant to the Orthopaedic Department of Perth Hospital. Besides Jenny they had another daughter Sonia, who later married Haden Lemann of Sydney, and a son Anthony, tragically killed in a car accident at the age of 19. I met and immediately took a liking to them all at the time of my first visit. After a further 18 months during which my naval duties again took me away from the Halls, I eventually married Jenny in July, 1951.

Linda's diaries cover the period from 1922 to 1974 and are a valuable historical record as well as a wonderful travel document. I have divided them into five parts covering her early travels with her father, her first visits to England and the Continent with Reg as a young married woman, her wartime evacuation and trips in the post-war period, later travels with Reg to America, Africa and Asia, and finally a series of trips throughout Australia in the 1960s and 70s. One of the things which strike the reader in this wide and varied chronicle is her common touch; she was at ease with, and interested in, people in all walks of life.

I first saw the diaries after Reg's death in 1991. In editing these lively and informative accounts I have tried as far as possible to let them tell their own story, providing only sufficient background information to connect the various episodes and make the context clear by explaining certain references where it seemed desirable. It is possible that not all her diaries have survived, or that they were not kept for all her trips; old photographs suggest that at least one trip is not recorded here. I hope that readers will find some of the same delight as I have done in journeying with Linda through her pages. My aim has been to try to communicate some of this pleasure and to pay a tribute to a wonderful lady whom it was my good fortune to know and love. Linny died of cancer in 1979 and praise of her from her many friends all over Australia and around the world paid moving testimonial to a generous spirit.

PART ONE

THE TWENTIES:
YOUNG SINGLE WOMAN

Linda with her friend Dorrie in South Africa, 1927

1. FIRST TRIP TO ENGLAND

The first diary begins on 7th. January, 1922 when Linda was 18 and living with her father at 28 Kooyong Koot Road, Hawthorn, a Melbourne suburb. The next day she travelled with friends by car to Lorne, a seaside resort on the Surf Coast, southwest of the entrance to Port Phillip Bay, for New Year holidays. She stayed there for a fortnight and the first 20 pages of the diary are taken up with an account of her social life. The main activities were tennis, swimming and dancing, and they centred around the Lorne and Pacific Hotels. Anyone and anything she liked is described as "bonza", and young men are judged by whether they are "thrilling" or not. Her first night there was not a very thrilling one. I can't see anyone down here who is likely to be thrilling for me.

However, things soon started to warm up and she attracted the attention of various men. The first was a Mr. Dunlop, who took me for a walk and tried to kiss me. I did not know what to do, however he didn't, I stopped him. At a dance at the Pacific Hotel two days later she met a young man who had been all through America. About 9 o'clock he suggested a stroll, so went and lay on the beach and we got on very well, he was quite thrilling, but I kept him at bay and would not let him kiss me. We went up and had supper about 10.30, then went out again and got on better still, this time he kissed me. He asked me was I cross, I said I did not know but I had meant to, he said that I was the first girl he had kissed for absolutely ages. I went to bed feeling rather thrilled.

Some would-be admirers were not so much to her liking. She went out with one like a silly fool, I don't know what I did it for, because I think he is a great big fat idiot. One she did take a liking to was an older man named Jack McFarlane, with whom I went down the beach. He is quite nice, said I was the only girl he had kissed at Lorne ... We got on wonderfully well, he was most awfully thrilling. On 22nd. January she returned home, to be met by all the family: Edith said that Jack McFarlane had rung up, they were all anxious to know who he was, in the end Edith and Hilda knew him down at Sorrento some years ago, said he was a Catholic and did not go to the war.

She became immersed again in family affairs and on 7th. February she and her great friend Dorrie Jefferies were bridesmaids at her brother Roy Anderson's wedding. However, she did see more of Jack McFarlane and one day took him home to meet the family: we went and lay on the croquet lawn and had a bonza talk. He told me that he thought of me an awful lot and that I was the only girl he had looked at since he had seen me. Anyway I felt very thrilled and excited. When he left after a chat and coffee with the family he asked to take her out again, but she tactfully declined, and Elsie was much relieved when I told her I had not made another date.

Linda's father had been making plans to take her to England in March on the Orient Line vessel S.S. Orvieto, and in mid-February it was proposed that her sister Ritza, of whom she was very fond, should come too: At afternoon tea it was suggested casually by Elsie that Ritza come to England with father and me, as she is run down with her catarrh. Phil took it up like a shot. I went home there to tea and discussed it, and it ended by Phil going to try and see if there was a berth on the Orvieto. I was terribly thrilled to think she might come. It was soon arranged and Linda enthused: Ritza is most frightfully excited and so am I, it all seems to be too wonderful to be true.

Preparations for the trip began to gather pace, interrupted for Linda one night when About 1 a.m. I was wakened out of a doze by my bed being violently shook, coupled with ominous creaking of the furniture. I lay in bed trembling and wondering what would happen next, then there was dead stillness. I could bear it no longer, I hopped out of bed and turned on the light and satisfied myself that no-one was in the room, went back to bed and slept comfortably till morning. It then transpired that the mysterious disturbance had been caused by an earth tremor.

Linda started getting going-away presents from her family and friends, and confided to the diary: **Everybody is so nice, it is worth going away to find out how much your friends mean to you.** There was a round of farewell parties, all her friends promising to write, and then on 25th. March she **Got up fairly early with the feeling that at last the day had come ... It was a wonderful feeling to think that I was going, I have so often seen boats off and longed to go.** When Linda and Ritza got on board the Orvieto they were given a big send-off, and later when they got to their cabin they found that a number of people, including Jack McFarlane, had left flowers, books and sweets.

They arrived at Adelaide two days later, where they went ashore to see the town and **walked through the Botanic Gardens, quite nice but not so nice as ours** and then the ship went on across the Great Australian Bight to Perth. The first morning they **Woke up and found we were in Australian Bight, and a very big swell on, Ritza and I both felt a bit sick** but they soon settled into the typical routine of a passenger liner, with the usual deck games, walks round the deck and dancing at night. On 31st. March they arrived at Fremantle and Linda went ashore for her first view of Perth, later to be her home. Back on board, **We said goodbye to Australian waters and now I had started on the unknown that lay before me.**

Shipboard life resumed in earnest and was chronicled by Linda in considerable detail. Playing bridge and reading helped to pass the time and a very hot passage across the Indian Ocean was enlivened by speculation about fellow passengers: **June, Ritza and I then had a long talk, chiefly about Mrs. Vandenberg and Miss Maitland. June had told me that they were professional bad women and had come from off the streets.** Two evenings later, while Linda was sitting on deck with a friend "in the part reserved for ladies", **Miss Maitland came up in a beautiful kimono ready for the night and did a Grecian dance for the benefit of the few stewards** that were round, showing just her pink georgette nightie.

The ship arrived on 9th. April at Colombo harbour, which was very busy, many big boats and hundreds of little steam launches darting here and there ... as soon as we landed we seemed to be surrounded by hundreds of natives of all nationalities and castes, following and chattering like monkeys. We walked up the main street, being Sunday all the European shops were shut, but the natives were all open and would rush out of their shops and ask you to buy, nor would they be put aside by a refusal. After walking round for a while they hired a car and toured the rest of Colombo: It was just wonderful. I felt as if I were seeing a play, Chu Chin Chow or something. I couldn't realise it was the real thing. We drove through narrow little dirty streets, native shops and hovels either side, and swarms and swarms of natives lounging round, in all different styles of dress, it was the East, without being marred by the West.

Later she saw the western part of the picture when they passed through the European quarters, lovely bungalows nestled in rich green foliage, coconut palms etc. and most glorious gardens. They made the obligatory tourist visits to Mount Lavinia (for a "real Indian curry") and to the Galle Face Hotel, where they watched a lovely long promenade called the Ladies' Highway, where all the elite take their rickshaw rides after the heat of the day before dinner. Finally they returned to the ship late in the evening, "a lovely ending to a wonderful day". Back on board Linda wrote: I felt I should love to be staying, I could understand the fascination of the East.

The first night out of Colombo the ship held its fancy dress ball and for the first of several times Linda went as a gypsy. She found that one of her partners "can't dance for knuts and it was pretty painful". But she made a new friend in a passenger named Arthur Baynes. They found a nice little secluded spot in front of the boat, and he took full advantage of it and kissed me most beautifully, I was thrilled because I like him most awfully.

The Orvieto arrived at Suez on 19th. April and she and Ritza and their father disembarked to drive to Cairo. She admired the famous Shepheard's Hotel, a magnificent-looking place, a huge open air terrace in front, a most beautiful entrance hall, all marble with rich Turkish rugs strewn about and an immensely high dome as ceiling ... The maids were all French and the stewards were Arabs. A Cook's tour included a visit to the museum: Most wonderful of all were the mummies, to see the embalmed bodies of these ancients lying perfectly calm, preserved through the ages, it almost seems they were everlasting ... saw the most wonderful jewels, of beaten gold, and mosaic enamel in rich colourings. The tour also stopped at the Citadel, on a hill overlooking the city: You look down and see minarets, domes and obelisks reaching up to the sky, the Nile wandering slowly through and far away in the outskirts the desert stretching, bordered by the Pyramids.

Another eye-opener was the mosque of Mohammed Ali, near the streets of the main bazaar quarter: It is an exact copy of St. Sophia in Turkey, only not so big. It is just sheer magnificence, the roof is one huge dome divided into five domes, all inlaid with mosaic enamel and beaten gold and silver, while it is supported by enormous pillars of alabaster and as a finale there was a trip by camel to see the Great Pyramids, where you could not but be awed by the hugeness of the Sphinx and the Pyramids standing there through time, almost to eternity in the middle of the hot desert sands.

They rejoined the ship by train at Port Said and headed into the Mediterranean, while Linda continued her friendship with Arthur Baynes. They admired Stromboli in action passing through the Straits of Messina: you could just see the pitch dark mountain outlined against the sky and every now and again spouting flame and fire up into the night ... then Arthur and I got comfortable in our same little spot with no lights. We got on most beautifully, I think he is an absolute darling. They arrived at Naples the next morning and sailed the same evening, just having time for a quick trip by car to Vesuvius and Pompeii. The ship got to Toulon on 26th. April, where Arthur disembarked after kissing Linda goodbye: I am going to have

a miserable time to London, cold and rough, all our nice old friends gone.

However, the weather proved better than she anticipated and she was on deck to watch the arrival at Gibraltar, though "passengers were not allowed to land". She "missed Arthur horribly", but was still able to enjoy the nightly dances. On 1st. May **we got our first clear glimpses of England, Plymouth, it was the sweetest old place, lovely green fields and quaint old houses.** Many of the passengers disembarked there, but Linda and her father and sister stayed on board until they reached Tilbury Docks the following afternoon.

2. ENGLAND, SCOTLAND AND EUROPE

On arrival at St. Pancras Station in London they were met by a friend of the family, Les Gray, and taken to their hotel, "a nice homely comfortable place". Arthur Baynes lost no time in coming round to see Linda: I introduced him to Les and we all talked for a good while, then went for a walk around London streets, which are terribly busy. We bumped into Jim Sharp and the Campbells, had a chat, then into a few more boat people, it was most thrilling. Arthur was a darling, told me all about his doings since we left each other. The next day Linda and Ritza went down Threadneedle Street, saw the Bank of England, the Royal Exchange, the Lord Mayor's house. Then we took a bus to Piccadilly Circus, had lunch at a funny little place, then down Regent St. ... we got into a lovely shop, Galeries La Fayette, and Ritza and I both bought a lot there, I bought a lovely knitted dress.

Another day they found the monument built to the Great Fire in 1673. Ritza and I climbed to the top, 365 steps, had a great view of London, quite close to the Thames, bridged first by the Tower Bridge with Tower of London on the left, then further down London Bridge and further still Westminster Bridge. We could see St. Paul's and Westminster Abbey in the distance. More times of meeting friends from the ship, window shopping, visits to the theatre and cinema and sightseeing followed; Linda was impressed with London society taking the air in Hyde Park: wealth and luxury abounded, beautiful cars everywhere, women with their pet poodles, most fascinating and wonderful men immaculately dressed from their toppers to their spats. A visit to Westminster Abbey also made a deep impression; it was filled with interesting history and romance, it filled you with awe and reverence for England and its great past, for there we saw the resting place of all the most illustrious of the land for hundreds and hundreds of years back ... we came out feeling inspired to live and do good for grand old Britain.

The next day Linda and her father "had a lovely day to ourselves", taking a Cook's tour to Hampden Court: **Cardinal Wolsey built it in 16th. century and presented it to Henry 8th. We saw the old banquetting hall, staterooms, pictures and tapestries, but best of all we loved the gardens, the lovely green lawns and the fine old trees. We saw a wonderful old grape vine planted in 1788 and now grown to an enormous size.** She went shopping again with Ritza and **we ended up in Selfridges where I bought a fur coat, £57/15/-. I don't know whether I like it or not, I bought it out of desperation.** They also discovered what was a novelty in 1922 when they **took the tube to Charing Cross and there found the moving staircase which we enjoyed immensely.**

During their final week in London they visited the Tower and saw the reminders of its bloody history, went to the Wallace Collection of paintings and antiques and had dinner at the Metropole, **a most wonderful hotel, plenty of life and we had dinner in a beautiful room with glorious pink tulips on the table.** They also went to Regent's Park Zoo, the Royal Academy, a play by John Galsworthy and by train to visit friends in Surrey, who took them for a drive, and **We stopped at one place to gather wild hyacinths, they were growing in thick masses under the trees ... then high tea about 8. The house was a typical well-ordered English home, a trained man servant to wait on us, everything beautifully served and no fuss or bother.**

On 22nd. May they all travelled to Dover by train and caught the Channel steamer to Ostend, and the next day did a tour of some of the World War I battlefields. At Ypres, **what a sight met our eyes, this fine old city of former days had not a solitary building standing ... the poor people had come back to their ruined homes and in most cases had built temporary ones of the scraps of iron on the old foundations and others were simply living among the ruins, too poor for anything else.** They went on to Brussels, where Linda was intrigued by a continental custom: **people sit outside drinking all day long. Everywhere it is the same, people eating and drinking** right out in the street. They visited the Town Hall, Law Courts, Houses of Parliament and Museum there. At Waterloo, they went inside the house which Wellington made his headquarters. We saw the bed he slept in and the original Times newspaper telling of the great battle.

On 27th. they crossed into Switzerland via Luxembourg, going first to Zurich: everything about the town looked good and clean and fresh, the houses are most artistic with their green shutters and bright window boxes of red geraniums ... I wanted to buy a Swiss cuckoo clock, but I had no room to pack it. At Lucerne they went for a boat trip on the lake, consumed large quantities of Swiss chocolates and visited the Casino, though only to watch. They took the funicular railway up Mount Pilatus, where they went on to the highest lookout and sat there watching the magnificent view ... we could see the snow clad Alps, peak after peak stretching up beyond the clouds.

Their father next took them to a hotel at Interlaken in the Alps: Mt. Jungfrau is just a white picture, it is feathery and majestic. Our hotel, the Beau Rivage, is a lovely hotel, the little mountain stream runs right at the back of it. Father, Ritza and I have got rooms opening on each other and share a lovely private balcony in front of hotel overlooking the mountains and especially to someone from Australia they were a magnificent sight, these great mountains where no habitation could possibly exist, just glimmering in their wonderful white. At Grindelwald we went to view the glacier ... there were the most wonderful blue green lights in it, they had tunnelled right through it, so we all went inside the glacier, it was quite weird, like being in a solid glass case. Another day they walked to the Trümmelbach Falls, where There is a lift that takes you right up inside the mountain, from where you can see this rushing tumultuous stream of water, falling, crashing, rushing down the rocks till it reaches the bottom, where it swirls round like a boiling pot.

On 9th. June the little party travelled by train to Lugano through the

15

St. Gotthard Tunnel, and Linda celebrated her 19th. birthday two days later on a boat trip to Porlezza on the Italian side of Lake Lugano. At Lake Maggiore they stayed at the Grand Hôtel des Îles Bourrées, a most palatial place, the front being all white Italian marble and glass, and most glorious gardens. They returned to Switzerland by train via the Simplon Tunnel to Lausanne, where they stayed at the Hôtel Mirabeau overlooking Lake Geneva. On a boat trip they walked to the old Castle of Chillon, which is built on a rock jutting out into the lake. It dates back to before the 11th. century and was used originally to guard the pass from Italy ... On the pillars were carved many names among which we saw Byron, Dumas and Hugo's names. It was all most romantic and fascinating.

They went from Lausanne on 15th. June by train to Paris, where they stayed at the Hôtel Moderne in the Place de la République. Linda loved Versailles, where the grounds are just beautiful, laid out in fountains, lakes and lawns, they recalled all the romances I had read of the French court, and I could picture the King flirting in the garden with a maid of honour. In Paris they saw most of the famous sights and went to a performance of "Faust" at the Opera. On a day excursion to Fontainebleu we saw the actual fields and church spire which inspired Millet to paint his famous pictures "The Gleaners" and "The Angelus". They also took in a show at Les Ambassadeurs: a display of female beauty, there were some beautiful scenes and dresses, the womens' attire gradually got scantier and scantier until at last they were quite naked only except a thin net thing round the middle. I was glad I had seen it, as I know now that tales of frisky Paris shows are not exaggerated. Another highlight was the Louvre, where we saw many art treasures, priceless old tapestries, the crown and jewelled sword of Napoleon, the pearls of Marie Antoinette.

They returned to England on 22nd. June by the Calais-Dover train ferry, and had another lovely tea on the train, ham and salad and hot buttered toast, real cream, ice cream, biscuits and cake. Back in London Linda went to the Royal Horse Show at Olympia, to Wimbledon where she "got a good seat for 2/-" and saw the legendary French player Suzanne Lenglen, and to a performance of "Decameron Nights" at the Drury Lane Theatre. With her father she attended a royal ball at the Albert Hall: the Queen entered the Royal Box, she looked very handsome and every inch a queen as she stood and acknowledged the greetings of the people, behind her stood the Prince of Wales looking so very youthful and a complete darling.

Mr. Anderson had planned a tour by car through England and Scotland, and now looked for a vehicle for the purpose: we espied a new little Swift, a darling little car, we enquired about it, £365, 10 horse power and altogether suitable. It is exactly what I should like. While he was debating the purchase, Linda went to Henley-on-Thames, where her friend from the Orvieto, Arthur Baynes, was competing in the sculls at the regatta: he looked just bonza, ever so much nicer than his opponent and he duly obliged by winning his event. Back at their London hotel, she and Ritza and their father met other friends from the boat: we showed them all our purchases and they showed us theirs, we were rather surprised they had such good taste as they had shown in their buying, as for the most part they generally look pretty aweful (sic).

Her father decided to buy the Swift and after Linda and Ritza went for "a trial spin" it was delivered to their hotel: then father came with us to drive it to the garage. I started it all right, put it into first, but every time I put it into second the wretched thing stopped, this happened several times till at last I had an audience watching, the policeman shouting at me and father getting irritated, cross and impatient. I was fearfully upset and felt like howling till at last I thought of adjusting the throttle, this did the trick and we sailed round to the garage in fine style. Their final engagement in London was when they went to Lord's to see a cricket match between Oxford and Cambridge. The place was crowded with most fashionable people, men in toppers and white spats and women in wonderful creations.

On 16th. July they set off for their tour in the Swift, starting at Oxford where they visited All Souls College and its chapel, which was a wonderful old place, the floor was of the finest inlaid Florentine marble and we saw the solid old carved oak seats and the lovely stained glass windows, some of which had been made from jewels. At Stratford they went to Shakespeare's house and at Warwick to the famous castle, a noble-looking place, a typical medieval home, built on the banks of the beautiful Avon, surrounded by lovely old trees, huge thick walls surrounding and an iron-studded gate through which we walked till we came to the remains of the old moat, walked over the drawbridge and under the portcullis and behold the ivy-walled castle amid green sloping lawns, it was all just like a story, the whole scene seemed so unreal, so unpractical in these extremely modern days. Linda and Ritza walked to the village of Shottery to see Anne Hathaway's cottage and saw the bench where Shakespeare actually sat in courting Anne.

The next day they passed through Worcester and Chester: it all looks very very old, many of the shops are built on the remains of the old Roman wall. At Blackpool she was impressed by the size: it is like St. Kilda only much bigger, the promenade stretches for miles and there are hundreds of amusement places, Luna Parks, dancing places etc. and three huge piers. They went on through the Lake District and crossed into Scotland on 25th., spending the night at the Dalblair Hotel in Ayr. At Alloway they went to see Robbie Burns' cottage: I bought a copy of Burns and we sat in the lovely gardens on the Banks of Doon with the little bridge in view and I read "Tam O'Shanter", how he drank late and long in Ayr, then rode out past the haunted church of Alloway, saw a ghost, then over the Bridge of Doon. It was so fascinating reading it all in the actual spot.

At the little town of Maybole, where his mother had been born, Father asked the registrar for the records of Grandma's birth, but found they were all kept in Edinburgh. At Prestwick they went for a boat trip round Ailsa Craig, and on 1st. August they reached Glasgow, where they stayed at the

Grand Hotel and made excursions to Loch Lomond, the Trossachs, the Falls of Clyde and Hamilton Palace, and went by boat to the Kyles of Bute, Dunoon and Rothesay. Glasgow itself Linda found depressing; she went for a walk in a big park in the middle of Glasgow. It was crowded with poor people, little red-faced girls minding mean-looking dirty babies, tired mothers, sullen fathers and oh the deformed and sick people everywhere, especially bow-legged children.

From Oban they visited Dunstaffnage Castle: its history most interesting, dating back to the earliest times. First held by Fergus I who came over with the Scots from Ireland, then the Macdonalds took possession and then the Campbells ... it sheltered Bonnie Prince Charlie and once held the Scottish coronation stone and has always figured a great deal in Scottish history, and many of the old Scottish kings are believed to be buried there. They also made an all-day steamer trip to the islands of Mull, Jura and Iona, where they saw various old crosses of solid stone and on them runic carving and also Christian pictures ... Next we came to the ruins of St. Oran and its burial ground which is held to be very very sacred, about 48 old Scottish kings and a few Irish and Norwegian and 1 French king are buried there ... to see these relics of ancient Christianity and hear of the noble lives of St. Columba and his followers just make the little island seem like a very hallowed sanctuary. Off Staffa they got the best view of the wonderful basalt formation of Fingal's Cave, the finest of all the caves in the island. It is futile to try and attempt to describe the wonderful formation of these great rocks, it just makes you marvel more and more at the wonders of nature.

On a boat trip along Loch Etive they walked to Glencoe: here the scenery was wilder and more Godforsaken than I had ever imagined ... on either side these great rugged barren mountains folded in one after the other, taking on all kinds of grotesque shapes. At St. Andrew's, where the local children seem to play golf as soon as they can walk they visited the famous golf courses and then drove on via Perth and Stirling to Edinburgh, where they stayed at the Caledonian Station Hotel. They saw the sights of the city, including the castle, **in a magnificent position on a very high rock overlooking all the city, we saw the Scottish crown jewels, Queen Mary's bedroom and where she lowered her son James VI down in a basket.**

They returned to England on 22nd. August and travelled via Durham to York, where they visited the Minster: **I was most interested in the tomb of William of Hatfield, brother of the Black Prince, and in the Chapter House where there are some very precious old glass windows dating from the 14th. century ... here and there beautiful colours shine out like precious jewels and they admit such a lovely soft light.** They then proceeded via the Yorkshire moors and the Fen country, arriving back in London on 1st. September. The next day the indefatigable travellers were at Brooklands race track, **a fearfully thrilling spectacle and the noise of their powerful cut- outs was like so many bullets going off.** They went to see James Barrie's play "Dear Brutus" and Gladys Cooper in "The Second Mrs. Tanqueray" and indulged in a final round of shopping, but **the girls are all so palavery that you can't tell them what you want.**

Another feature of the end of their London stay was the gastronomic delights. One day they **all went to lunch at Ye Olde Cheshire Cheese in Fleet Street. It is the quaintest old place founded in 1667, it keeps the same customs as it did then, the floor is strewn with sawdust, the same hard wooden benches to sit on and the same old famous dishes. I partook of pigeon, oyster, mushroom, steak and kidney pie.** Another day they dined again with their friends the Humphreys, and **a more excellent dinner I have never had. We had the loveliest tomato soup, then beautiful fillet of fish, then chicken and pork sausages, steak and kidney pie, potatoes, cauliflower, beans and then 4 most glorious sweets, meringues, peach Melba, sweets and devilled almonds and all kinds of wine.**

The time had now come for them to return to Australia, and Linda **felt**

ever so sad to think it was my last day in London. On 30th. September they rejoined the S.S. Orvieto at Tilbury and sailed for home via the same route as they had taken on their outward journey, and following a similar pattern of activities. The voyage was comparatively uneventful, although recorded by Linda in her usual detail. This time her chief admirer was an older Englishman, Mr. Tanner, "an absolute darling", and she also became friendly with Percy Chapman, one of the M.C.C. cricket team travelling in the ship. She, her father and Ritza reached Melbourne on 8th. November and thus ended her first overseas trip. She was soon immersed in family life again.

3 . ENGLAND AND ITALY

By the time of her second voyage to England with her father in 1925, Linda had become very friendly with a young man named Joe Gullett. The diary starts with her first morning on board ship on 6th. May, en route from Melbourne to Adelaide. She met the English test cricketer Percy Chapman again on board, and also a young married couple, the Oldmeadows: They seemed so happy, I couldn't help feeling a bit envious, if only it could have been Joe and I. Between Adelaide and Perth a Dutchman, Mr. Belmonte, introduced himself, prompting her to comment: I seem to have a mania for foreigners, or at least they have for me, Lord knows why. She was soon busy with the usual round of deck games and dances, and she and her father played a lot of bridge. Their first game was with Mr. Belmonte and a Miss Carey: a harder or more unattractive face I've never seen, she looked like a retired boarding house keeper, however she wasn't such a bad old stick.

The ship reached Fremantle on 11th. May and Linda went ashore for lunch and "a nice old chat" with a family friend, Joan Hislop. After an uneventful trip across the Indian Ocean, the next port of call was Colombo, where she and Mr. Belmonte went by car with friends from the ship to Negambo, a little seaside place 22 miles out. We saw a native do the mango trick and make a fight between a cobra and a mongoose. The first day out was a simply frightful day, we have struck a monsoon and it does nothing but rain and blow a gale, but conditions soon improved and they arrived off Suez at the end of the month, where it was wonderfully interesting passing Suez and entering the canal, a long straight bit of blue water and hot burning sand on either side. Occasionally we would pass another boat, some camels on the side, a signal station, a palm plantation. I spent the day rushing from one side to the other, looking at points of interest.

At Port Said she went ashore with Mr. Belmonte: the night was just too wonderful for words and I felt all exalted ... we sat down at one of the street cafes, just like the continent, and had real Mokha coffee and smoked Egyptian cigarettes, while the seething native life entertained us. At the Casino Hotel the scene was wonderfully fascinating, most frightfully cosmopolitan, French, Greek, Italian, English, half breeds etc., while the Mediterranean lapped the shore in front of us ... The music was feverish, hurried, pulsating and the people danced in the same way. On 3rd. June they were at Naples, where they got a car and drove along the coast through Posillipo, Pozzuoli to Dolfatara, where we went down the crater of Little Vesuvius, saw boiling lava, mud etc., we crept along a boiling hot tunnel called the Dogs' Grotto, right inside is supposed to be the Lake of Avernus and the entrance to the River Styx.

The ship made brief calls at Toulon and Gibraltar, where Linda and her father went to some very pretty gardens where we heard lots of wild canaries singing most beautifully. They were off Plymouth on 10th. June, where they disembarked and travelled by train to London, arriving at their hotel to find the city in the grip of a heat wave. Linda lost no time in visiting some of her favourite London shops: went into Galeries Lafayette and bought a sweet little chiffon dress for 7 guineas and wrote my first cheque. Over the next few days they visited Buckingham Palace, Hampton Court, Westminster Abbey and the Tate Gallery, and went to the opera, Carl Rosa Co. at the Lyceum, saw "Lohengrin" which was very heavy. That night she heard the bad news that her niece Gwenda had polio, then becoming prevalent in Australia: When we got home we found our precious Australian mail ... I opened Ritza's and heard the horrible news about poor little Gwen having paralysis.

Towards the end of this short stay in London, Linda discovered a new shopping Mecca, a place called Walker's Court off Shaftesbury Avenue. A very quaint place, a tiny little narrow street and a regular market going on. I bought 5 beautiful pairs of stockings for 25/-. She went with her father to see "The Barber of Seville" at Covent Garden and the polo at Hurlingham: the elite had treated it as a garden party, I think poor old father was the only man without a top hat ... Afternoon tea was set on the beautiful lawns under the superb old spreading chestnut trees, while the band played. I think we really saw England at its best, not really one dowdy or shabby person. They also visited friends at Maida Vale, eliciting an interesting comment on domestic service at this period: Mrs. Thom was a dear, quite young and charming with 3 bonza kids and only 1 maid.

The day before she left London Linda was invited to dinner by Reg McKellar Hall, a young Australian surgeon who had just obtained his F.R.C.S. at Edinburgh and was in London briefly studying orthopaedics: had my hair trimmed, shampooed and waved and only cost me 6/- ... Then I got dressed in my new pink chiffon dress and Reg called for me about 7.30 ... He took me to the Piccadilly, we had dinner and danced in between the courses, and I just loved it all. Reg was a dear and we talked of all sorts of things, he asked me about myself, whom I was engaged to, I had Joe's ring on my finger which I can't get off. Three years later she and Reg were to be married.

On 25th. June Linda and her father travelled by train to Scotland, where they stayed for a month at a hotel near Gleneagles in the Ochil Hills and had a dear little table for two right against the window and can gaze out onto the Scottish hills now ablaze with yellow gorse. Here she played tennis and golf, went swimming and dancing and started the long solo walks which became a feature of her diaries: went for a lovely long walk right over the golf links, saw tons of wildflowers, wild foxgloves, pansies etc., also some rabbits. I found a baby rabbit and picked it up in my hand. A few days later, although it was raining, I set out for a nice long tramp, I never feel lonely on these occasions. I love the feel of the soft rain on my face and my thoughts are good company as they are mainly of Joe ... I must have walked about 10 miles today.

She continued to play regular tennis, golf and croquet, and accompanied her father on various expeditions. One was by coach to the Pass of Killiecrankie and Blair Atholl, where they walked to the River Garry, which **is full of salmon and we could see them leaping out of the water.** Another was to Taymouth Castle Hotel, **right on the head of Loch Tay ... it is wonderful, everything is left as near as possible as it was when owned by the Marquis of Breadalbane, one felt rather like an interloper.** She drove to Gleneagles with a Mr. Singer: **he has a ripping car, a Ballot, and we did over 50 most of the way, sometimes 65.** A final highlight was a visit to Glamis Castle, a **most picturesque castle and the most interesting one I've ever been in ... saw Bonnie Prince Charlie's saddle and riding boots ... the family portraits of all the Bowes-Lyons, saw King Duncan's bedroom and the place where Lady Macbeth murdered him.**

She and her father returned by train to London and the Rubens Hotel on 20th. July. Then followed a series of excursions around the south of England; one was by coach to Canterbury **to the Cathedral, a truly glorious sight, looking so venerable and timeworn, and behind it part of the old town wall and the great gate.** Another was by train to Bournemouth, where they stayed at a beach hotel and made day visits to Salisbury and Stonehenge, the New Forest and by ferry to the Isle of Wight. At Southampton they visited the Cunard liner "Berengaria": **the magnificence of the lounges, smoke rooms, ballroom etc. were a revelation. We saw the suite "The Prince", a perfectly wonderful thing with a glassed-in sun parlour. Its price is £1000 a day ... There was a Pompeiian marble swimming bath.** Back in London they went to the Ballets Russe at the Coliseum and to see Marie Tempest in "Hay Fever".

On 17th. August they travelled by train to Torquay and stayed at the Hydro Hotel. Linda hired a gown, cap, towel and tent to undress in, all for 1/- **and had a lovely bathe. There was no nice sand, only pebbles all the way down to the sea.** From there they had "a wonderful drive right over the

Devonshire moors", including a stop at Princetown, which is right in the highest and wildest part of Dartmoor and is a little village collected around the great Dartmoor prison ... a dreary formidable place in wild and lonely surroundings. On a walk from Torquay Linda discovered the village of Cockington: Cockington itself is the sweetest little old thatched village, with an old thatched forge 900 years old. I am told it is one of the prettiest villages in the whole of England. She sampled a village fair there, where she went into one of the side shows, saw an awful creature in pink cotton tights. I went on a spinning jenny thing and won a huge doll.

At the end of the month they moved on further west: At Barnstaple we got into a tiny little train and we were met at the station by a very old horse conveyance which took them to Lynton, where huge thickly wooded mountains seem to rise right out of the sea and Lynton is on top, the quaint little village of Lynmouth down below ... from our table in the dining room by the window we get a lovely view of both mountains and sea and the little village. From there they explored Clovelly: The one street of the village goes right down the side of the hill to the sea. It is cobbled and so steep that it goes down in steps ... There are donkeys to take people up if they find it too steep to walk. In a teashop there they had lovely home made scones and cakes and huge bowls of Devonshire cream and blackberry jam, very delightful but ruinous for the figure. Another day they took a bus to Exmoor, where Linda admired the "Lorna Doone country".

They returned to London on 31st. August and she plunged into her exploring and shopping again, and went to her first "Hamlet", performed in modern dress, which appeared funny at first, but the acting was so superbly good that it didn't seem to matter much about the clothes. She also saw Binnie Hale and George Grossmith in "No No Nanette", and a military tattoo at Wembley. On 23rd. September they took the bus to Croydon Airport and flew across the Channel to Le Bourget: The engines made a terrific noise which made me a bit nervous at first, but I soon forgot to be nervous

27

in my excitement at being amongst the clouds and seeing the world thousands of feet below ... Father and I had lunch baskets, we enjoyed our lunch, then I began to feel violently ill and had to use my lunch box as a receptacle. I had rather a nervous twinge actually crossing the channel but I was too sick to care much.

In Paris they stayed a night at the Grand Hôtel in the Rue Royale and then caught a train for the Riviera at the Gare du Lyon. They stopped at Mentone and booked into a hotel on the seafront, and the next day Linda walked into the town, sheltered by high steep mountains, the slopes of which are terraced up as far as can be with grape vines, olives, trees etc. It was so beautiful with the white continental houses and the cypress trees, just as I had always imagined it. Another day she took the train to Cap Martin and walked right out to the point and feasted my eyes on the view. The sea was so blue and inviting that I took off my shoes and stockings and dangled my legs in the water. She went on by bus to the casino at Monte Carlo, where the atmosphere inside reeked of stale scent. The baccarat and roulette tables were crowded, I didn't understand the games at all so did not play.

Back at the hotel, Linda Explored the old town of Mentone in the morning. It was rather like going into a native quarter, the streets were so dark and narrow and the smells were so bad. She noted that All the women are always asking the good-looking concierge all sorts of questions. I flatter myself, I hope not wrongly, that he rather favours me, as he always takes me up in the lift. On her last day there she went to Monte Carlo again and Walked home along the Quai Bonaparte and sat for awhile on a seat overlooking the sea, an Italian workman came and spoke to me and we carried on a conversation in French for over an hour, I was quite pleased with myself.

On 2nd. October she and her father took the train to Genoa: a good-looking young Italian got on, I felt him staring at me the whole time, I tried not to bother about it and go to sleep, then I looked up and caught his eye and he gave me a most disarming smile, so I smiled back ... he then handed me his card with "Je vous aime" written on it ... I hardly knew what to do, so I just smiled and said "Non". He asked me for his card back, I gave it to him and he gave me another without "Je vous aime" written on it. From then on we held quite a conversation in French with a little Italian here and there. At Genoa they did a Cook's tour and saw where Christopher Columbus was born, also the violinist Paganini and we saw the old gates and city wall and a very wonderful Cathedral di San Laurenz, where the ashes of St. John the Baptist are supposed to be ... went to Campoganto to see the famous cemetery. The statuary there is truly marvellous and world-famed. They went on to Milan, staying at the Hotel Europe, right by the wonderful cathedral ... went inside it, it is most enormous, the biggest I have ever seen and the stained glass windows shine out like precious jewels. Another Cook's tour took them to the pagan temples and the art gallery, where they saw many wonderful old works, most beautiful and all dating from the 14th. or 15th. to the 10th. century.

Their next stop was at Venice and they got straight into a gondola and were taken along the Grand Canal to our hotel. I cannot say how great the thrill was of actually seeing the Rialto, the Doge's Palace, the Piazza San Marco, the Bridge of Sighs all for the first time ... Venice has always been my city of dreams. Linda found to her delight that "Our hotel is the old Doge Dandalo's palace", and lost no time in visiting St. Mark's Church, which stands alone among other churches for the richness of its basilica and its wonderful mosaics, and then too it has the famous four bronze horses standing on top of the basilica and also the Doge's Palace, intensely interesting, first for its wonderful gothic moorish architecture and then for its wonderful pictures. They took a steamer trip around the lagoon and another to the old fishing town of Chioggia: we took a gondola and went over the water to the Sorenata. It is a brightly lit boat where they sing accompanied by guitars and mandolins, and people come out in gondolas and moor all round to listen. I loved it, with the view of St. Mark's, the Campanile and the Doge's Palace in front of us, the lapping of the water against the gondolas, and then the real Italian music. It was all so lovely that it made me ache.

After that they travelled by train to Florence, to a hotel where "we overlook the Arno with the old Ponte Vecchio" and where their Australian mail finally caught up with them. An evening stroll took them down all sorts of little narrow streets which at every turn showed us some interesting old medieval building standing out in the moonlight. They visited the Pitti Palazzo and the Uffizi Gallery: The pictures were wonderful, I was especially enraptured by Raphael's Madonnas ... I bought a print of one with my last 8 lira.

They also went to the hill town of Fiesole, where they saw the remains of an old Roman theatre, an old Franciscan monastery and an old cathedral built in the most interesting Tuscan style. In Florence Linda was enchanted with the cathedral and wonderful campanile, it is all built in green and white marble. Opposite is the baptistry with its wonderful old bronze doors, one by Pisani, the other by Ghiberti, they are famous in the history of the world's art. Another day she found the house where Dante Alighieri lived and the old parish church next door where he married, Beatrice also used to attend there, her family arms are to be seen over the high altar.

On 14th. October they went on by train to Pisa, where the famous leaning tower was much more extraordinary than in pictures and looks just as if it were in the act of falling down. Her father met a mysterious Italian at Pisa who persuaded him to accompany him to London on a money-making venture, the details of which are not recorded. So she was left to travel by train to Rome on her own and "felt very forlorn and deserted". However, Rome soon cheered her up: wherever I walked was full of interest, old churches, beautiful monuments, fountains, palaces, villas etc. ... Rome to me is so overwhelming, there is so much, every inch oozes with ancient history and civilization. There too she saw again an Italian, Ugo Ballelli, who had met the family on a previous visit to Australia. He sent his card to her hotel and came to see her: he was very nice, wanted to show me all over Rome etc., but I said I had a Cook's guide. He says he wants to marry me and if I won't live here, he will come to Australia with me. Of course I didn't take it seriously, explaining again that I loved somebody in Australia. She did a Cook's tour to the Colosseum and the Church of St. Paul, where There are 2 most wonderful altars with alabaster, malachite, lapis lazuli and agate used for their sole decoration. It also went to the Capitol, the Forum and up the Janiculum Hill, where St. Peter was said to have been crucified. From this hill a most wonderful panorama of Rome was had. The old Sabine Hills in the background, the Appian Way, the Vatican with all its large estate, the Dome of St. Peter's etc., in fact all of Rome was stretched before our eyes.

Another day she visited the Vatican, "full of the most priceless treasures", and the Church of the Capucines, which has a cemetery underneath, we went down and found it full of heaped skulls and bones, the walls all decorated with skulls and bones, even lightshades made of them, while several old skeleton monks leered at us in their preserved monks' clothing. Ugo took her to dinner: I am improving in my French and Italian and can understand him much better, our conversations are getting quite fluent. They went on to the theatre to see a Neapolitan comedy which was "quite beyond me". More Cook's tours followed, to Nero's house, the baths of Caracalla, the catacombs and Hadrian's villa, where I sat with a priest and 2 women from Dublin. They took me for a Catholic and talked freely to me, the women seemed on excellent terms with the priest and were making all sorts of unpriestly remarks. The Villa d'Este was very wonderful, the garden exceptionally so, all laid down with lovely vistas showing through tall cypress trees and fountains of all shapes and sizes.

On her last two days in Rome Linda went to the Pantheon, the Palatine and the Villa Borghese, "full of the most wonderful works of art", including Raphaels and Titians. She also attended a mass at St. Peter's: Inside the church were soldiers in full dress uniform keeping the crowd in order ... all of a sudden silver trumpets burst forth and the Pope arrived held aloft on a gilded throne, bowing from side to side, with cries everywhere "Viva la Papa", certainly a wonderful sight and I was so glad that I had not missed it. Ugo sent her a goodbye present: there was a parcel from him and a letter, a beautiful souvenir of Ancient Rome and a sweet note saying it was a talisman of prosperity, good fortune and love.

She caught the train to Naples on 21st. October and stayed at Parker's Hotel, where I have a most lovely front room and the whole beautiful bay stretches before me crowned by Vesuvius puffing out volumes of white smoke. Her father returned from London the next day, but instead of having made money he told her he had lost £5000, and was not surprisingly depressed. They went to the Blue Grotto at Capri by boat: the entrance is so low that you must lie flat down in the boat, the boatman has to be very adept shooting in a wave. We got very bumped about and wet. Inside was wonderful, it is quite impossible to describe the wonderful blue and crystalline clarity of the water. Afterwards we had lunch at a fascinating little place on a terrace overlooking the Bay of Naples with wonderful old Vesuvius as background and ripping Italian music ... I don't think I ever felt so in love with Italy as I did then, I just adored it with every particle of me ... Capri itself was the quaintest, most picturesque place I think I have ever seen, it would be an ideal haunt for artists.

The time had now come for them to return to Australia in the S.S. Ormonde, and Linda "spent my last 50 lira on a dress at La Rinascente". Ugo came to bid them goodbye and was very eloquent about the poetry and romance of his beloved Italy, he made me feel it all intensely ... he gave me some lovely red and white carnations, red for his heart and white for my soul, he said. The ship sailed at midnight on 24th. October, and the diary describes Linda's fellow-passengers as usual, including **old Chisholm, who dances like a draught horse ... he imparted a lot of unsavoury gossip to my ears.** But generally they had a happy voyage, with brief stops at Port Said and Columbo, where she **bought 2 raffia bags, some green beads supposed to be Ceylon coral for 10/- and a white sapphire for 3/- which I didn't want but he inveigled me into it, saying it would bring me luck.** They reached Fremantle on 18th. November, where her mail included a **lovely long one from Joe saying that he had failed in one subject and had to do supps, oh I was frightfully disappointed and awfully sorry for him because such a long time more of work and suspense, I just can't bear to think of him failing again, it makes our little affair seem so hopeless.** A week later the diary ends with their last day on board: **I felt quite a little sad as we have been an awfully happy little party.**

4. SOUTH AFRICA

Linda's next overseas trip in 1927 was to South Africa in S.S. Ulysses, again accompanying her father, this time with her girlfriend Dorrie Jefferies. In the meantime she had seen more of Joe Gullett and Reg McKellar Hall. The diary starts at Fremantle on 30th. May: no news from Reg so decided he was a dirty hog and dismissed him from our thoughts and went to Perth to see "Trial by Jury" and "Pinafore" at the Savoy Theatre. On their return to the ship, however, he was waiting: Reg is really a dear, so gentle and understanding, he told me that he had always had tickets on me and made himself very sweet. The next day he took them for a drive around Perth in his Fiat, and when they got back he and I had a nice chat in the cabin and I kissed him goodbye.

The voyage across the Indian Ocean was uneventful; Linda duly recorded the details of shipboard life: made up some topical verses to sing at the concert tonight, they were chiefly about the food, which is the last word. On 11th. June she noted "I am 24 today which doesn't give me much pleasure". They arrived at Port Durban in rough weather three days later and It was a very thrilling sight watching the poor pilot come aboard, as the sea was raging. We berthed about 6, it was dark and wet and miserable, very different from what I had imagined. They went to the Marine Hotel, where Father got a nice letter of welcome from Auntie Bella saying she had arranged for some friends to show us around.

The next day Linda made tracks for a hairdresser, had my hair done which took about an hour. The others hadn't waited for me so I then chose the most elaborate Zulu rickshaw driver and lolled around for 1/2 hr. The Zulu rickshaw men are most picturesque. Later they all took a tram through the residential quarter: It was absolutely beautiful, the white houses and red roofs set off by luxuriant tropical vegetation. The following day "Bella's friend Mrs. Storm looked us up" and took them for a drive round Durban;

they were "thoroughly fascinated with all we saw". That night there was a dance at the Marine Hotel: **They dance in a square courtyard which is open to the sky, here and there tall coconut palms stretch up and in the middle of the floor is a huge palm and all around are pergolas covered over with tropical creepers etc.**

They caught the ship on to Capetown on 17th. June, but **Dorrie and I hate our new cabin, it is a pokey little hole for two.** They were met on arrival by Auntie Bella and Uncle Alf, whose surname is not recorded, and escorted to another Marine Hotel, where they **mapped out our tour with Cook's. It sounds most fascinating and I feel wildly excited about it all.** Their first visit was to Parliament House, **where an interesting debate was going on about the flag, the Boers wanting to do away with the British flag and they are now in power. We saw General Smuts but did not hear him make a speech.**

Linda found that **Uncle and Auntie are just dears and have given us the most wonderful welcome** which included a visit to their new house in the suburb of Claremont and a drive around Table Mountain: **the drive home was glorious, Capetown has the most lovely surroundings, mountains and sea.** Auntie Bella had a son named Les, and Linda soon reported that "Dorrie and Les are having an ardent affair". They went for drives to various parts of the surrounding country, including Cape Point: **the scenery equal to anything I've ever seen, we followed the coast all the way, the road cut out of the side of steep mountains ... I believe this drive to Cape Point is one of the finest in the world.** She also went on several shopping expeditions: **bought myself a nice light silk raincoat at Fletcher and Cartwright's for 69/6 ... bought a sweet little crepe-de-chine dress, 87/6 ... a very nice coat and jumper suit, 10 gns. the lot, very cheap I thought. Clothes seem to be much cheaper here.**

On 30th. June they made a trip to Cecil Rhodes' memorial at Devil's Peak, and saw Groote Schuur, the home of prime minister Herzog, once

Rhodes' house ... built in the Dutch style. It is filled with priceless old furniture, and marvellous treasures and antiques from all parts of the world. A few days later they set out to climb Table Mountain, with "marvellous views of Cape Town": Then the thrills of rock climbing began. My heart went a bit watery when I saw the sheer rock we had to get up, however I said nothing ... then I got the rope and after some time got up. However that wasn't the worst, the next bit we had to climb a rock with a sheer drop of 3000 feet yawning below us. They called it sensational but not difficult. I felt very windy but tried to compose myself by admiring the wonderful view while waiting my turn to climb. I got up and felt very pleased with myself ... It was very tiring and tedious coming down and took about 2¹/₂ hours. However we got home about 6 and I didn't feel so tired and felt I had had the most wonderful day. I soaked in a hot bath for about ¹/₂ hr.

The next tour took them into the bush and they drove along the Veldt, passing old caravans with their bullock teams, then through lovely mountain passes, the longest and steepest being the Omlini Pass. The wildflowers and flowering shrubs were wonderful all the way along. They ended at a remote village named Knysna, where The hotel was extremely homely and not at all comfortable. It was very cold at night and no fire so we lighted a chip stove which smoked so badly that we had to go to bed. To get a hot bath you have to muck round with a chip heater and the ladies is right outside, so five days here will be more than enough, I think. One day they drove to a forest called the Garden of Eden, where they took a launch up the Keurbooms River: we landed for a while and the forest was so dense and the atmosphere so still that it was just like being on a desert island, it seemed a little spot completely lost to civilization. At Knysna Heads they saw ostriches, rock rabbits and small bok on the wooded slopes of the harbour.

They drove back via the Prince Alfred and Montague Passes to the town of George, where they took the train to Oudtschoorn and then Bloemfontein in the Orange Free State. They were met there by friends of Auntie Bella, the Juras, and Linda got her first Australian mail, including letters from Joe and Reg: **Joe's letters didn't please me very much, he seems to be doing no work and wasting his time very stupidly.** A few days later they went by train to Kimberley to visit the diamond mines, and **saw all the various processes of getting the diamonds out of the stones. We saw them getting some wonderful diamonds, one huge yellow one as big as a walnut and a beautiful white nearly as big, worth about £2000 ... The natives who work in the mines sign on for a certain length of time and during that time are never allowed to leave the compound ... When the natives have finished their contract they are put 4 or 5 days in detention before going home and given salts in case they have swallowed any.**

On the alluvial diamond fields on the Vaal River they saw a diamond called "the Star of Zion, worth £10,000". In Kimberley they went to tea with Sir William Creswell, famous in the early naval history of Australia, and Lady Creswell, who were living there. At their hotel the next evening **it was a dance night and all the tables were lavishly decorated with exquisite flowers, we saw all the elite of Kimberley in their ball attire.** They travelled on by train to Mafeking and Bulawayo in Rhodesia: **all along the line we saw natives in their natural state. We had several stops and bought all sorts of wood carvings from the natives.** After an overnight stop at the Grand Hotel at Bulawayo and then a third night on the train, they reached the Victoria Falls and a "beautiful hotel overlooking the Zambesi Gorge".

The next day they walked to the Falls: **They are of course marvellous, enormous volumes of water just hurling themselves over this sheer rock drop into a swirling whirlpool at the bottom.** They also drove to Livingstone, which was "swarming with most picturesque natives of the Barotse tribes", and walked to a place called Silent Pool, where **I took my shoes and stockings off and paddled in the Zambesi ... saw one enormous crocodile asleep on the bank and one little chap in a tree.** Another walk was to the Big Tree, which is an enormous Cream of Tartar or Baobab tree ... set off in a canoe paddled by 4 lusty niggers ... landed on an island and got lots of lucky beans.

On 31st. July they returned by train to Bulawayo and the Grand Hotel, and the next day drove to Rhodes' tomb in the Matope Hills: very rocky and solitary, they reminded me of an old Pagan temple ... it is on the highest rock with huge boulders all round, it is just a simple tomb blasted out of the granite, commanding a wonderful view all round. His friend Dr. Jamieson is buried just near and a little further away is a big monument to those who fell in the Matabele War, it rather destroys the picture of solitude and nature, I think. Travelling on to Salisbury they were again met by friends of Auntie Bella and taken to Meikle's Hotel. The town is very small but has lots of nice shops, natives swarm everywhere ... they aren't allowed to walk on the footpath, the Rhodesians are very strict about the colour line. On the second day there, Dorrie and I arrived late for breakfast, about 9.30, and father came in and ticked us off, he was in a very bad mood, I was sorry because I hate upsetting him.

They drove to a place called Gwelo on 5th. August to visit an Australian friend, Bruce McKenzie, who took Linda and Dorrie to see his "very lovely" farm at Happy Valley, where they stayed for several days. The weather was idyllic and Linda found that the glorious sun every day makes one very lazy. One evening Dorrie retired early and left Bruce and I, we got rather matey and stayed up till pretty late. I think Bruce is ever so keen to have us here as it is really rather a lonely life. The next day after tea we took our stroll, it is a glorious part of the day when the sun is going down ... we had our cocktails on the stoep and all got quite sentimental with the charm of it all ... after dinner Bruce and I had a ripping night, talked about everything, marriage etc., we both got quite confidential. Soon it was time for our last walk round the farm, every evening came down in the same wonderful gentle caressing way and we watched the sunset glow ... I drank it all in for the last time, I felt greedy about it all as if I couldn't take my fill, I want to keep that memory for always. Bruce drove them into Gwelo on 10th. August and as the train left, clutched me almost feverishly and went off with a very quick goodbye. I went to bed feeling horribly sad, I hated leaving Rhodesia. I think Bruce has disturbed me quite a lot.

They travelled by train to Johannesburg, buying odd curios from the natives, father bought me a jackal skin rug after great pressure on my part, £6/10/-, terribly cheap I consider as it is quite a beauty. They stayed at the Carlton Hotel and went to see a kaffir war dance: It really was the most wonderful spectacle. Hundreds of Kaffirs attired in the most weird and grotesque get-up making their weird music on the tom-toms. Linda enjoyed some more shopping: got the taffeta evening gown I saw yesterday at Blinman's for 14 guineas ... got 3 ripping bags for 51/- and a lovely filled-up dressing case for 65/-, which I made a present of to myself. They went by car to Pretoria to visit "Aunty Bella's friends the Becketts" in a lovely old house called Merton Keep ... Prince Christian died in this house during the Boer War, so we saw the room and his photo.

On 23rd. August they returned by train to Durban, where Linda received letters from Bruce: I opened the letters with great excitement, hoping for I don't know what, however all through they were both very sweet, that was that and I somehow felt I could howl and howl. She also got 2 from Joe and a sweet one from Reg asking me to stay with him and his mother in Perth. They stayed with Auntie Bella's friend Mrs. Storm until they rejoined S.S. Ulysses, which sailed for Lorenco Marques on 29th. and was delayed for a day there when two crew members were jailed.

The ship anchored on 3rd. September off Mozambique, which looked quite a picturesque little place with a grim old fort on one end and a few quaint foreign-looking buildings, while all around were the picturesque old Arab dhows. They were not allowed ashore, but spent an interesting hour watching the flocks of Indians embarking with all their weird collection of worldly goods. They come on board as deck passengers and bring their own bed and bedding with them. On the passage to Zanzibar she met a mysterious author, who wasn't very edifying to talk to and I wasn't surprised when he said he wrote mystery stories and got his plots from "The News of the World".

They went ashore by boat at Zanzibar and found it the most fascinating place, like a bit of old Baghdad completely unspoilt by European touch. It is a very old Arab town and the streets are narrow and windy and the architecture most interesting, all Moorish or Arabian. Most of the houses had most wonderful old carved doors, many studded or inlaid with heavy brass. Shopping in the bazaar, I bought 6 strings of seed pearls for 22/-, 2 ivory cigarette holders 5/- each and a rather beautiful little ivory box for £2/5/-. They drove to the other side of the coast where the Sultan has his summer residence. We passed on the way all the clove fields for which the island is famous, we could smell them very strongly.

Their next port of call was Mombasa, where we went round the old Portuguese fort which looked very timeworn and battle-scarred, I believe it has been besieged and captured 16 times and has been the centre of many fights between the Portuguese and Arabs. Linda and Dorrie went exploring on their own: It got dark about 6 and we were far away from everywhere, we got very tired and nervy as we thought we should never reach the hotel and there were native huts all around us and no white people for miles. They made it back safely and sailed on 7th. September, with hordes of Indian passengers embarking ... there are now only about 12 1st. class passengers.

En route to Bombay she again met her author, Louis Martyn, who told her he wrote under the pseudonym of Riley Raine and that he had put her in his new book: he said he knew he had no chance, but that he had fallen in love with me. I went to bed feeling rather fed up, in fact horribly fed up, it seems to be my lot in life to have people I don't want fall in love with

41

me, whereas when I do the falling in love things aren't nearly so easy, life is a horrible muddle. The next day he told me a great secret, he is in the Secret Service going on a very dangerous mission in northern India ... he seemed a different person altogether, a thousand times more interesting than the rather smug stereotyped Englishman I thought he was. Well he made the most wonderful and ardent love to me but I could not respond.

The ship reached Bombay on 16th. September and Linda saw 5 towers where the dead bodies are put and all the vultures sweep down and devour them. She bade goodbye to Louis Martyn, who had been telling me the plans of his mission ... all I could tell him was to hope ... he sent me a map and plan of the route he is taking, also a key to the code he will write to me in. Her father, Dorrie and she also disembarked and travelled by train to Madras: it is a very interesting place quite unspoilt by tourists, gardens and Hindu temples everywhere. It is called the City of Gardens. They crossed by boat to the north of Ceylon and had a nightmare train ride in intense heat to Colombo and so spent our last night of a very terrible journey.

They stayed for a week at the Galle Face Hotel, where on the first day Linda and Dorrie met a Mr. Corbett: he asked Dorrie and me along to his sitting-room, some other rather extraordinary women and 2 other men. We danced and drank and chatted and had quite a matey night ... Corbett and I went out on the terrace and stayed there till nearly 2. I said hundreds of times I was going to bed and meant it, but somehow the tropics sap your determination. Of course he tried to make love which I didn't encourage but I had the most extraordinary conversation with him that I've ever had with a man. He escorted her to a fancy dress party and dance: he is so attractive, an absolute man of the world and quite a naughty one, but terribly attractive and nice ... I stayed till 5.30 a.m. and crawled up to my room feeling a very bad egg. His ship sailed next day and she got a glorious pair of satin pyjamas with a sweet little rose from Corbett.

They played golf and visited Nuwara Eliya and Nan Oya, returning from the latter to Colombo by train, one of the most beautiful train journeys I've ever had. The whole way the scenery was glorious, first we passed through all the tea plantations, then the rubber, then the coconut and lastly the paddy fields, all most beautiful in their different ways. Letters from Louis Martyn "make me feel that I have a great responsibility". But this was the last time he figures in the diaries. Mr. Chandler, the manager of the Galle Face Hotel, asked them to his home, the most marvellous flat filled with rare old ivories and porcelain from China, old brass, old furniture, everything, it was a veritable Christies, but all beautifully arranged. He presented Linda and Dorrie with "an ivory powder box each". At her final party she attracted another resident: Arguello and I took ourselves off and sat by the lovely old sea ... it was ripping sitting on his balcony listening to very nice music and we danced in the dark ... when I got to my room I found a nigger and I suppose I caught him in the act of rummaging for loot.

On 1st. October they boarded S.S. Cathay, a ripping boat, beautiful deck space and we've got a lovely big cabin. She received two letters from Reg asking me to marry him, that he had loved me ever since he met me. Of course it wasn't a surprise although I was hoping he wouldn't say it so soon till I really know what I want to do. She noted in her diary: I am not going to bother to recount the doings of the boat as we have led a very uneventful life, making no effort to be sociable.

They reached Fremantle on 10th. October and I dressed up in my new clothes and then waited with mixed feelings to meet dear old Reggie ... then the question had to be faced and all I said was that I couldn't make up my mind as we didn't know each other well enough. Reg said he quite understood and that was that. He took her home for dinner to meet his mother, who is extremely bright and nice but terribly deaf ... Reg and I sat in the garage and talked and decided that as he couldn't leave his practice and come and see me, I must come and see him. Back on board she tried to persuade Dorrie to come over with me ... told her our plans and she was very pleased and anxious to help. On the passage to Adelaide she recorded: I still feel very disturbed and unsettled. I like Reg so very much and I feel I could be happy with him as long as he loved me very much, but he wasn't at all convincing on that point. Her last entry in this diary was: I'm dreading getting home, my feelings are in such a muddle.

5. JAVA AND SINGAPORE

Linda's final overseas trip as a single girl was in 1928, just before her marriage to Reg McKellar Hall. Immediately prior to it she had travelled to Perth to stay with Reg and his mother, and they had become engaged. Once again she accompanied her father; her diary starts on 26th. July: After six beautiful happy weeks in Perth, left by the "Gascoyne" for Soerabaya ... Reg and Mrs. Hall came down to see us off. She found that the boat is very tiny, not quite 3000 tons, no deck space so we shall have no games to divert us, the servants are all Chinese so that lends an Eastern touch. The first evening on board she met a congenial fellow passenger, Dr. Clendinnon, and then retired to my cabin to indulge my loneliness and feel thoroughly miserable.

The ship arrived at Geraldton the following day, where after a walk to the town she returned to lunch on board, noting that "the food is horrible". On 28th. July they anchored off Shark Bay and the day after berthed at Carnarvon, where we reached the town by a train which ran along the pier for about 2 miles. At Onslow there were just a few straggling buildings on a sandy, desolate, uninteresting looking coast. The next port of call was Port Hedland, which consists of white galvanised iron buildings ... all looked sun-baked, with not a sign of green anywhere. She had met a Chinese, Limchun, who seems to have been one of the ship's engineers: The wind died down at night and it was most glorious and full moonlight, Limchun and I went for a walk and it was fascinating, the dry drab little town seemed quite mystic and beautiful by night. We walked along the mangroves and climbed out onto a branch overhanging the water, it was all so still and quiet that we could hear and see the fish leaping about ... the wonderful night worked its spell, I'm afraid, and Limchun got very ardent and I had to remind him that we were both engaged ... we went and sat behind the wool bales and watched the pearling luggers come in.

On their second day at Port Hedland we had to take on 2000 sheep and large amount of wool bales. The ship then went on to Broome, where the water was the most beautiful pale green colour and there were lots of pearling luggers ... found the town most interesting. It has a distinct atmosphere of its own compared with the other little ports we have called at. Here we saw the first sign of tropical vegetation, picturesque bungalows and dwellings of natives, abos, Malays, copangs (sic), Chinese, Japanese, all sorts. After her day ashore, Linda got back to the boat about 5, found it high and dry on the sand, an extraordinary sight, the tide falls here 30 feet and at low tide you can walk miles out to sea.

On the passage from Broome to Derby there was drama on board: Dr. C. has run foul of Mrs. Beresford who has turned out to be a snake in the grass. He decorated her chair and put "weight limit 2 tons" and she has retired to her cabin, had hysterics and deputations with the captain, chief steward etc., so it will be very awkward when she emerges. They got to Derby on 5th. August: the tide is so forceful here that it stirs all the mud up from the bottom of the sea, and the sea for miles round is a horrible muddy colour ... To get to the town you have to traverse about 2 miles of mud flats. The town itself reminded me of a small Rhodesian town, there were plenty of huge Baobab trees that grow so much in Rhodesia. She and her father met there a man called Rose who has a station some 65 miles out. He had driven a team of bullocks in to ship away ... he told us all about the country round about here and was most interesting. We watched them drive the poor old bullocks on board. It all seemed cruel because they were terrified and stubborn and the natives seemed to take delight in prodding them.

The ship now crossed the Timor Sea to Lombok Strait: In the afternoon we began to pass high mountainous islands, Lombok between which and Bali is supposed to be the old original division of Asia and Australia. The island of Bali looked mostly high mountains precipitating right down to the sea and we could see that they were cultivated practically up to the summit. There was one perfect cone-like mountain standing out above them all - the Peak of Bali, over 10,000 ft. high. The last event on board was the fancy dress ball, but Linda felt it was pathetic to see the stodgy passengers trying to have the spirit of Carnival.

They reached Soerabaya on 9th. August, where Thomas Cook's staff drove us in a superb Studebaker to the Oranje Hotel. We shall have the same car all through Java and also a very nice little guide boy called Jimmy. That day Linda went for a walk down the main shopping street ... Pasar Besar it is called. The European shops are wonderful, especially furniture shops, glorious rugs and antiques. They also took a drive round the town and were most impressed with all we saw, it beats Colombo to a cocked hat as far as houses, shops, tidiness etc. are concerned ... I was charmed with the Dutch houses, the grandest sort of architecture all with the doors and windows flung wide open and inside one could see glowing wonderful lamps of all shapes and sizes and the most lovely colours.

Their next trip was to the Bromo Hotel in the mountains to the southwest of Soerabaya, and Linda found the country much like Ceylon, densely populated with natives and every ounce of land under cultivation. At the hotel she had "the most delicious coffee I've ever tasted." The next day they were up at 3 in the morning to go to the Bromo Crater and see the sun rise ... rode in sedan chairs and had 8 native bearers each ... freezingly cold. After two hours' travelling they arrived at the top of the Livloeng Pass ... had our first view of the Bromo Crater smoking away ... The descent from the Pass down to the Sand Sea, the name given to the volcanic plain which is the floor of the old original crater, was terrifically long and steep and we walked down, it would have been too dangerous in the chairs. At the bottom we got into the chairs again and the most unpleasant part of the journey began, travelling over the Sand Sea which is really all ash from the volcano. We jolted across this for several miles and the dust was dreadful.

At the foot of the crater they had to climb very steep steps to gain the very top ... There had evidently been a recent eruption because the ash was all fresh and the steps totally covered with it, and our feet sank up to the ankles in it ... At the top we had a wonderful sight, a perfect cone going down 400 ft., we could see sort of boiling mud at the bottom. Huge volumes of smoke were belching out and occasionally we heard great rumbles ... got back to the hotel about 11, very tired, stiff and dusty.

Later that day they walked down the mountain as far as the Grand Hotel ... the view was marvellous, the clouds had lifted and we could see the coastline and Soerabaya. At the Bromo Hotel Linda found that all the meals are very heavy and many courses, but I can't appreciate the Dutch food yet, only the coffee which is delicious. They drove on to Songgoritti, where they stayed at the Bath Hotel, with hot mineral baths ... very pretty, surrounded by high hills ... all terraced up and every inch under cultivation. Travelling west over the mountains they passed teak forests on either side, through coffee plantations, the coffee plants were in full white bloom and the smell was delicious. They went through Madloen to Djokjakarta, where they had a very nice hotel in the same plan as all the others, dining room and lounge in one building, then all the bungalows separately. All the bungalows have a little open air stoep and at night they are all lit up with gay coloured lamps.

From there they visited first the Water Castle, which is now in ruins, it was built in the 17th. century for the Sultan of Djokja and then a batik and brass factory; it was most interesting to see them beating the brass and making the designs for the batik and then filling them in with the vegetable dyes. It requires infinite patience and skill. The factory also worked buffalo hide, which they dye in all beautiful colours and decorate with real gold leaf. I bought a beautiful brass lamp and buffalo hide shade for 29.50 guilders, about £2/10/-, also a lovely hide belt and brass buckle for 13.50 guilders and a brass bowl, 9.50. On their last day there they drove to the Pambanan Temples, once a holy city of the old Hindus dating from about 8th. cent. before the Mohammedan invasion.

Continuing westwards on 15th. August they passed through Mandret, where there is rather a lovely old ruin of a Hindu temple, we climbed up some steep steps and in a chamber at the top was a wonderful statue, very well preserved, of Buddha, about 3 times life size, on either side of him were other big statues. A few miles further on and we came to the famous Borobodur, dating from the 8th. century and practically intact, as it had been covered over by earth all those years, till it was discovered in the 18th. century. It was much as I had imagined, I had seen so many pictures of it. All round the bottom is carved the entire life story of Buddha. At Warasobo they stayed at the Hotel Dieng, a pretty little place in the hills about 3000 ft. high, so quite nice and cool.

The following day they made an early start: away by 1/4 to 7. For the first few hours it was lovely driving in the coolness. The scenery all the way is so beautiful and the native life so interesting. We passed through numerous market towns and for miles beforehand we would pass the natives all making their way to the market carrying all sorts of wares, huge loads on their heads or in baskets Chinaman fashion. The women do practically all the burden bearing. For about 10 miles we ran along the banks of a canal, and the natives were bathing in it all the way along and we were treated with all sorts of sights of them in their birthday clothes. They arrived at Cherbar, a hot seaport town, clean and very well kept and laid out with gardens as all the Dutch towns here are and broke their journey at the Hotel Retblink. The next day they continued right over high mountains ... all the time through the rice fields, through forests of luxuriant palms, coffee plantations etc. ... all the time there is the absorbing native and his toil, father and I call them the human ants ... we saw them making beautiful fine hats out of pandanus, a leaf that grows here. The hats are sold for about 1 guilder and working all day [they make] 30 a week. They are sent

49

away to Paris, where they are blocked, trimmed and sold for several guineas. At Saroet they stopped overnight at the Hotel Doese, and drove next day to Lake Bojenart, where the natives make music out of bamboo instruments and all the little children dance to it. Nearby was Lake Leles, "so beautiful that it looked like a painting", from where they drove on to Bandoeng, a very nice large town with beautiful shops. It's the official centre of Java. There they stayed at the Hotel Preanger and a fellow-tourist who had accompanied them thus far from Soerabaya, Mrs. McBean, left: quite a good old sort but very self-righteous and boring and I don't think we'll miss her overmuch. On a visit to a quinine plantation, Linda sampled Rijstaffel for the first time. The foundation is rice and then you have about 20 other dishes ... I had in mine chicken soup, fried bananas, cooked peanuts, fried egg, rissole, fish and various other oddments.

On 21st. August they arrived at Batavia, where she went shopping: had my hair shampooed and water waved at "Salon Louis Quinze", cost 4.50 + 50 cents for tips. I then had a chocolate ice at a very nice delicatessen shop, purchased a 50 tin of De Reske cigs for 1.25, about 2/-, very cheap. The next day they drove round Old Batavia, through the Penang Gate ... through the Kali Besar, once the famous residential part, now just insurers' offices ... at an old Portuguese church near here, we saw the whitewashed human skull of Peter Eberfeldt. He was a half caste and had planned a massacre of the Dutch, was found out and executed and his skull has been there ever since, about 200 years, as a warning to all other might-be traitors. Later Linda took a walk right down Ryswyk, the European shopping part, along the Pasa Bawe, the Chinese part ... Batavia is rather an interesting place, a mixture of the continent and the East. In the Dutch fashion, a canal runs down the middle of all the streets and the natives bathe and do their washing there.

Another day she visited the museum, and found it very interesting, wonderful old Chinese furniture cabinets, chests, screens, porcelain, statues and carving, all sorts of relics from the old Hindu temples, vases, horns, jewels and pottery, all sorts of beautiful things from Java, Sumatra, Bali etc. Afterwards at their hotel, two Dutchmen came and made themselves most agreeable ... from Soerabaya, Abandanon and Breidveld were their names, Mr. Abandanon is coming on the boat to Singapore. They took her to a dance and she went for a drive to Tandjong Priok after with Mr. Breidveld, the drive was lovely and we sat on the beach and watched the sea, and then of course the almost inevitable happened and he started to get amorous ... When we got back he was so insistent that I became tired of arguing, gave him the slip and rushed in safety to my room, I didn't turn on the light but hid behind the bed in case he had seen and followed, just as well because he looked in the door, my heart gave a jump, but I was undiscovered and after a few minutes standing there in uncertainty he went away and I went to bed in peace. The next day she wrote: foreigners I suppose don't understand that we can enjoy a drive late at night without any ulterior motives.

Her father was indisposed and that evening Abandanon and Breidveld asked her to dinner and on to the "Perroquet" for dancing: Mr. Abandanon interests me very much, he is a dear to talk to and dances beautifully. On 25th. August they all lunched together at the hotel and then went on board S.S. Optenhoort for passage to Singapore: father shouted an excellent bottle of champagne, so we had a cheery farewell ... a beautiful boat, quite the best I've been on. The first day out Linda found that the passengers were a strange and interesting lot, few women, many men, Dutch and English, many Chinese, half castes and all sorts. She and her father played bridge morning, afternoon and night for 25 cents a 100 and I won about 8.50 guilders ... We finished bridge about 11.30 and I sat and talked to Mr. A. who is a most charming personality, and also I must admit indulged in a little extremely light but quite artistic lovemaking.

They arrived at Singapore next day and stayed at the Europa Hotel: to my great joy got 2 most lovely and quite thrilling letters from Reg, he is a darling. Linda walked to the famous Raffles Hotel and gazed at the fascinating scene. The terrace is on the seafront and in full view of one's gaze is a myriad of all sorts of ships ... After lunch went up to my room and found a lovely bunch of red carnations from A. On a car tour of the city they saw beautiful Chinese and Arab houses, the Chinese form 90 percent of the population here and are enormously wealthy ... went for a wander down High Street where all the lovely Chinese and Indian shops are, I bought all sorts of things. She unexpectedly met her old friend Kath Wright: we went down and lunched together and told each other all our history. She lives on a rubber estate near Johore.

One evening Linda and her father went with friends to the Southern Hotel in Chinatown for a Chinese dinner, which consisted of many courses and in between times cigarettes were handed round and hot steaming towels with which the Chinese rubbed their hands, neck and face most vigorously ... shark's fin soup most delicious although rather heavy, then varnished duck, skin also most palatable if a little greasy, then Bird's Nests, not so bad, then some sort of chopped up liver which I really couldn't tackle and several other courses. Their host, Pung Su, was a highly cultured good talker quoting Shakespeare, Longfellow, conversant with all the philosophies and sciences. Afterwards, Mr. A. and I went for a drive to the Gap and had a most interesting conversation - life and love of course, the same old subject with fresh points of view and from different aspects. He really is a most charming personality and a very fine character, I'm exceedingly glad I've known him.

The next day Mr. A. presented me with a beautiful little jade brooch with a dear little note to the effect would I wear it as a souvenir for the so many hours of exquisite delight he had had in my company, he really is a charming galant. On his last night in Singapore, Mr. A. talked to me in the most wonderful way, we both realised what a delightful friendship we've had ... we promised that we shouldn't let a year go by without just sending a few lines to say how we are.

Next day Linda saw him off in S.S. Optenhoort and "felt quite sad saying goodbye". To console herself she went to a little French shop, Janine in Battery Road ... The woman was most awfully nice, Australian ... I bought 2 dresses and a little pair of satin corselettes, 126 dollars altogether. She had a very social time during her last few days in Singapore, starting with morning tea at John Little's, "the great Saturday morning meeting place in Singapore". At Raffles Hotel we had foie gras, delicious, caviar, not so delicious but eating it gave me a nice expensive feeling, iced consomme, then sole meuniere, pheasant, strawberries and cream while at the Dutch Club, on Queen Wilhelmina's birthday, "never have I seen champagne in such lavishness." After her final shopping expedition she walked languidly home, a yard's walking seems like a mile in this climate.

On 3rd. September they joined their ship, S.S. Marella, for the return trip to Australia. This time "our cabins are small and dark inside ones". She had been introduced in Singapore to a young Englishman named Hurst travelling in the same ship, who has completely taken charge of me, he is quite nice, but a bit tiring to have him planning your every movement. They called back at Batavia for a day, where she went to a native exhibition: a sight well worth seeing. The buildings were all in native style of architecture and brilliantly illuminated. There were thousands and thousands of Javanese there, all wandering around but never a sound from them, they are a most gentle, passive people. We wandered round seeing the various exhibits of native work, wonderful beaten tin from the island of Banka, wonderful embroideries in rich colours from Tonkin. She also watched some dancing, practically all Eurasians and how they danced, with wonderful rhythm and abandon. It was a curious sight to see full whites mixing quite happily with practically 90 percent black. The Dutch of course have no scruples about intermixing.

The ship anchored off Semarang on 7th. September and Linda went ashore by launch with Mr. Hurst for a lovely drive round the hills ... I realised afresh what the Dutch have done for Java, they have made it a thing of beauty, cleanliness and order. At Soerabaya she met Mr. Abandanon again, this time with his wife: I sat next to Mrs. A. at lunch and found her charming, quite nice and slim and smart for a Dutch woman, a sweet face and very nice manners ... I had no time alone with A. at all, which was a disappointment as I wanted to talk to him about lots of things ... I felt quite sad to think I might never see A. again. Crossing the Timor Sea she met a young Frenchman, Henri, and they agreed we are going to talk for an hour after lunch each day, so it will be good practice.

They reached the Australian coast at Darwin on 13th. September: I've never felt so hot in my life, Singapore or Colombo was nothing to it ... The town was very drab and unlovely like all inland (sic) Australian towns, wide streets, notices, unsightly veranda posts etc. ... it was interesting to hear the American and the Frenchman's views on their first Australian town, they both said they'd never seen anything so drab and dreadful in their lives ... We took on about 40 passengers at Darwin, sailed about 9 p.m. with 7 stowaways on board. The next day she was feeling rather depressed owing to a most evil-looking eruption of red spots on both my arms and back which is very hot and irritable. Soon the spots were "growing like wildfire", and though she got several letters on arrival at Thursday Island, "even they didn't cheer me up much": Dorrie was a bit sad that our single days were nearly over and Ritza was a bit peeved that I was rushing the wedding so.

She went ashore after dinner at Thursday Island and found it the most depressing, sordid place, far worse than Darwin. There is no electric light, the whole town is more or less in blackness except for a feeble lamp here and there ... A hideous hotel, a few straggling shops kept by evil looking Chinese ... little memorial church which was partially made from the wreck of the "Quetta" in 1890. Going through Albany Passage, We passed the old homestead of Jardine ... He helped a lot in the rescue of people from the "Quetta" and in that memory ships when passing the homestead always slow down and blow the siren, all of which the "Marella" duly did. Soon her rash cleared up, and the diary ends on 21st. September in the Barrier Reef with blue seas, blue sky, warm sun, the wonderful Australian colouring again.

Linda was married to Reg McKellar Hall at the Presbyterian Church at Toorak in Melbourne on the 23rd. October, 1928.

PART TWO

THE THIRTIES:
YOUNG MARRIED LADY

LINDA AT HER FATHER'S IN MELBOURNE WITH JENNIFER, 1932

6. ENGLAND AND FRANCE

Linda first travelled overseas with Reg in 1932. He had just been appointed Senior Honorary Orthopaedic Surgeon at Perth Hospital and was undertaking a year's post-graduate study in Europe. Their first child, Jennifer, was nearly two years old and was left in the care of Reg's mother and a nursemaid. They left Fremantle on 1st. August in S.S. Orsova, but her diary does not begin until they disembarked at Toulon on 26th., where they caught the train to Nice and stayed at the Terminus Hotel: **Reg trailed me all over the town looking for a cheap old haunt of his, but alas I weakened before he'd found it and insisted on dining at the first place we came to, which of course was most expensive.** The next day there was a "great display of bathing belles" and they went by bus along the coast to Mentone, which was "very dead after Nice and extremely hot". After lunching on snails they returned to Nice: **We sat on the promenade and watched the bathing. Nice seemed to be teeming with life, all beautiful sun-tanned beauties.**

They then set off to travel to Aix, where Reg had arranged to visit the local hospital and meet his cousin Lillias Gordon who was staying there. They went first by bus to Aix-les-Bains, passing **the most wonderful scenery, all the part through the awe-inspiring Gorge du Mesela ... passed Entre Vaux, the quaintest old fortress town I've ever seen. It was perched high up on a rock and the old drawbridge is still there leading over the moat.** They stayed the night of 28th. August at the Hôtel aux Savoie at Grenoble and next day, en route to Aix, stopped at "the lovely little village of La Piève de St. Chartreuse", where they turned off to visit the old Chartreuse monastery: **it was founded in the 12th. cent. and was abandoned in the early 19th. when French law made all monasteries illegal. The famous Chartreuse liqueur is now made in Spain. Further on, we passed through the indescribably wonderful Gorge de Grazers, on through the tunnel of**

Échelles and thence to Aix.

There they were met by Lillias and taken to the Hotel Bristol, where we sat under the gorgeous old trees, sipped our coffee, listened to the excellent music and watched the life of Aix. The next day they went by steamer across the Lac du Bouget to the old Abbaye D'Haute Combe. Before Savoy was sold to France, Haute Combe was the burial ground of the Italian Kings of Savoia. They made an all-day trip to Mont Blanc and Chamonix, in a valley bordered by 2 rows of majestic alpine ranges. It is a great centre of alpine climbing and the little shops are full of mountain sticks, boots, knapsacks etc. and it fills one with a feeling of adventure ... that wonderful range of peaks all snow- covered was a truly dazzling sight.

On 3rd. September Linda and Reg travelled by train to Paris, where they stayed at the Terminus Hotel overnight before crossing the channel by boat train to Dover. It was "a great thrill being in London again" and they found "digs" with a Mrs. Coonan at 75 Westbourne Terrace. At Simpson's in the Strand they had a marvellous lunch for 2/- in quaint circumstances. All the diners sat round a half moon table, at the head sat a venerable old chairman, who said grace and served us all. He said grace again, told us an amusing story and then invited us to guess the weight, height and girth of a tremendous old cheese. The next entry in the diary reads: After this I cannot remember my daily doings. I know we spent our first 2 weeks in London digging up people ... Then Dr. Paton arrived on the scene and put Reg on to a marvellous free trip of the Italian spas for one fortnight, arranged through the B.M.A.

Linda wrote this after her recovery from a critical illness. After Reg left for Italy she went to hospital for a pre-arranged curette, and after coming home suffered a haemorrhage and "quite the most agonising experience I have ever known". She had to return to hospital: It seemed the end of everything to me and I felt so lonely with Reg away ... I am told now that my life flickered in the balance, I had absolutely no pulse for a while. Her friends, especially the Mays, rallied round and sent a wire to Reg, who arrived back on 29th. September, and **Oh, wasn't I glad to see him. I felt I had battled on alone so long.** The poor darling had had an awful journey, just the wire saying I was worse and to come at once and no other information. However, the sad story ended well, I got better and better every day and came home the following Wed. For a short while she felt very weak and feeble ... spent the next week getting back strength and seeing the shops again.

On 15th. October Reg bought a new car, a Standard 9, for £155, and they started to make excursions, the first one to Kent: **the autumn tints of the lovely old trees and the vivid vermilion and scarlet of the Virginia on the old grey stone houses make it a glorious time of year in the country.** They found Rye, where they looked for friends, **a delicious old town snuggled up on a steep hill which rises from flat marshy country. We entered through a lovely old gate and immediately had a view of the ruins of an old fortress on the top of the hill ... a young man from a nearby old 15th. cent. cottage came to our rescue. He told us the Bendalls were weekending at Keston near London and invited us into his cottage. It was a fascinating old place with its wonderful oak-beamed roof and great old fireplace. He regaled us with cigarettes and ginger wine.** He recommended the Mermaid Inn, where they lunched, and afterwards explored the town: **it is one of the old Cinque Ports and has been the scene of many a foreign invasion. The houses are all old and quaint with the loveliest old doors I've ever seen in England.**

Back in London, Linda **lunched with Mrs. Chenery at her club, The Old Victoria in Sackville Street, it was once the London house of Mrs. Fitzherbert, George IV's mistress and has some lovely old furniture.** She and Reg went to the Caledonian Market and found it **a huge and amazing place, old clothes and junk of all sorts, antiques, old silver, old jewellery, old furniture, absolutely fascinating and to our inexperienced eyes marvellously cheap. We had a wonderful old poke round and I spent about**

£3. Bought 2 lovely little miniatures, £1 each, an old silver candlestick, 5/-, a pewter teapot, 5/- and a pretty old jug dated 1840, 5/-. They returned to Rye, "a great haunt of writers and painters", to visit the Bendalls and saw the inside of their house. They've got lovely genuine old furniture and the place is an absolute delight. At the Mermaid Inn again, we slept in a wonderful room and a still more wonderful old carved mahogany 4-poster bed.

On 23rd. October they drove to Canterbury: very wet and cold, still nothing could dim the beauty of the grand old cathedral ... it was fascinating to read a list of the archbishops, St. Augustine was the first, in 597 I think, then other names that are so linked with early history, like Lanfranc and Anselm and St. Dunstan. It is a graceful cathedral, its piers are so tall and slender and the wonderful rich 13th. cent. glass shining through is most beautiful. We found the spot where A'Beckett was murdered, admired the old part of the cathedral with its rounded arches behind the choir, saw the old stone chair where the archbishops are crowned and have been for centuries. They completed a round trip via Chatham, Rochester and Cobham, a beautiful, peaceful little village with an inn celebrated by Dickens and so back to London.

A few days later she met Reg at the Overseas League after his hospital work and went to have cocktails with a Mrs. Eastman, a charming soul he had met at Salzo Maggiore. She had a marvellous house in Connaught Square, with heavenly furniture. She herself was very attractive and beautifully dressed in black velvet and lovely lace. I felt very shabby and ordinary, she however was so charming that I soon forgot it. Another girl popped in who was also at Salzo Maggiore, Eva Turner, a great singer. She has lived so long in Italy that she talks broken English ... Mrs. Eastman had suddenly lost pots of money and is heartbroken, as she must now let her beautiful house. At Harrods Linda saw displays of Christmas toys and of corsets: they showed the corset worn through the ages, the dreadful iron affairs that looked like instruments of torture.

At the end of October she and Reg set off by car on a northern tour. They travelled through the Cotswold Hills to Gloucester, where we had a good look at the cathedral and its famous cloisters. The nave of the cathedral is pure old Norman, while the lovely cloisters belonging to a demolished monastery are 13th. cent., fine tracery carving. Going on through the Severn and Wye valleys to Hereford, they saw another fine cathedral, which is of red sandstone. It has a lovely old Norman nave like Gloucester and one of its chief treasures is the Mappi Mundo, one of the oldest maps in the world, dating back to the 13th. century ... Jerusalem was in the centre, the Garden of Eden was shown, Asia and Ceylon were shown with drawings of crocodiles and tigers. They also went past the Auld House, a lovely ½ timbered 17th. cent. house, now a museum of Nell Gwynne, David Garrick and other famous people who have been born here.

At their next stop, Leominster, we inspected the lovely old Priory Church, it has a fine Norman nave and north door. The chief interest for us was a ducking stool, used for ducking nagging wives, dishonest tradesmen who gave short measure and other such malefactors. They then drove through Ludlow, "one of the loveliest old towns I've seen", and Shrewsbury to Oswestry, where Reg visited the orthopaedic hospital. From there they went to Liverpool, which they found "enveloped in smoke and grime", to investigate accommodation for the period Reg was shortly to spend doing courses at hospitals there. They returned to Oswestry and booked into the Old Boot Inn at nearby Whittington. Reg spent two days working at the orthopaedic hospital and Linda went on walking expeditions across the border into Wales, where she discovered Llanfair, a lovely little village with a mountain stream and a lovely old bridge in the centre of it. It is called the Switzerland of Wales.

On 5th. November they drove into Wales for the weekend, passing through

Llangollen to the really wild mountainous country of North Wales. Our little narrow road dug out of one of these grim slate mountains was really thrilling. We got to the top and had a marvellous view of all the great mountain peaks, chief of which were the Arans. Further on they came to Dolgellau, down in the hollow right at the foot of precipitous mountain peaks, the highest Cader Idris. Every little chimney pot of that quaint old stone village was pushing out lovely blue smoke. Eventually they reached the coast at Barmouth, carved out of the side of those grim old mountains and faces the Atlantic, which today was as blue and calm as the Mediterranean and continuing along Cardigan Bay, they sighted Harlech and its grand substantial hoary old castle standing out on a high rock overlooking the bay ... we had our first view of Snowdon and her inspiring companions from Harlech Castle.

From there they headed for Snowdon Peak and stayed the night at the Castle Hotel, Llanberis, at the foot of Snowdon and in fact is hemmed in on all sides by grand mountain peaks. The next day they came to Caernarfon, silent and asleep, it was Sunday. The Welsh Sundays are worse than the Scotch ones. The castle was a splendid sight of great and imposing strength and the outside is in wonderful repair and looks much as it must have when built by Edward I. Another fine castle was at Conwy, a fascinating medieval town surrounded by enormously strong walls punctuated here and there by great fortress towers and then of course there is the grand old castle, so strong and proud looking. They returned directly to Liverpool via Llandudno and Denbigh to start Reg's study period.

7. LIVERPOOL

Reg had arranged to do post-graduate courses in orthopaedics at Alder Hey and Leasowes hospitals at Liverpool, and on 6th. November they booked into a boarding house at 142 Upper Parliament Street. The next day Linda explored the town and discovered the great new cathedral en route and visited it. It stirred me very much, there is something noble and vast about it. I felt thrilled to think that this most beautiful and quite wonderful building was being created in our lifetime. They found that "Dinner in the boarding house is rather like being at school" and that Liverpool suffered from a grey pall that hangs over everything, so that you can only see a few hundred yards around you. She found a local golf links and started to practice, and then Reg came home with the news that he is going to do a course here that will last 6 months. It seemed an appalling prospect for me. I had screwed myself up to bear 3 months, but 6 - ugh!

The next time she went into town, she thought Liverpool seemed dirtier and more depressing than ever and sought distraction on the golf course and at the Overseas League. She made excursions to several neighbouring areas and "struggled with all my Christmas cards for Australia". On 16th. November she lunched at the Overseas League, where a Miss Miles had lots of people for me to do things with, at which prospect I rather recoiled as I hate being dragged into doing things with people who have been found for me and they are all so busy and efficient ... All the same it is very kind of Miss Miles. Afterwards she had my hair permanently waved in the hope that it will improve me. My hair has been motheaten in the extreme and has given me a great inferior complex. The next day she was In despair of my golf, had a lesson, 3/6 for an hour, but as usual the lesson took from me my old style and I failed to grasp the new one.

Linda and Reg had met a Dr. Edelstein and his wife, and she started sharing activities with Mrs. Edelstein, going ice skating and to a play at the

Playhouse. On 23rd. November, The event of the day was the Prince driving down our street, of course we all rushed out and saw him. He had no smiles for anyone and looked tired and worn. He is having a strenuous 2 days' visit to Lancashire seeing what is being done for unemployment. Miss Miles had arranged for her to play golf with a Miss Loveday, but Miss L. couldn't play at all, so we had no game and the wind was penetrating. I never got warm and was thankful to give up when it got dark at 4 p.m. Once again I am forced to realise that golf is not an English winter game. She went with Mrs. Edelstein to the ice-skating rink, where she was "filled with great enthusiasm" for skating, and also to Southport, a fine place, but unfortunately the sea has receded and the grand promenade and the pier etc. grace only a few sandbanks, the sea being vaguely discernible a few miles away.

She and Reg played bridge with Dr. Bell and Dr. Sweetapple, two fellow-students of his, and she discovered the Public Library, where she went regularly to read and borrow books. She went with Miss Miles to a Sir Henry Wood concert at the Philharmonic: the audience was interesting, all the old families of Liverpool attend these concerts, they are the thing to do. I don't think I've seen such a collection of well dressed old dowagers before. Mrs. Edelstein drove her to see Eaton Hall, rebuilt about 100 years ago and is a very magnificent place, rather on the style of a French chateau and to Chester with its old Roman walls where they explored some of the famous old Rows. We went down into some of the old crypts over which all the shops are built. This particular one was used as a large wine cellar. We discovered God's Providence House, it was a place of refuge during the Plague and so got its name. It has a marvellous carved black and white front which is all restored work of 100 years ago. It is now an antique shop and we wandered round and found some lovely old Chippendale and Hepplewhite chairs. They also visited the cathedral and met a playful priest who tweaked my hair and patted my back.

Another day Linda lunched with Miss Miles at the 1918 Club, where we were addressed by a Miss Tunstall of Cheshire, where she says the villagers still practise witchcraft and believe in magic and images. While Reg played golf, she went for a 12 mile walk to Halewood and back, through old farm houses sheltering in the bare but beautiful trees. The country landscape seemed quite beautiful with the mist settling down and softening the outlines, all just like an English Xmas card. On 6th. December their Australian mail arrived and they had "good news of Mrs. Hall and Jenny". She walked to the nearby Sefton Park, where the scene was glorious, so Christmassy. The ponds are all frozen over and Peter Pan's pirate ship on the pond was truly icebound.

Linda went by train with Mrs. Edelstein to London for a week on 9th. December, visited her London friends and did some Christmas shopping: The shops are thronged and packed with lovely Xmas goods ... past Bradley's, a most exclusive shop, the atmosphere was too aristo for words, we walked in and walked out ... In spite of my determination to keep away, I got drawn into a shop by the sight of a lovely old mahogany Georgian sideboard, £12. It was a bargain, but just a little massive-looking for a modern house. In the end I bought a set of 8 Chippendale chairs, genuine, for £20. She also explored and discovered Adelphi Terrace, where David Garrick and the brothers Adam lived, also saw where Sam Pepys had lived and thoroughly inspected and admired all the Adam doorways ... It is a fascinating part, survival of old London.

Before she left Liverpool the guest house had had a new boarder who left without paying, and on her return detectives came to interview us about the strange boarder and the disappearance of my cheque slips and Reg's gold lighter. On 21st. December Reg started his Christmas holidays and they "set off in the car for our Christmas tour". They travelled through Lancaster, an old town with memories of John of Gaunt. There is a really lovely Middle Ages castle, well preserved, set up high overlooking the town. They stopped at Windermere, a "beautiful town on the very lovely long narrow lake", and further on visited Furness Abbey, set in a lovely peaceful valley and like Tintern was a Cistercian abbey. The ruins are very beautiful and we wandered round trying to piece it all together. At Coniston they stayed the night at the Sun Hotel: the scenery is grand and lovely, the lake is set in much wilder and more interesting country than Windermere. Behind Coniston great jagged peaks loom up, and as there are no roads that traverse these mountains I think it must be all very wild and mountainous.

The next day they passed through a lovely mountain valley called the Little Langdale. The scenery was truly gorgeous, we went over the top of Bled Tarn, here we were warned the descent was dangerous and impracticable for motorists and to return the same way. Reg however, in fact we both felt adventurous, so we made the descent, which wasn't so bad. They went on through Grassmere, Thirlmere and Derwent Water, all "truly beautiful", and climbed to the top of Honister Pass, where they were again warned of the dangerous descent: However, we were both filled with the spirit of adventure and down we went. It was indeed very steep and narrow and twisty and the road very rough and in parts washed away into great deep furrows. However, we managed all right and were well rewarded as the scenery was very inspiring, great forbidding slatey crags and peaks looming up on our flank. At Calder Bridge we saw the beautiful ruins of Calder Abbey, then to Gosforth, where we saw a wonderful old carved stone cross alleged to be built by the Norse about 1000 years ago ... we ran along West Water. It was now growing dark and the scenery around was grim and forbidding but quite thrilling. West Water seemed very black and from the other side of it rose great jagged peaks.

After an overnight stop at a little hotel where climbers from the peaks of Skiddaw and Scafell were much in evidence, they went on through the Eskdale Valley: we came to the foot of Hardnott Pass, we could see far, far above a funny little road winding and twisting its way over and through the towering mountains. We decided we must try it. This decision resulted in the car stopping in pouring rain, and they had to turn back. Another stoppage later necessitated a tow into Penrith, where they spent part of Christmas Eve waiting for repairs. But they reached Hawick over the Scottish border on schedule and stayed with friends, the Turners. On Christmas Day they had a "great feast" and listened to the King's speech. They visited Dryburgh Abbey: I adored Dryburgh, it is in such a wonderful setting on the banks of the Tweed, amongst lovely hoary old twisted gnarled trees as old and older than the abbey itself. The abbey was started in 1162, Walter Scott and Earl Haig are both buried there. At Hawick Cottage Hospital We were given a most sumptuous dinner and a lovelier decorated table I have never seen. We feasted and drank and made right merry. As they warmed up they danced their reels and sang their splendid rousing Hawick border songs.

Linda and Reg drove to Edinburgh on 29th. December and stayed at the Grosvenor Hotel. They visited Edinburgh Castle, that wonderful old place oozing with history and romance. The shrine is magnificent, blending in with the castle surroundings perfectly. There is so much that is wonderful and lovely to see inside that it is quite hopeless to attempt to describe it. They also went to Craigmillan Castle: It dates from the 13th. cent. and is in a good state of preservation, as there are many rooms still standing, the kitchen and dungeons, the huge banquetting hall with a splendid old carved stone fireplace and a minstrel gallery. Various bedrooms, one of which Queen Mary of Scots used. Returning to Hawick, they were taken to the chapel of Rosslyn Castle, the most exquisite thing I've ever seen in stone. Every inch of it seems to be carved in exquisite carving and the inside has the effect of a fairy cave almost. With their friends we celebrated New Year's Eve in real Scotch style ... all had a magnificent dinner party at the hospital once more ... at 12 we all left to do a bit of first-footing. On their last day there they had an enormous Scotch high tea, scones, Bannock cake, shortbread and lord knows what.

They reluctantly returned over the border, stopping briefly at Chevy Chase, the scene of great Scotch and English battle in 1314, where Percy Hotspur was wounded and Earl of Douglas killed. At Newcastle they met an old friend, Dr. Bromhall, who took Reg over the hospital while Linda explored the town, with its splendid new bridge over the Tyne, from which Sydney Bridge was copied, I believe ... lots of Roman things which have been dug up all along the walls round here. They reached Durham on 4th. January and went again to the cathedral: This time I admired the lovely Rose Window and was impressed by the end transept, called "The Transept of the 9 Chapels", here it is St. Cuthbert was brought and buried in about 10th. cent. At the west end is the Lady Chapel or Galilee Chapel and here it is the Venerable Bede is buried. At Stokesly they found "the most inviting old world inn", the Golden Lion, and stayed overnight. Next day they stopped at Ripon, said to be the 2nd. oldest cathedral city in England, so we inspected the cathedral, dating from Norman days.

Driving over the Yorkshire Moors they saw Bolton Castle, which is in the best condition of any I have seen in England. It was built in the 14th. cent. by the Scroope family and was besieged by Cromwell and since then has been unoccupied. It now belongs to Lord Bolton. They climbed up Wensley Dale to the top of the pass, and were completely in the heart of the snow region, nothing but snow- capped hills to be seen for miles around. At York they visited the famous Minster: It is lovely inside, belonging to the Perpendicular Decorated Period, 13th. to 15th. cent., but I think its chief beauties are the glorious glass windows, the west window nicely mullioned and the long slim five sisters, a beautiful rose window and some glorious old glass are at the side of the choir. York is famous for its old glass, containing more than any cathedral in England, some dating from Norman times. We climbed right to the top of the main tower and had a good view of the city and parts of its old Roman wall ... took a short walk round some of the fascinating little narrow streets, the tops of the old houses bulging so much that they are nearly meeting from opposite sides of the streets.

After that they headed over the Cat and Fiddle Pass across the wild Derbyshire Moors ... passing the lovely old town of Knutsford where lived Mrs. Gaskell and about which "Crawford" was written and got back to Liverpool on 7th. January, to find it "transformed by snow". Reg resumed his course and Linda her previous activities. On 25th. Reg returned to Oswestry and she went for a gorgeous walk, never going on the main roads at all. I walked through the grounds of Chirk Castle ... then on through a lovely path through the bracken fern, crossing the river at Castle well, then right over the hills at the back. Snow was thick everywhere and the sunshine out and everything seemed glorious. I actually got warm climbing the hills and took my hat off to give my hair some sun and wind. I found a poor little frozen robin, there are lots of them dying for want of food and water just now when everything is frozen hard ... followed the stream all the way back to Chirk, having done 3 1/2 hours solid walking.

The next weekend they took the car up the Pennine Chain to Buxton, buried deep in snow ... went up the hill at the back and watched the crowds tobogganing and skiing. Linda continued her golf and walking and on 12th. February drove to Wales with two fellow-boarders: I was itching to walk in all this lovely country, but Miss C. and Mr. W. are not good walkers, so I gave in gracefully and we drove all the time. Back in Liverpool, seeing children in the park "made me homesick for Jennifer so badly". At tea with Mrs. Edelstein, two of the guests seemed very well read and intelligent. Conversation flowed on all topics - Russia, reconstruction of Palestine, homosexuals, etc. Going home Mrs. R. said that she was amazed at it all, she said she couldn't imagine English women talking on these subjects to people they didn't know. On another walk she went over the fields to Thornton Hough. It was snowing heavily and I revelled in it, it was a lovely glorious feeling alone in a silent snowing world. It was fine and powdery and didn't wet much, so indulged in my romantic feelings with no undue discomfort. I got to Park Gate about 2.30 having been walking for 2 hours.

On a drive with Mrs. Edelstein on 21st. February they found Lower Pevery, with a lovely little Parish church. We went inside and found it heavily timbered with wonderful old oak beams and all the pews were enclosed like railway carriages. She went skating again and learnt to waltz, at which she "got on splendidly". Going home in a snowstorm was very thrilling and I felt joyous and elated as I battled my way home. On 4th. March Linda caught a train to Calderstones and walked to Woolton, about 6 miles away: Spring was in the air, the hedges were sprouting and the skylarks were in full song, and walking out in the fields amidst it all I felt so mellow and peaceful, and how real the truth and joy of nature is. That evening she had a talk with her fellow-boarder, Mr. W.: We started to talk about sex and in the end he poured out his soul to me. Sex revolted him, apparently. I tried to put things right for him as best I could and when I saw his poor troubled soul in his eyes I waxed quite eloquent. I think I must have helped him, he said I was the most sensible person he had ever known, that he never really talked about it before and felt that he could now think differently about things.

She went skating again and waltzed with her instructor, Santall, who told me all his love affairs, he is a nice lad and very handsome. She and Reg drove to Blackpool to see the sights: of course it was empty at this time of the year. A ghastly place, hotels, boarding houses, Luna Parks etc. stretch along for about 3 miles. All sign of sand and sea seems entirely obliterated by the huge concrete boulevards and promenades. Another day they went to Aintree to see the course where the Grand National steeplechase was shortly to be run: There were thousands there and I heard much good Lancashire and had a good foretaste of the big day itself, as all the tipsters and sideshow men were there. I liked seeing the barges on the canal and was interested to see one being towed by an old slow horse. On a "gorgeous spring day" they drove to a place called Rivington, on a chain of pretty small lakes and behind which interesting hills rear themselves up ... Lord Leverhulme seems to own much land around here and has built himself a lovely house in the hills and down on a point jutting into the mere stands a half-finished copy of a medieval castle which he started, but death raced him to it.

On 21st. March, at tea-time, I was seized with awful cramping pains in my tummy. They increased in violence and I was glad to get home and take some brandy. Didn't feel sick, just great pain. Went to bed and Reg treated me. She spent the next two days in bed, but was soon well again and walking with Miss Cossens from the boarding house: It was heavenly, a wonderful soft evening, the air so fresh and the thrushes and all the birds so joyous. I could have thrown out my chest and walked for miles. I couldn't as poor little Cossens can't walk at all, so we had to go at what seemed a snail's pace. On April Fools' day, as she was driving through lanes in Cheshire, Gazing up at the signposts and not looking, bashed into a huge furniture van and pushed it over. The front of our car was smashed to atoms, but by the grace of God no-one hurt ... I hated having to tell Reg but he was marvellous, always rises to the occasion in big things.

The car was towed to a garage at Northwich for repairs and they got a lift there next day: It looked a sad wreck, but the garage man was most efficient, said he'd work night and day to get it finished by next Saturday. He was as good as his word and had it ready just in time for them to return to London on completion of Reg's course. Linda went for a final walk to Hale, where she found some nurseries full of tulips out in all their glory, it might have been Holland, then we came on fields of daffodils, an amazing sight. We lay full length on the grass and feasted our eyes on them. They packed and said their farewells to their Liverpool friends, and on 8th. April collected the car to drive back to London.

8. ENGLAND, FRANCE AND ITALY REVISITED

Reg had arranged a series of visits to clinics and hospitals in London and on the Continent, combined with a driving tour. On the way back to London they passed through Shrewsbury: the Shropshire country was glorious, all the beautiful white blossom right out, spring is very far advanced. At Stratford they had a look over Ann Hathaway's cottage at Shottery, Shakespeare's birth and deathplace and of course the new theatre, beautifully situated on the Avon. We had a drink at a very old inn called the Garrick. Back at their "digs" at 108 Westbourne Terrace, they visited Harrow and walked up to the church on the hill, stood on the spot where Byron stood and wrote famous lines. This time Linda found that London is bewildering and tiring, one sees so much that I feel I'll never decide on anything ... Reg and I went to see my man about the Chippendale chairs and Reg roared them up and they promised faithfully to get the guarantee by Thursday.

On 13th. April they took a driving test for their licences for the Continent: I went first unfortunately, and when the man told me to brake I braked suddenly and a taxi ran into me. Policeman arrived and I had to go through the same old harrowing formalities. Later they drove through the Stowe Valley, which is Constable country. It was glorious, the loveliest in England, it is so unspoilt ... country so lovely that it seemed unreal, almost as if we were in one of Constable's landscapes. At Melford they stopped overnight at the Bull Inn, which has been an Inn for 350 years, and before that was a house of a wealthy weaver. Melford was in the 16th. cent. a centre for a big woollen weaving industry ... The dining room and lounge have still the old beamed walls and ceilings and wonderful old fire places. Next day they visited Bury St. Edmunds and spent a fascinating hour prowling round. There are remains of the old monastery building where the martyr St. Edmund was buried, he was killed by the Danes in 8th. cent. We went to a lovely old church, St. Mary's, where on the same spot a church has stood since 633 A.D. ... it had a wonderful carved oak roof, said to be the finest in the world.

Linda and Reg then drove via Yarmouth, where we saw hundreds of little fishing boats berthed along the river, all the herring fleet having a rest on Good Friday, I suppose, to Norwich in the Norfolk Broads country, with very old narrow cobbled streets and funny old crooked houses. One of these was the Maid's Head Inn, which has been an inn for 400 yrs., they have just unearthed an interesting old 15th. cent. fireplace, with great stone seats on each side. Queen Elizabeth once slept there. At Sandringham they passed the Royal residence: The surroundings were perfect, the lush parklands were alive with great fat pheasants and they spent the night at the Duke's Head in King's Lynn, which was a flourishing prosperous town in the days of the Flemish woollen weaving.

On 15th. April they reached the estuary of The Wash, where the country was dead flat, lots of windmills working and every now and again we came on fields of daffodils growing in the open, a lovely sight. There they came across the village of Boston, which was once a flourishing tea port and has a wonderful church and a still more wonderful decorated and carved steeple 286 ft. high. Their next stop was at Lincoln: we had a wonderful view of Lincoln Cathedral about 4 miles out of Lincoln, it is magnificently situated on a hill, somewhat like Durham ... It is magnificent, the West font especially so, and parts of it are original Norman ... the nave and choir pens Gothic, while the chancel part is more the decorated period. It is all very richly carved. At Melton Mowbray We went into all that remains of Oakham Castle, the old banquetting hall. It is lined with all sorts and shapes of horseshoes given by different Royalties and peers of the Realm, from Elizabeth, Prince of Wales, Duke of Wellington etc.

They travelled on to the Fen country, where at St. Ives they admired the 19th. cent. bridge over the Ouse, it has a small chapel in the middle of it. At Ely, the enormous cathedral stands out from the surrounding Fen country. It is a magnificent building outside, with its exquisite lantern towers. Heading back towards London they stayed a night at the famous Blue Boar Inn at Cambridge, where they visited the colleges and wandered in the courtyards and through the lovely "backs". St. John's, Trinity and King's are the 3 most imposing colleges ... had a look at the little round church of St. Sepulchre's, solid Norman and very old, one of the 4 remaining in England of round churches of Knights Templars.

On return to London they arranged their passage back to Australia; "booked our passage, Moreton Bay, July 19, £58 each, best cabins." After visiting their friends the Illingworths at Sidcup, they stayed the night at Folkestone at the Pier Hotel and had a feed of steak and eggs and chips, 3/ 10 the lot. It was a matey place, we gathered round the bar after and chatted and others played the piano. Reg thought it was a potential brothel. They crossed the Channel by car ferry to Boulogne on the 21st. April and drove to Berck-sur-Mer, where they Chose a moderate-looking hotel, Hôtel de la Paix, en pension 45 francs per day each ... We called on Doctor Jacques Calvé, the great orthopaedic man. He spoke hardly any English but we got on well and fixed up a good day for Reg tomorrow and asked me to have tea with his wife, who is American. The next day Linda Dressed up in my new navy blue clothes and went at 5 o'clock to take tea with Madame Calvé. She was extremely nice.

They drove to Rouen: It is very ancient, has been an archbishopric since 3rd. cent. It is full of narrow streets and quaint old bulging houses and wonderful churches ... The outside of the cathedral was truly wonderful, all the beautiful stone carving so fine and exquisite that it looked like lace. It is one of the finest specimens of Gothic architecture ... It was here that Joan crowned the Dauphin King of France ... we admired the wonderful Gothic carving of the Palace of Justice and the old town clock forming a gateway across a street, then we went to the Market Place and saw where

Joan was burnt at the stake. After another day working with Dr. Calvé and an old friend, Dr. Tucker, Reg drove them to Paris, where they stayed at the Hôtel des Marevaux.

Here by way of contrast they went to the Folies Bergères: The Folies were as usual, but we both agreed not nearly so magnificent as formerly ... I enjoyed watching all the prostitutes plying their trade, they work tremendously hard and the place is alive with them ... Reg took me to a place in the low seamy part, Rue Blondel, called "Au Bel Poulet". It is just a very low brothel, the women being the lowest of the low. As soon as we entered Madame clapped her hands and we were surrounded by about 30 naked women all pressing in on us ... We sat and drank our beer and watched. I couldn't believe my eyes, women of all shapes and sizes. We sat for about an hour and saw plenty. Next day Reg took me down by the Markets to the Cap Pharamond, Rue de la Grande Turanderie, and there we had the famous Tripes à la Mode de Caen. Afterwards they walked round the city and watched the gay Parisians, oh how smart and chic the women are, it is the way they manage their hair and hats, their neat feet and their gloves.

Their next excursion prompted a reference to the Great Depression, then nearly ended: to the Casino de Paris to see the famous Josephine Baker, but Reg and I weren't impressed. The places have lost their dash, they seem passé now, how Paris must miss the tourists, specially the Americans. While Reg visited another hospital, Linda had a look round the Galeries Lafayette, bought a navy blue beret for 15 francs. Met Reg and his little girl friend Jean Something, the one he met crossing over coming back from Italy ... we walked along the gay Avenue de Clichy, round the Place Pigalle, past the "Moulin Rouge", it was all most amusing and interesting. We went into book shops, looked at all the salacious French literature, postcards etc. I bought Lawrence's "Lady Chatterley's Lover" for 18 francs. It is banned in England and this is supposed to be unexpurgated.

On 28th. April they walked across the beautiful Pont Alexandre III to the Invalides where we inspected again Napoleon's tomb. It is a marvellous thing, I had quite forgotten how wonderful with the soft blue light playing through the windows and the gold light shining on the marvellous altarpiece with the Chapel showing through behind and then sunk down below the most inspiring massive porphyry cenotaph which I suppose actually contains Napoleon's remains. It is the Holy of Holies for France, we saw a gendarme rudely tell a man to remove his hat. Later that day they watched the students of the Latin Quarter thronging by. We sat fascinated for ages, there were all types and descriptions, we were just near the Sorbonne ... We dined in the Boulevarde Montparnasse, finding a wonderful cheap place with the most marvellous variety. It was called St. Cécile. I had turbot vol-au-vent and champignons and chocolate mousse all for about 10 francs. Finally they wandered along Rue Pigalle and had a beer in Fred Payne's bar, a most extraordinary little place. A nigger playing the piano, a fille de joie staring into space, Fred playing some gambling game and so on.

The following day they drove to the Salon, it was the first day it was open to the public and there were thousands there. Inside it is a huge place like Olympia ... The people there also were most interesting, I've never seen such weird hats, the artists with their sombrero touch while the women stick any sort of weird shape on their heads and carry it off with inimitable French chic. That evening, Reg took Jean and me to a marvellous place to dine near the Folies called "Au Pere Luiz". It was an artisty sort of place, check table cloths etc., chickens roasting in front of an open fireplace and the wall covered with signed photographs of actresses and well known artists etc. We had a marvellous feed including the most wonderful fresh asparagus.

On 1st. May they set off to drive to Switzerland, passing through Fontainebleu forest, where they found a lovely secluded spot in the forest and had our repas champêtre ... passed through Dijon, a lovely old town and old capital of Burgundy. They spent the night at Dole, "birthplace of the great Pasteur", and next day Did our shopping for lunch, 1 kilo of apples

3.40, 2 loaves of bread 60 cents, and a refill of vin de pays 4.50 ... another lovely day, climbed up through the Juras to the Swiss frontier ... came into sight of the snow-topped Alps. We stopped and sat in a field and lunched and gazed upon them. They went up the Rhône Valley: The valley in spring was a sight, the fruit trees all in blossom and the lush green fields gay with wildflowers and on either side towered up the great snow topped Alps ... arrived at Hilary Roche's sanatorium about 7. He and his wife gave us a warm welcome and showed us to the loveliest room with a superb view ... They have just built this wonderful new place about 2 yrs. ago, it cost £70,000 all subsidised by T.B. people and their relatives.

Linda and Reg stayed two nights with the Roches and then returned to France en route to Monte Carlo. On 5th. May they passed through Briançon, a wonderful drive right through the mountain fastnesses ... quaint old town surrounded by mountains, all of which are heavily fortified ... had a puncture and Reg found his wheel brace had been stolen. They arrived at Nice next day and took the Moyen Corniche road to Monte and what a drive it is, it surely is the most fascinating and beautiful coast in the world. At Monte Carlo they stayed at the Hotel Windsor and met Reg's cousin Lillias and Aunt May, who were living there. They visited the Casino, which was full of awful people and the atmosphere was asphyxiating as usual, we watched the Baccarat, Roulette, etc. Another trip was to the Palace: I have been reading Sir Frederic Treeve's book on the Riviera and the history of Monaco is fascinating as are the Grimaldi family, part of the old Guelph party which was thrown out of Genoa by the Ghibellines and have reigned there ever since.

On 7th. May they drove to Gorbio, a glorious old village perched high up on a spur of rock in the middle of the ravine. We had to leave the car in the only flat place, the square. The houses were all huddled close up together and the steep narrow streets went up in steps under old archways. Picturesque and malodorous. From there they continued to La Turbie, almost as old as the hills it is perched on, the Romans had it for a long time and there is still a great tower built by the Romans to commemorate their victory, also 2 old Roman gateways ... wandered about and found it was all a mass of fortifications, as are all the other hills round about and obviously new since the war ... walked along to another huddled up picturesque ancient village called Eze. It is built upon a spur of rock and has known a violent past. We climbed right up through its winding steep narrow arcaded streets to the top, where there were remains of the old tower and here we sat and drank in the beauty for an hour or so. Their last evening was a glorious moonlight night and Monte with all its lights twinkling right up the mountain side was like a fairy land. The Casino being a brilliant patch of light in all the twinkles.

Linda and Reg crossed the Italian border on 9th. May; when they stopped for lunch Our Italian was out of practice and we didn't manage very well and got stung over 30 liras for a very poor lunch, however we travellers buy our experience dearly. They went to Milan and stayed at the Rosa Hotel. While Reg arranged to see a Dr. Galleazzi work, Linda went to the castle of the Sforzas ... wandered through the Ducal apartments where the ceilings and walls were marvellously painted. They certainly lived in great splendour ... Coming back to meet Reg I saw the streets were lined with people and glorious looking soldiers, asked what it was and was told the King was passing after having opened an exhibition in the park. I met Reg at the cathedral where there was a great crowd and about 2 minutes later the King passed in an open carriage and drove on to the Palazzo Reale.

Afterwards they visited the cathedral: it is a glorious inspiration inside and out. Huge gothic columns, wonderful windows. The ceiling is painted to look like carved stone, it is a wonderful effect. They also went to Sant Ambrosio, a funny old church rich in frescoes, mosaics etc. and full of pagan symbols alongside Christian. We paid 2 lira to see the Altar of Gold, a magnificent thing studded in pearls and precious stones of all sorts. When

81

Reg returned to work, Linda walked on to the Chiesa Della Grazie and gazed on Leonardo da Vinci's fresco of the Last Supper ... As I was going home ran into another huge crowd outside the Palazzo Reale so clambered up on the side of the cathedral and presently the King came out and bowed to the populace. At night they gazed on the cathedral which was floodlit. I think it is quite one of the loveliest sights I've ever seen. We were lucky as it was only lit for one night in honour of the King.

On 11th. May they travelled to the Cartosa di Pavia about 17 kilos from Milan. It was once a Carthusian monastery and was fostered by the Visconti and Sforza family. To describe its wealth of beauty and art treasures would be impossible. Some say it is the finest building in all Italy. The facade of the church is patterned in different coloured marble, mostly richly carved and it makes you gasp with wonder when you first see it. Inside are treasures upon treasures, altars of mosaic in marble and precious stones, paintings by all the famous men of the day, bronze work, woodcarving and ivory carvings. Next day they drove to Cernobbio on Lake Como, where they stopped and had a drink at the famous Villa D'Este Hotel, they charged us 15 lira for coffee and beer but it was worth it to see the place. We drank on a beautiful shady flowery terrace right on the brink of the lake with most gorgeous view. Further on, As we got to the head of the lake the mountains got higher and higher and closed in more on the lake and it is really more beautiful, only there are no villas or pleasure resorts up that end, only quaint little old villages.

At Pavia There was only one expensive hotel there so chose a local albergo ... got a room for 12 lira, quite nice and clean and overlooking an inner courtyard. We had great fun using our Italian and we managed to get all we wanted and our hosts were smiling and friendly. The following day they explored the town again, it has an old cathedral and a university founded by Jean Visconti in 1300 and something, also a Visconti castle of 13th. cent. ... wandered round the markets, bought some lunch, saw the old women skinning the frogs alive, a horrible sight. Moving on to Genoa, they found Its lovely pinky reddy yellowy houses rising up one on top of the other from the beautiful blue harbour from where they drove along the Ligurian coast which is equal to the Riviera ... left the main road and went down to Marghanita and Portofino, about 8 kilos. Portofino is a dream place, quaint and colourful. The women were all making wonderful lace.

The next stop was Massa, where we camped the night at the Ristorante Florentino, it was a simple local inn and we had great fun with the Italian, all the inmates helping us by making signs. We got a clean room but no running water. On 14th. May they reached Pisa, and climbed the tower and went into the cathedral, they are both built of beautiful pink marble like alabaster. Nearby was Lucca, an old Tuscan town in the hills with lots of wonderful churches ... on to Pistoia, another famous Tuscan town, we walked up the main Piazza where there are wonderful red medieval buildings, a touch of Florence. They stopped that night at the Corona D'Or Hotel in Bologna, where Reg had arranged to see a Dr. Potti.

Next day Reg and I took the tram up to San Michele in Bosio where Potti's hospital is and I left Reg to go to work and I wandered round the hill where there were lovely villas and gardens and a great view of Bologna ... after lunch went into the old University, which is supposed to be the oldest in the world. It was here that they first dissected on human bodies. The following morning "Reg went off at 7.30 to work with the great Potti"; later they went to tea at the Poggiolis'. There were many Italians there including the Principessa Greoloni and her very nice daughter who talked English and Josephine Adami (Hardwick of Perth) was there so I talked to her most of the time. While Reg worked again, Linda next day Took the funicula up to San Luca to see the famous virgin, she is being brought down today for her yearly visit to the cathedral. It is a great procession and all the peasants from near and far follow her down the hill. They have built a huge covered arcade all the way down the hill to bring her in case it rains. I walked down the arcade, it is quite a mile long. After lunch she called on Mrs. Poggioli and we went up to Josephine Adami ... Reg came about 7 and we stayed on to dinner and met the dashing John. He is a darling, gay and handsome. We had a cheery dinner, drinking lots and lots.

On their last day in Bologna, they Got a lovely fat mail from Australia which Reg and I devoured ... down Via Mazzini poking into all the beautiful red courtyards. Went into San Stephano, which is built on an old pagan temple and dates from the 4th. cent. We saw a real old sacrificial pagan altar. They travelled on 19th. May to San Marino, a tiny independent republic perched right up on a rocky crag, lord of all it surveys. That night they reached Ravenna, where they stayed at the Albergo Capello, and next day set out to explore the town. First to the fine old town square where on 2 great columns are perched the statues of the 2 saints, Sant Appolinare and S. Vitale (a soldier). We passed the house Byron lived in and wrote "Childe Harold", near Piazza Byron, where also is the tomb of Dante who died here. Later they went into the Archbishop's Palace, where amongst many old Roman and Byzantine relics and works of art was a famous chain of ivory all exquisitely carved, said to belong to Emperor Maximilian in about the 4th. cent.

Another experience there was a visit to the jewel of Ravenna, Church of S. Vitale, where we got a guide. It dates from the 4th. cent. and the mosaics there are the earliest and the loveliest, being Roman in soft lovely greeny colours and the figures so clear and full of life. I had never imagined mosaics could be so lovely ... The church itself is a gorgeous building, octagonal in shape and full of the most beautiful marbles, wonderful Roman and Byzantine columns.

Linda's old friend from her previous visit to Italy with her father, Ugo Ballelli, had contacted her and arranged to come to Venice to see them, so they duly went on there via Padua, "a lovely old town teeming with interest" and with a university "next oldest after Bologna". At Venice they stayed at the Hotel Vittoria, where "we got en pension terms for 40 lira each".

They met Ugo the next day: He had got quite fat and had a very bad breath and on the whole I wasn't pleased to see him. However the poor thing had travelled all night on the train, so had to put a good face on things ... poor Ugo, I think his expectations far exceeded the realisation. Afterwards they went sightseeing: had an hour's gondola with a charming gondolier, Armandi, who grossly overcharged us of course, 15 lira instead of 12. However, we loved it, it was just evening and everything was so still and lovely. We glided down the Grand Canal and he pointed out all the famous palazzi, where Browning died, Byron lived and Gabriel D'Annunzio and his love Eleonora Duse, Don Carlos of Spain and many others. We went as far as the Rialto and came back through the small canals under the Bridge of Sighs. Later they went for a stroll through the Piazza, crowded with people and music everywhere, it is always a fascinating scene, it is the centre of Venetian life ... to a serenata where there were 2 or 3 gondolas lit with gay coloured lanterns and the Italians singing and playing mandolins ... oh, it was all so lovely and enchanting.

The following day they bumped into Ugo again, he had missed his train to Rome, and he joined them in a visit to the Palazzo Papadopoli: the old family majordomo showed us around. It was an enormous place and had priceless old things, paintings by Tiepolo, Gobelin tapestries, Spanish leather, French and Italian brocade on the walls, Venetian glass chandeliers, etc. He showed us too a few of the private apartments, I was most interested in the photos of various members of the family, also an autograph which was signed by the Kaiser, 1914. At the Frati church they saw a huge picture, the Assumption by Titian and a really lovely one of Virgin and Child by Bellini. They visited a glass factory and watched blowing and fashioning beautiful glass things by hand ... saw all sorts of marvellous glass, eventually bought 2 strings of crystal, green for me, blue for Mum, 155 lira the two. Reg also

bought me a green ring in a nice old setting for 65 lira. The next day they bid farewell to their Italian friends.

9. Austria, Germany and Holland

Linda and Reg now headed for Vienna. Entering the Dolomites, they crossed the Austrian frontier on 23rd. May near Villach, spending the night at the Post Hotel there. Next day they were held up for 2 hours while we had a new axle pin made ... things seem very cheap ... all the people in their funny clothes, men in shorts, little jackets and quaint hats with feathers. En route they stopped at a country Gasthaus while Reg had a pot of beer. Reg had another pot when we got to the top of the Semmerang Pass.

At Vienna they stayed at the Graben Hotel, where they "got a large room for 15 shillings". Reg had arranged to work with the American Medical Association and later accompanied Linda by train to the Schönbrun Palace, the old winter palace of the Emperors, begun by Charles VI of Austria, finished by Maria Theresa ... lived in by Franz Josef who died here in 1916, Carl and Zita abdicated there. The gardens are truly beautiful, more so than Versailles, we wandered all round and feasted our eyes on the statues and wonderful vistas and beds of the most colossal tulips I've ever seen. They found that The coffee houses are great places, you are supplied with all sorts of papers and people sit reading for hours like clubs. Reg spent a day at a Dr. Behler's clinic and Linda visited the shops: they are really exciting, much more so than Paris, I think ... walked right along the Ringenstrasse. A wonderful street surrounded by gardens and trees, mostly chestnuts now out in gorgeous pink and white blossoms. They met their old friend Dr. Tucker again and dined with him at Pataky's Hungarian Restaurant, where "the zigeuner music is glorious, so rich and mellow". He and Reg worked again at the A.M.A. and later took Linda to the Rathaus Keller and the Dorotheum, a huge auction place filled with rubbish and beautiful old antiques of all sorts.

On 28th. May they started a day of sightseeing at the Spanish Riding

School in the Hofburg, where they saw a magnificent display of marvellous horses, all white and silver grey, and then Baden, a lovely old town on the slopes of the Wiener Wald ... it was near here Beethoven wrote the Moonlight Sonata. Next they saw Mayerling, where Rudolph the crown prince had his unhappy end, his mistress taking an oriental revenge so he shot her and himself. Finally they went through Mödling, a very old town in the Wiener Wald and the ancient seat of the Battenbergs. There were ruins of old castles all round the hills ... we had a magnificent view of Vienna at our feet and the great Danube carving its way through the plain to the Black Sea. From here we went to Kahlenburg (an old castle) which is still higher up in the forest. There is a great tower here built for the Crown Princess Stephanie from where she could see over the Hungarian border and all the peaks of the Alps. We climbed up, it was dusk about 8.30 and we had one of the loveliest views I've ever seen. Linda went home to bed after a perfect day. I feel I've done Vienna now.

They drove the following day to Kreuzenstein Castle: it hasn't been lived in since 1645. It has all been restored and is furnished with marvellous old antiques. Back in Vienna we had some coffee and Viennese pastry at a cafe in the heart of the chestnuts, the white blossom of which was gently falling all the time and looked like snowflakes ... wandered into the Stadt park after. It is a marvellous place, beautiful statuary and terraces wonderfully lit. On their last day, while Reg worked, Linda packed and went shopping: they had such wonderful toys I'd like to have bought a German toyshop, but it was the carrying of it around. I then took the train over to the Belvedere Palace, once belonging to Prince Eugene, famous statesman, warrior etc. in Austrian history. The palace is a marvel of Baroque art.

They said their goodbyes and set off for Budapest: The Hungarian plain is supposed to be the most fertile in the world, and certainly they had cherry trees growing along the roadside. They found a pension just off the

Main Promenade on the Danube ... Buda is the other side, the old town built on a steep hill, and all the most important buildings were floodlit. Pest is the new part and flat, and has a length of wonderful hotels, restaurants, gardens etc. along the Danube gazing over to the lights of Buda. Next day they went to the Royal Palace, a magnificent building on a plateau-like hill overlooking the Danube and Pest ... the ballroom was specially lovely, all of a beautiful soft marble and silver. They visited Central Park, "famed as a spa and bathplace": all round the baths are fountains, gardens, tea tables, music, dancing, we had an ice in these beautiful surroundings.

On 1st. June they drove to Lake Balaton: The country is amazingly fertile and the vegetation so luxuriant that it looks quite tropical. The villages were very primitive, the houses made of mud and straw with thatched roofs. On the chimney of one was a stork's nest and 2 great storks perching on it ... I picked a huge bunch of red poppies and blue cornflowers, all the way along was ablaze with them and they look so lovely growing with the white daisies. They crossed back into Austria, but next day Found the car had another broken stub axle, so had to wait 2 hours while a new one was made. Had a lovely walk meanwhile along the banks of the swift-flowing River Mur. They continued on Through mountain valleys all the way, the fields were ablaze with wild flowers ... I gathered gorgeous wild pansies and forget-me-nots ... We passed through Bad Isehl where Franz Josef had a summer villa, where Elizabeth went from Bavaria to stay with him.

At Salzburg they stayed at the Hotel der Löve, where they got "a room for 8/- and mine host knew a few English words". They walked round the town: The River Salzach flows through it and on either side rise steep rocky crags, on which are perched grand old Schlossen. The town seems to be all old archways. Next day they climbed up the steep hill behind to the great massive schloss which is perched on top, Hohen-Salzburg, it was the palace castle of the prince archbishops of Salzburg. We had a magnificent view all round ... wandered round the monastery of St. Peter into the beautiful

Collegium church ... Haydn is buried there and Salzburg is the birth place of Mozart.

They entered Germany on 3rd. June and travelled to Munich, down the great Maximilian Strasse and parked in the Josef Platz. We lunched at the Hofbrauhaus, a huge beer hall, plain tables round an open courtyard decorated with beer barrels. People were drinking the biggest pots of beer I've ever seen. Reg and I polished one off between us. Afterwards they had decided to drive slowly round to see the main features of Munich. However, going slowly along Ludwigstrasse a maniac on a bicycle dashed into us, wasn't hurt but beat up his machine. A crowd collected and one nice man gave us his name, they all knew it was his fault. However, we made a getaway before police and formalities of delay would occur. They then pushed on to Rothenburg and I'm glad we did, it is quite the most enchanting place I've ever seen ... The old walls and towers and gates are perfectly intact. The old pointed houses are perfect gems.

After that they headed west, passing through Heilbronn, from where we followed the Neckar down to Heidelberg. It was a beautiful drive and the river a pretty sight crowded with gay canoes, it is Whitsunday today. At Heidelberg they drove round looking for hotels, all full, a holiday weekend. At last we dug in with a funny old girl who let us have her best bedroom ... quite nice and clean but crowded with all her treasures, gas light and no running water. After dinner they had an early foretaste of the ominous rise of the Nazi Party: drove up to the old ruined schloss on the steep hill at the back of the town. There was a big firework display on and they put flares in the castle and made it look as if it was burning and had a mock bombardment ... They had a huge swastika as a firework and the people all sang about Hitler and made the sign ... we had a beer in the Biergarten where the students have their duels once a week. Next day they explored further and came to a little white gasthaus nestling in shady trees and garden, Gasthaus Hirschgasse. This is the famous place of Heidelberg, the headquarters of their duels. Mine host took us all round and showed us everything, the swords, where they fight, the floor of which was much bespattered with blood where they had their wounds dressed after. They have been fighting here since 1090.

Passing through Ludwigshafen and Mannheim they reached Mainz, where every house seemed to fly the German flag and the Swastika, I've never seen so many flags. The roads were crowded with holiday makers, hikers, bands of youths and girls, carrying flags etc., they seem to delight in flag waving ... had a meal on the terrace of a very famous and old restaurant, the Krone. This part is celebrated for wine, so we had a bottle of good Rhenish wine and gazed out onto the Rhine and the lovely wooded hills and castles.

They crossed the border into Holland on 6th. June: The country from here was delicious ... just like one beautiful garden all the way ... Canals, windmills and the villagers actually wearing their clogs. They made for Leyden to visit Linda's friend Mr. Abandanon, but found it entirely devoid of decent hotels. In desperation we put up at the Hotel au Commerce opposite the station. We got a poky room into which we could hardly get our luggage and for which we had to pay 4.50.

The following day they moved to the Pension Zaese, where Bandy rang up about 9 and asked us to come and see him in the afternoon ... found Bandy's abode. He was waiting for us with Anneke who is 11 now and very tall, slim and lovely. Bandy is much the same, though a little older looking. Mrs. A. is just quiet and sweet and then there was a wonderful great big son with a nice good face. It was good to see him again. Reg went to work next day with a Professor Jansenn in The Hague, while Linda met Bandy and we went for a walk in the woods. He told me all about himself, he has no job and is eating his heart out with impatience, pent-up energy, has all sorts of schemes and does a little writing. They visited Amsterdam and stopped at Haarlem on the way, which is a lovely old Dutch town surrounded by woods and with a nice market square. All round here we could see the remains of the tulip fields. In Amsterdam they had a bun in the Ryks Museum, saw Rembrandt's famous "Night Watch" ... saw a little of old Amsterdam, it is more Dutch looking than The Hague.

On 11th. June they drove to The Hague and had lunch at a lovely little place in the woods, the queen mother has a house just opposite, returning to the Abandanons for dinner. Linda's birthday was next day: Well, my birthday was over and I hadn't realised it, however I'm glad as Anneke asked me my age and I was able to say 29. They lunched with Professor and Mrs. Jansenn, and had an hour's tramp in the sand dunes, it was glorious, the earth and trees smelt so good in the rain. We went to a pretty little village called Warmardt and had tea at a delightful Dutch restaurant that had gardens going down to the banks of a big canal, it was called Den Meerast. They had a Hungarian band there to add to the delights. On the way home they went round the old canals and back ways of Leyden and found some wonderfully picturesque spots, the Vischemarkt and an old red house called the Burcht, which was originally an old castle.

Their last day was spent at The Hague, where they had lunch at a place run by an ex-flunkey at Wilhelmina's court, he had grown too fat to be a court man any more. He was enormous but still had his courtly bows and manners and gave us an excellent lunch. Linda found that It was sad to say goodbye to Bandy, I feel I have not seen nearly enough of him. They drove back to France: It was a slow journey as we had to pass through the enormous city of Rotterdam, over bridges and 2 ferries, then over the border and into Belgium and through Antwerp, which is a large and beautiful city, then we had to take a ferry over the Scheldt. From there on the country was very pretty, but we had those rotten paved roads all the way.

En route they stopped at Ghent, which "looked marvellous, beautiful square and buildings", and at Bruges: enchanting, we crossed over the canal and entered the city through a medieval gateway, drove through narrow streets and found the main square with the Hotel de Ville and great belfry tower ... stayed the night at a cheap pub, St. Hubert, bed for 30 francs or 2/6 each. Next day they "left by another marvellous old gateway" and so on to Boulogne, where they caught the Channel car ferry on 14th. June: being first on we were last off. The customs were quite disagreeable about my dresses, suspecting that they were bought abroad, which they were not, however I wasn't charged any duty ... stopped at Sidcup with the Illingworths for the night.

The diary ends here, although they were not due to sail from London to Australia for another month. It was the last overseas trip Linda would make until after World War II.

LINDA (LEFT) WITH HER SISTER RITZA AND FATHER IN LONDON, 1922

LINDA (CENTRE) AND HER FATHER (REAR) ON BOARD S.S. ORANA
WITH FRIENDS EN ROUTE TO ENGLAND, 1925

RIGHT
LINDA'S FATHER IN HIS GARDEN WITH HER
FIRST CHILD, JENNIFER, 1930

BELOW
LINDA'S HUSBAND REG DURING THEIR VISIT
TO ENGLAND, 1932-33

LINDA AT THE GWALIA MINE, 1942

REG AND LINDA WITH JEANETTE DE NIO AT VINCENNES, 1951

LINDA WITH THE ABANDANONS AT DELDEN, NETHERLANDS, 1951

LINDA WITH THE BENSONS (VIOLET, L. GEORGE, R.) AND GUESTS
AT THE ENTRANCE TO HER HOME AT 5 BAY VIEW TERRACE, MOSMAN PARK, W.A. 1951

LINDA AND REG IN THEIR GARDEN, 1952

DINING WITH LADY DOLLIE BRUNTISFIELD, (RIGHT), KENYA, 1958

SAMPLING A HOOKAH AT ISTANBUL, 1963

RIDING A MULE AT LINDOS, 1963

POSING WITH FRIEND IN MEXICO, 1964

REG ON NORTHERN SAFARI, 1965

At an outback camp, 1967

In the bar at Fitzroy Crossing, 1972

WITH WILDFLOWERS AT BOWRAL, 1974

PART THREE

WARTIME AND
EARLY FIFTIES:
MOTHER

On holidays at Augusta, W.A. with her children
(L. to R., Sonia, Jennifer, Tony).

Early in 1942 the Japanese threat to, and bombing of, northern Australia caused such concern in Perth that some families decided to evacuate until the situation clarified. Linda, now with three children, was one of those who took this decision, and in March she set off by train with two close friends, Jean Cuming and Margot Frayne and their children, to travel to Leonora, a small country town north of Kalgoorlie and about 600 kilometres northeast of Perth. If she kept a diary of this period it has not survived; this chapter consists of extracts from the letters she wrote to Reg at the time.

Her first letter was undated and written from the Gwalia Hotel: **This is the first more or less free moment I've had since we made up our minds to flee from our homes ... From the moment we left the Perth station the children were in the seventh heaven of delight and excitement. They rushed from one end of the train to the other, opened and shut windows, inspected lavatories, cupboards etc. ... The night was a bit hectic, Jennifer, Barbara and Ken were up all night, I'm told, getting out at each station. Sonia and Tony apparently slept fairly well. I ended up in a top berth with Jean and the baby below me. Margot had Gillian Ainslie and Julian in with her.** Their stop at Kalgoorlie savoured somewhat incongruously of luxury, thanks to kind friends: **We arrived at Kalgoorlie about 11.30 I think. Bernice Thorn and Rosalind were there to meet us. Bernice had packed us a most beautiful hamper of cold pigeons, chocolate cake etc. The Railway Hotel hamper was delicious, lovely cold chicken all carved up, fresh brown bread and butter, lettuce, tomatoes, hard boiled eggs and a huge box of fruit.**

After that conditions started to deteriorate: **We had about 3 hours to wait at Broad Arrow owing to washaways and things. We quite enjoyed the break, Julian and Tony were shown all over the engine by the engine driver ... The worst part of the journey was the last part. The children were worn** to a frazzle with excitement and lack of sleep and having to wait till 11.30 p.m. seemed endless. When they arrived at Leonora, it was pouring with rain and we had to rush the sleepy children over to the hotel and then go back for all our innumerable packages ... Me and my family are all on the verandah and oh how we slept that first night. Linda had hoped to visit, and perhaps stay with, her friends the McKinnons at their outlying property, but Dan sent us a wire saying they were flooded out and the road would be impassable for 2 or 3 weeks.

She and her fellow-travellers had mutual friends living in Leonora, the Taylors and Gawlers, and they "found the Taylors' house right in the main street". From here they inspected various accommodation possibilities, including the nearby mining settlement of Gwalia, and we decided to hold a conference at night after all the children were in bed. After thrashing everything out we all decided on taking the place in Gwalia over the road. Acting on this decision, We inspected the Gwalia place again this morning. The woman is very nice and is already painting and cleaning and we feel we can make a good do of it. In fact we feel we are luckier than any of the other evacuees in Leonora in their stuffy little houses ... the place is a collection of semi-detached iron buildings. In the centre is a kitchen, large dining room and veranda. There is an open air laundry with 3 troughs and a copper. There are at least 10 little separate bedrooms with 2 beds in each and a chest of drawers. There is a large shower room and a bath room with a chip heater. There is also space where we can make a garden and 3 pepper trees, and there is also electric light.

They accordingly prepared to move in, and Linda let the McKinnons know; "we rang Dan this morning ... I feel sure he is very relieved". They visited the mine: The Sons of Gwalia mine is just behind the hotel and looks most lovely at night as it is brilliantly lit up, but by day the heat was "intense". Seeking relief, they went for a picnic to a water hole in the Taylors' trailer, and also found the mine had a lovely swimming pool, concrete bottom and sides. The kids are dying to swim in it, we have our doubts as to cleanliness as it is for the mine employees and their families and they are all the dirty dog type. Their white tin houses with chooks and goats and children everywhere remind me of Malta or any other Southern Mediterranean country. At the end of her first letter she wrote: I still think Margot the ideal person to evacuate with and so does Jean, her sense of humour is superb and she is magnificent altogether. We all agree having each other is the only one salvation ... J. and S. both swore they were going home to you on the next train (there are no trains at present owing to washaways). However, they've had a weep and a grizzle and feel much better now.

Her second letter was written from their Gwalia encampment, which they had christened "La Hacienda", and dated 1st. April: at the moment we are all feeling a bit jaded. It is a hectic life with so many young to be fed, bathed and disposed of ... I feel very far away and out of touch with you ... I hate to think of you sleeping in the house alone and all of us up here for heaven knows how long. On Tony's birthday she took the children for a "jaunt": The locals hanging round the pub gaze at us in fascinated wonder. I decided to take them to what looks like a huge dried up salt lake, but is really the sludge from the mine, I thought the kids could dig in it and pretend it was the beach ... eventually found a pipe gushing with filthy grey water which made sort of a creek. They wallowed in the grey slime having a glorious time. One wonders what the sludge actually contained, and after a while so did they: Binkie suddenly said there would be cyanide in the water as they use it to treat the ore. We leapt up in horror and grabbed them all and rushed them grey and filthy back to the hotel ... put them in the wash troughs.

They moved from the hotel to the mining settlement: We moved into the house on Sunday and it was high time we left the hotel, as I caught Tony having a large swig of beer from one of the most disreputable of the thirsty hotel clients ... The bill was quite reasonable, £12/7/6 for the 4 of us for 11 days. She described their routine: we start the day early as the mornings are glorious and we feel full of energy and rush round and do all our jobs. About noon it is very hot and a great langour sets in ... everything gets filthy with either the red dust or the red mud. The adults agreed to share the cooking week about, but Linda admitted I must say I have a few qualms about my prowess at cooking for this mob and with a wood stove ... six months with Jean and Margot will be as good as a 2 years' Domestic Science course at Invergowrie. She ended by discussing the children and saying "It will be a great relief to get them to school".

The next letter is dated 9th. April and starts by describing how they try to keep up to date with the war news, though their wireless has limitations: the volume is very low and it is really only possible for one person to hear by sitting close up to it. The daily round continued: Jean and I are struggling through our cooking week ... things get very hectic and it gets boiling in the kitchen at mid-day and we have a good old grump and grizzle, but we always cheer up, and we are getting on famously. We've all agreed to be absolutely frank and speak our minds so that no-one suffers in silence. Concerning the children, she felt The state school is going to be a marvellous experience for them ... toughen them up no end and they will get out of all that soft indulgent life that they had when we were at home and things were going well. She ended: I'm glad you are happy and busy, we are too really and feel we could be quite happy if we knew we could come home in 3 months.

However, in her next letter dated 17th. April, Linda wrote: I've got a feeling we are going to be up here for a long long time, I think the news is ominous and threatening to us although there is a temporary lull over Australia ... you must prepare yourself for a big bill to foot as the price of our safe evacuation. She had letters from friends in Perth who were "enjoying life": I must say we get a little sour when we read these letters. Our life is certainly not a bed of roses, what gets me most is the hecticness of all the children together. I long sometimes to have my own family to myself. She was also worried that I'm not a good worker, Margot and Jean are splendid and I feel that they both do much more than me.

When the roads re-opened she went to stay for two days with the McKinnons at their station "Pinnacles", a dear old homestead with a nice big lawn and garden and a perfectly marvellous vegetable garden, they pump about 20,000 gallons of water daily ... Dan says it has never looked better, he has never known such a good season. She found that Dan and Angie are feeling the strain a bit of having to share their home ... we feel we are the best off of all the evacuees up here ... They took me out to see the shearers' quarters, where we might have been living and honestly Reg I think we'd have all gone mad in a month if we'd stayed there.

In her fifth letter, written on 23rd. April, Linda reported: our spirits go up and down like a barometer, the weather plays a large part and this week has been very hot. The children come home roasting from school and turn up their noses at the food that we have sweated over the hot stove to cook, and we all get a bit downcast, however we cheer up as the cool of the evening descends, but then we seem to get eaten by mosquitoes and sand flies. She was concerned about her finances, as I think it will cost at least £6 a week for me and my family to live here. Everything is so expensive. Their daily activities kept them fit: Jenny, Sonia and Barbara have ridden into Leonora on their bikes to get some books they need for school ... today I scrubbed the kitchen floor, after which I was black and dripping with sweat ... Jean, Margot and I chop a bit of wood each day ... Mulga is the hardest wood imaginable. On the subject of the future, she felt that It is the uncertainty that is getting us now I think. However I suppose we can stick it till the spring and by then something ought to show us which way the wind will be blowing ... anything in the way of papers will be most welcome, and you and Jimmy will be welcomed with open arms when you come, may it not be too long.

When she wrote again on 29th. April the weather had changed: thunder and lightning, a good old blow then blessed rain, which found its way in odd places through our hessian lined walls. And for the first time we had to close down our open air stove ... Sunday was the most gorgeous cold almost frosty day. We all nearly baulked on the cold shower but were glad after that we had been brave as we felt so marvellously exhilarated. The other two husbands arrived for a visit, and I must say I felt very jealous that you weren't with them. They have both had a lovely time, the weather has been perfect, fresh morning and evenings and lovely moonlight nights. I really have had a big ache that you couldn't have been enjoying it too. On the credit side, The children are all settling down very well and getting used to school ... I feel we could happily stay here till September, we might as well have the benefit of the lovely crisp frosty winter, having got the hot weather behind us.

News was in great demand: Thanks sweet for the Bulletin. I really appreciate it as we hardly use the wireless at all, just to get the 9 o'clock news, so it is good to read up a bit. Mum sent me 2 most interesting Australasians and had all the known facts about the Java naval battle and it was interesting to get your titbits as well. The Battle of the Java Sea, in which the cruiser HMAS. Perth was sunk, had taken place at the end of February. Locally, because of the war, The talk is all about the closing of the mines, but they say this mine is in a good position, having lots of older men and also a large stock of chemicals. If it did close I suppose it would be goodbye to the town of Gwalia. Fresh food was sometimes a problem: Vegetables, fruit and eggs have been very hard to procure, none seem to come up on the trains lately. We have managed to get a few local eggs and we'll soon have our own beans, they are in flower already.

Linda's seventh letter was dated 7th. May and heralded an easing of the war situation (the Battle of the Coral Sea was just then taking place, effectively ending Japan's immediate threat): The train arrived up here last night about 8 o'clock, all the children stream over to see the fun ... Reading through the lines of your letter I thought you seemed tired and in need of a bit of fussing up and looking after. She had sounded out a Perth neighbour about a return: I wrote to Moll this mail ... asked her if she thought I ought to come home as I suppose there is no urgent reason now why we should remain here. With the change of season she was warming to Gwalia, and Sometimes I'm burstingly happy, I just can't help it. I really love this simple life, I adore the beautiful fresh sparkling mornings and getting up early and having a cold shower and being hungry for breakfast. I also adore the evenings and walking out on the desert plains and watching the sun set. The financial position was now clearer, too: I think it costs us roughly £1 per week per person, that is with electric light, very expensive here, water also expensive, wood also expensive and rent thrown in.

Her next letter was undated and anticipated a visit by Reg: We are all excited that you are coming up and hope to plan everything for the best ... I was full of plans for the childrens' holidays, however nothing has developed. However, their life was not without its excitements; one day Jean and I, Barbara and Ken, Jennifer and Sonia set out on our bikes to find some salt lakes about 6 or 7 miles along the old Menzies Road. We were full of the spirit of adventure, topees on head and knapsacks on back ... then Jen had a puncture which we could not fix. Anyway we sat down under the mulgas and ate our lunch and were happy except for the non-stop attack of flies. Then we explored 3 deserted mines ... got a lovely miner's lamp ... Then the question of getting back. I decided that Jen should ride my bike and I would wheel hers and walk home, not a pleasant prospect as about 4 or 5 miles at least and very hot. However as luck would have it at that moment a huge truck came along, the first sign of anything we had seen on the road since we set out. It gave me and the bike a lift into Leonora.

Linda arrived home to find that Tony had a temperature and was vomiting and in great pain. I got Dr. Wilson thinking it was appendicitis. However it proved to be some sort of a tummy germ ... He had 4 rotten days, lots of pain and very tender tummy, however we got him onto grated apple and boiled water and he has recovered and almost himself again. Anyway I haven't been able to go out, so that was the end of the holiday expeditions. Reg had replied to her overtures and she ended her letter: You feel we should stay here and the other husbands do too and we really feel it is the right thing ... we'll be counting the days till your arrival.

She wrote again on 22nd. May with suggestions for Reg's visit: To make your arrival more exciting than ever you might get a few comics for the bigger children and some sweets or something for the littler ones. The weather had become unseasonal: we have had 8 dull wet days running, with absolutely no sunshine, it is something that no one up here remembers before ... we have to slosh around in thick red mud. Two of her friends from Perth, Mabel Barrett and Margot Bunning, came to visit and it was the first time I've had a walk with other grown-ups and without children ... I took them up the hill round the mine to the ridge of rocky hills that lie at the back of the mine. Here are found the most incredible hovels of bits of tin and sacking, all round are chooks, goats and empty tins, it looks like something on the outskirts of Bombay or some awful native quarter. In fact all Gwalia looks a bit like that, but this part is just a bit worse, they even have to cart water.

Linda's final letter from Gwalia was dated 8th. June, after Reg's visit: You have come and gone again and I am feeling a bit adrift, the time just flew, that it now seems like a dream that you were ever up here with us ... it was glorious to have had you, you were so sweet and we all did love it. Jean Cuming was returning home in a week's time and I feel a bit miserable, in fact I feel as if I'd love to pack up and go too. However, I'll give it a fly with just Margot and I here together and if we can make a do of it I'll stay as I said I would until the end of the school term. Actually Jennifer and

Sonia will miss the Cuming family even more than I shall and I'm afraid Jen will be very sad without Bar and Jean. The weather had been a factor: the wet weather yesterday and today finally decided her. It is so difficult for her to find anywhere to put Hamish, as our yard is just a sea of mud ... You were lucky to get away yesterday as the rain started about 11 and kept on steadily and depressingly all day.

This caused various problems: Our wood position is acute as no-one can get out on the roads to bring in any wood and we are completely out ... Mr. Rowe told us to approach the hotel as he had let them have wood. Jean went over and asked them, they will let us have enough till the roads dry up. The damp also worsened any skin infections, and Poor Jenny has a nasty area with her Barcoo rot ... She got the plaster off last night and under it were two big sacs ... Jean opened them with a sterile needle and made them into flat open sores on which I laid thick your ointment. They look quite clean and much better this morning, but her arm is very swollen and painful. Her letter ended I must stop now as the news is on and I believe Sydney has been shelled or something ... I love you very much and would love to come home to you. You'll have to be prepared for an arrival back anytime I think.

Evidently they returned to Perth shortly after this. Linda's reference to Sydney is probably to the Japanese midget submarine attack on the harbour on 31st. May.

In the autumn of 1950 Linda made her first trip through the centre of Australia, travelling by bus with her son Tony to visit the childrens' ex-nanny, Noni Starke, in Darwin. Her diary starts en route on 16th. May at Ti-Tree Well on the Stuart Highway, north of Alice Springs: **Overnight at Aileron Station, owned by Fred Colson ... talked with Mrs. Colson, grew up in the Murchison, husband worked on railway sinking wells, lived in Alice Springs, bought Aileron 12 years ago. Fred went out with Lasseter to Reef.** A little farther on they "passed Central Mount Stuart, then got into very poor country" and afterwards **Passed Sterling Sand Plains Station ... Barrow Creek for lunch, interesting, surrounded by flat top hills. We saw over the Repeater Station, Telegraphman lives there for 3 years ... only in the last 7 years, before that relayed by hand with Morse Code. Saw the graves of 12 telegraph men shot by Blacks, Warramunga tribe in 1870.**

They then went on through arid country, dead cattle here and there, at Wycliffe Well saw a beautiful vegetable garden and a short time later **Got to Wauchope Hotel for afternoon tea, lovely cool cement building owned by Mrs. Lenderdam, daughter-in-law of Alice Springs Lenderdam. Green lawn, oleanders, Parkinsonia trees, Black Babies, rock melons, an oasis in the desert ... had a beer in bar, met a dear old pioneer English owner of the Whopper Mine in Tennant Creek.** After this Linda and Tony **went on our way and came to the Devil's Marbles, very impressive, great balls of red granite perched one on top of the other ... arrived at Tennant Creek, large town, 800 people and like an American midwest town, galvanised iron houses but 2 large modern hotels. We had gone 253 miles that day.** Next morning they were **Up early, lovely cool morning, walked to the hospital, saw the E.S.A. bank open up, man in pyjamas sweeping it, red tin building. After breakfast, steak and egg, went over the Government Battery, where** they crush ore, then on to Edna Beryl Mine, 5 men working shaft 167 ft. deep, gold 8 oz. per ton, most primitive, lived in mud hut.

Shortly after leaving Tennant Creek they came to Banka Banka, met Ward who owns the station, 1000 square miles, 11,000 cattle, bought 9 years ago, £17,000, now worth £120,000. Had just shipped 1100 cattle, got £25,000 and very pleased with life, employs 14 natives. A little farther on the country changed on the right side, Barkly Tableland stretching to Queensland. Rich grass, Mitchell and Flinders, bigger trees, dark green with big black pods, acacias in bloom, wild hibiscus, wild ti-tree, big sprouts of purple flowers like Geraldton wax, also lovely red bushes like flowering gums. They stopped for tea at a place called Elliott, an artificial town since the war, big aerodrome, a road going off to Mt. Isa, lots of new building going on, over 6000 houses, some government scheme ... Met old Mac, Scots publican and station owner at Newcastle Waters, said the whole thing was absurd, all government drones. Afterwards they pushed on 98 miles to Daly Waters, good grassy country and trees getting bigger ... a nice cool hotel surrounded by interesting garden, sat out in the garden and had cold beer under a shade house of paperbark ... They are building a big new Post Office. Tony and I found pure white lizards, Daly Waters very crowded and busy with lots of young men. After dinner took a stroll ... played snooker in the air force hostel.

On 18th. May they left Daly Waters and passed through thick spear grass, poor old trees, lots of deserted old army camps ... passed Birdum, the terminus of the Darwin Railway. Next they passed a lovely lagoon with water lilies and pandanus palms and crane-like birds, the scene of the old Elsley Station. We went into a graveyard where the bodies of the Waluka and Aeneas Gunn buried in 1902, there also the grave of the Wizzer and the Chinese cook, as well as unknown travellers. The references in the above passage are to the book "We of the Never Never" by Mrs. Aeneas Gunn, who lived at the station: The present station is 5 miles away, a tourist centre now called Mataranka. We lunched at Mataranka Hotel, a charming little place, nice open air rooms and a good garden, lovely poinciana trees, paw paws, custard apples, various lovely bougainvilleas and we sat in a greenhouse where there was a cage of galahs and finches.

Later that day they got to Katherine for afternoon tea, ugly old sordid-looking town ... We passed peanut fields and then the Katherine River, quite pretty and flowing with a good deal of water, lined with pandanus palms. We had a paddle and took snaps. The country from here was dreary and monotonous, poor country, rocky and hilly, stunted gums. They stayed the night at Pine Creek, where they "had a cold beer and a shower". The following day found them in very hot country, dry and uninteresting, except for the odd creeks we passed which were lined with tropical growth. Much evidence of the Army, huge airstrips all along the side of the road, with runways into the bush and remains of great camouflage nets. They lunched at Adelaide River, where they found the "same type of iron building surrounded by nice tropical vegetation", and arrived at Darwin in mid-afternoon: the approaches very dirty and untidy, a great collection of discarded army material.

Linda and Tony were dropped off "by the bombed Bank of New South Wales" and walked to the sea front, past Government House, a lovely old stone building in a beautiful garden, lovely position overlooking harbour ... then on round the sea front to the New Darwin Hotel, a magnificent white building. They stayed at Ludmilla House in the suburb of Nightcliffe, in a glorious position on a point overlooking the Timor or Arafura Sea ... huts not furnished but had their own shower and lavatory ... A pleasant dinner facing the blue sea and the setting sun. A message from Noni Starke awaited them, and after dinner she and her husband Clyde arrived and they all walked back to their bungalow, where they had "cold beer, much chat and lovely letters from Reg".

Next day they took a bus into town, where **Noni joined us ... out to**

Fanny Bay, very lovely, saw the famous gaol and golf links, past the relics of Vestey's Meat, £1,000,000 down the drain and emblem of all the many blasted schemes for Darwin. After lunch they walked round the beach to a coconut grove. Great fun selecting coconuts. We wandered home along Ludmilla Creek, lovely tropical growth, saw kingfishers and brightly coloured parrots, ate wild passion fruit, saw the green ants nest in the trees. On 22nd. May they took a trip on the harbour with Noni and went round all the submerged wrecks from the bombing raid ... we passed Channel Island where the lepers are ... went right through the heads. The following day Noni took Tony to explore Rapid Creek, while Linda "went to Mrs. Reid for morning tea", where she met Mrs. Edwards, "ex-matron of Darwin Hospital, married to the owner of Newcastle Waters Station", and a Mr. and Mrs. Lucas. They all went to Flagstaff House, Military O.C., Brig. and Mrs. Fullerton. Lovely garden right on the point, masses of women there doing archery. She dined with the Lucases: "Lucas is Minister of Works and Housing ... lots of fascinating chat".

Another day they went to Berry Springs, A lovely place, beautiful clear fresh water surrounded by tropical growth, lots of birds and fish. Tony and I swam all the morning. Later they visited a Mrs. Flynn at "one of the old houses" and met the Broken Hill flying doctor and the local Vestey's manager and had more "Fascinating chat about the great interior and the strange personalities it breeds." On 25th. May, their last day in Darwin, they went shopping and Called on Mrs. Edwards who gave us a cold beer. Her house one of the oldest in Darwin, falling to bits but fascinating. She has 2 black boys and a small girl, Mary. Afterwards they had lunch with Mr. and Mrs. Hudson, he is a Stock Inspector ... A beautiful garden, lettuce, beans etc. as well as lovely tropical ferns and looking right onto Fanny Bay. They had hens, bantams, goats etc. Next door was Dr. McKenzie, dietician, lovely garden, 2 crocodiles and a big carpet snake and some interesting birds. Their last visit was to an aboriginal burial ground ... in a beautiful spot by Ludmilla Creek, lush vegetation, a lagoon with cranes and many beautiful kingfishers. The graves were marked by carved totem poles, the designs quite fascinating. Saw lots of wallabies.

Linda and Tony said goodbye to Noni and Clyde Starke and left Darwin next day: made Adelaide River for lunch, visited the soldiers' war cemetery there, the graves of men who had died or been killed in the area. They found Pine Creek full of interesting characters, it is the centre of mining, buffalo and crocodile country. We talked to a young buffalo shooter arrayed in cowboy clothes ... He showed us some hides he had brought in, worth about £5 each. Farther along the track they went for a walk down to the creek bed, some sluggish water and pleasant trees, interesting stones, there were some old pensioners living there growing tomatoes. We saw their salted beef hanging from the rafters. There were buffalo horns around the tin walls. They also met Two crocodile men with beards we talked to. They had come in for a few days. Loved the life and lived like kings out in the bush on geese and barramundi. Had got into trouble down South. All very fascinating, every man is worth talking to and one longs to be an artist to sketch the odd types that live in these parts.

Next day they arrived at Katherine, where Linda found the "nights cooler and fresher than in Darwin": had a long stop at the beautiful river lined with pandanus and the banks of beautiful fine white sand, lots of little striped and spotted fish. After that we went to the Headquarters of the experiment farm, in charge of a man called Arnott. It is run by the C.S.I.R.O. and they are trying to find out what can grow best in this country, and also to try and improve the pastures ... trying out cotton, sorghum, peas etc., hoping to work out a scheme for mixed farming. They had lunch at the Katherine Hotel and dinner at Mataranka. The following day it was A lovely fresh morning, woke to chatter of hundreds of birds and parrots ... on a bush track about 30 miles to a lovely spot, Bitter Springs. Paper barks, pandanus, wild cotton, sandpaper trees all made a glorious setting. The water was clear, deep and fast flowing and very warm and bitter. After a swim went to Waterhouse Lagoon, it empties into the Roper River. We walked all round, lots of bullrushes and water lilies. After lunch they went on to Daly Waters: lots of men there again ... Tony rushed in to say there was a carpet snake, it had been found in the bar, it was about 8 ft. long and still alive. We tried to take a photo but it climbed up a tree.

On 29th. May they had morning tea at Elliott and arrived at Banka Banka Station about 12 for good lunch, largest slice of cold beef I've ever seen served. We had lost all the tropical vegetation and got into Central Australian country again, passed lancewood trees from which the natives make their spears and they got to Tennant Creek at 4 p.m., where Tony and I went over to the opposition hotel and I had a beer there as you could drink at tables on the pavement, shady side of the street and watch the town go by. The bar was full of wonderful types as usual - had a chat to a nice old boy, Polish, couldn't understand his name or the mine he worked in. Next morning they Heard half-caste had been murdered at Pine Creek last night ... saw about 1 doz. emus on the track ... passed some huge road transports, some construction company with caravans, cooks and machinery going out to build dams in the big stations. Stopping at Barrow Creek for lunch, they heard that They have found more gold out west, say it is a good thing, probably Lasseter's Reef.

They arrived at Alice Springs, the terminus of their road journey, that evening: great bliss, a single room to myself ... Tony and I had a good walk round, down to the Todd River. Next day they awoke to a Lovely fresh sunny morning, up early and watched the mist roll off the red and purple ranges. They took a bus to Connellans' airport, where they saw the map of their routes, they do 2 routes a fortnight of over 3000 miles, and 2 other smaller ones. Tony had a flight in a Tiger Moth, 15/-. After lunch they went in a taxi to the foot of Mt. Gillen ... we went up a saddle back, fairly rough going, had wonderful views. The others only got so far, Tony and I pushed on for the top. Hard work, had to go on all 4's, very steep, very rough. Got up to where the great red rock rears up out of the shady sides and had to give in. Had magnificent views. The descent was fearful, however we made it.

On their final day, 1st. June, Linda and Tony woke up to a foggy damp morning, disappointing as we couldn't see the ranges ... had a look at the Residency, an old stone building, then talked to a lot of schoolgirls who had been stuck on the way to Hermannsburg Mission. They were bogged for 3 days and had enjoyed the experience. They walked round the town and found the house of the artist Rex Battarbee: It is going to be modern and interesting. Big studio overlooking the Todd and the Range. He was a nice unassuming sincere man, showed us some of his paintings and had interesting talk about Namatjira and others. They were driven out to the airport by friends to fly to Adelaide via Oodnadatta and Woomera; security was imposed on the aircraft because of the classified trials being conducted at the Woomera rocket range. Linda's diary concludes with the entry: curtains were put on the windows and we had to sign papers and we couldn't get out, most war-like.

Linda and Reg had planned a trip to England and Europe in 1951 accompanied by their elder daughter Jennifer. However, on my return from the Korean War Jenny and I decided to get married at short notice. Linda and Reg bravely agreed to travel to Sydney and hold our wedding there on 21st. July; ten days later they sailed for England in S.S. Strathmore without Jenny. The first entry in this diary lists the fellow-passengers at their table: 1st. Officer, Thompson, Harry Anderson, bachelor, Fred Alexander, ex-speedway rider, now in theatre business, actress Billy Pons from New Zealand. En route to Colombo they met Matthew and Janet Weeks, shipping people, Scotch, live near Liverpool, Sir Charles and Lady Lloyd Jones, Sir Charles gave me lovely books. When the ship called at Colombo they spent day with Mavis Montgomery and Gwyneth and Wilfrid Adamson. Baroness Chanteaux nee Betty Dyson got on at Colombo, daughter of Babs Lindsay and Will Dyson, friend of Betty Bunning and George and Violet Benson, who were artist friends of theirs in Perth.

At Bombay, The Lloyd Jones got off and we were moved to Captain's table, Janet and Matthew Weeks, Captain and Barbara Anson, nice English girl from Madras. Their third port of call was Marseilles, where Linda and Reg took car to Aix-en-Provence, lovely old ancient French town with an old cathedral built like a fortress. After we drove to Cassis on the coast and had bouillabaisse for lunch, didn't like it much. Sailed out past the Chateau D'If, lovely view of Marseilles and famous cathedral on the hill. We passed Corsica, Sardinia, Majorca and Minorca, Gibraltar at night and arrived at Tilbury early on Monday August 27th. Once there they took Daimler car costing £4 up to London, it took all our luggage and we enjoyed the drive, specially East End of London, Poplar, Limehouse, Stepney, we noticed all the bombing.

Linda's brother Roy and sister-in-law Florence Anderson were then staying in London, and Linda and Reg Dined that night at the enchanting London house of Roy and Flo in Pembroke Square ... after dinner had a drive round flood-lit London, saw the Festival all lit up. Next day they went over the Festival, Dome of Discovery, Lion and Unicorn Hall, Skylon etc., dined there overlooking the Thames and all the lovely Westminster buildings, which were floodlit. We looked over the amazing Festival Hall. Reg's cousins Gertrude and Isobel Gordon and Linda's cousin Margaret and her husband Gordon Darling were also in London and they visited them. The following day they had drinks and food at the Park Lane flat of Margaret and Gordon, then Roy and Flo took us to 'Waters of the Moon', Edith Evans, Sybil Thorndike, Wendy Hiller, wonderful show. On 1st. September, their last day in London, they went to Battersea Gardens Festival, very attractive, like the Tivoli Gardens on a smaller scale, also saw modern sculpture in the Park, Henry Moore etc., strange and odd but rather lovely, all in the open air.

Linda and Reg then flew to Copenhagen to attend a medical conference and stayed at the Palace Hotel, a lovely old fashioned building, with green copper roof and dull red bricks, typical of many Danish buildings. We settled in, then walked along the Osta Gade Stroget, long narrow fascinating shopping street of Copenhagen. The shops were magnificent, the silver especially caught my eye, so plain and elegant and exquisite. We arrived at the magnificent Hotel D'Angleterre, here we registered for the International Poliomyelitis Conference and I put my name down for 2 excursions and 1 visit to the Ballet at the Royal Opera House. At the reception, About 600 delegates all in day dress were received in utter splendour, beautiful room, flowers, flunkeys with gold braid, soft music, champagne flowing and food that beggars description. They met a friend and fellow orthopaedic surgeon from Australia, Claudia Burton-Bradley, and some others they knew: Claudia was there, also young Dr. and Mrs. Betts from Adelaide, Sister Kenny whom I had a few words with, found her like a dead stone.

Next day, Reg, Claudia and I went to the old University for the official opening ceremony, performed by the Queen of Denmark, Queen Ingrid. She was very stiff and straight and good-looking, really a Swedish princess. Afterwards they wandered round the lovely old fairy tale town, went up the Runde Tur and had a glorious view, the roof line is the special feature of Copenhagen, so many are of brilliant jade green copper and so many spires, domes and turrets in queer and fascinating designs and shapes. While Reg and Claudia attended conference sessions, Linda went to a tea given by a Mrs. Morris Fishbein: the same super food, the Danes are artists in patisseries and confectioneries ... met the great American Dr. Howard A. Rusk and his adoring secretary. He had just come from working in Israel, said it was a terrific experience, they were attempting to do so much with so little and achieving great things ... Met Dr. and Mrs. Van Zwol and we talked together till Reg and Claudia joined us. We all got on well. He was a great handsome tall happy creature, champion tennis player of Holland and she was English. That night they were received in the Raadhus by the Mayor and the Burghers. A lovely impressive building, but the feast was more so, beautiful beautiful food in such plenty and served on the old Royal Copenhagen china, everything to match, dishes of all shapes and sizes ... After that we went into the Tivoli Gardens, music, lights, beauty everywhere, restaurants, dance places, concerts all in this magical setting of trees, coloured lights and exotic buildings like Eastern palaces and temples. We had beer etc. in a student inn packed with young men and women quaffing beer and singing rousing songs, led by the Innkeeper we thought. On 4th. September, Valerie Van Zwol and I went down the Stroget together, looking and longing and I bought a silver brooch and earrings ... to a place where they had an open air museum of all the various types of farm houses up to the Industrial Revolution. They had types from the most primitive up to very rich farms, all most interesting.

Next day Linda Went to the Institute with Reg and Claudia and saw the way International Conferences are conducted, somewhat like the League of Nations in 4 languages, earphones and interpreters. Afterwards she wandered round fascinated by all that I saw, specially the lovely old medieval Borse building ... orange brick and its incredible jade roof with the main spire fashioned like a huge coiling dragon. Took a Motor Bade along the wharves, saw many beautiful yachts including the yacht of the King. Chatted to a young French student in French, all the other passengers were school children who swarmed round me and asked for my autograph. I landed at Lidingo, found the famous mermaid statue, had some tea and lovely pastries, wrote a few letters in the autumn sunshine and then walked back to the hotel. That evening they went to another splendid reception at the Medical Institute. Then we dined at the famous Goldener Lam Restaurant, all had Rijstaffel, then to the Opera House to see Ballet, magnificent Opera House packed to the last degree, we felt very hot and couldn't enjoy it. Saw Les Sylphides, then a modern one.

Linda took a bus trip to Elsinore Castle on 6th. September: it was a lovely drive all along the water that separates Denmark from Sweden, beautiful villas, trees and gardens, past the great Tuborg brewery. Tuborg and Carlsberg Breweries have been great benefactors to the Danish people. Elsinore is right on a point and less than a mile separates it from Sweden. In the olden days it was a grim fortress that held up all the passing ships and collected taxes from them. It is a great square massive place with 4 huge towers on each corner, enormous moat and ramparts and a huge beautiful courtyard where they have Hamlet played in the summer by various famous Shakespearean actors of different nations. Afterwards the bus took them on through beautiful rich country to the great Frederiksburg Castle, once a royal one, now a museum presented to the people by Tuborg. It was packed with treasures, Gobelin tapestries, portraits of all the Royalties of Europe.

The same evening she and Reg went to Professor Preben Plum's to a buffet dinner party, long train journey through beautiful woods, met in cars at the station and driven to his enchanting elegant French style villa. It was glowing with bright light from scintillating chandeliers ... right on the water overlooking Sweden and in the winter they skate from their door to Sweden ... wonderful food and wine including Scnapps which I tasted. After we went down to the water's edge, lit a bonfire and sang songs of the various nations. On their last day in Copenhagen, Linda Did some shopping at Den Permanente where all the best of Danish arts and crafts are to be seen, silver, pottery, furniture, textiles, all of the highest levels in artistic creation ... magnificent dinner for all the delegates to conclude the conference. On 8th. September, Reg and I had a last wander round past the Fish Market, into the famous Thorvaldsen Museum and then flew to Stockholm, where they stayed at the Hotel Malmen.

They registered for another medical conference at the Nordbacke Institute: at night to a high tea reception at the Institute, Swedish style, tea, plum cakes, apples, speeches etc., then outside to watch Swedish folk dancing. While Reg attended the conference next day, Linda wandered round the town, beautiful city, glorious shops, series of islands connected by many bridges, canals etc. The old town with the King's Palace is on a separate island, lovely old Dutch type houses with richly decorated facades, some from the 13th. and 14th. century ... In the afternoon went in a party with all the wives over the King's Palace, then over the famous Royal Church and Hall of the Nobles and round the old town. In the evening she went with Reg, Claudia and Gell to the National Gallery for a lovely orchestral concert of Scandinavian music, Sibelius, Grieg etc. ... Went for supper to famous old Restaurant Bern's, where Strindberg and all famous poets and troubadors etc. used to gather. It was very big, much gilt and opulence characteristic of last century.

On 11th. September she took a bus to the Summer Palace, then over a real French theatre that had been built in Napoleon's time and fallen into disfavour. Elegant theatre and wonderful collection of theatre decor and sets etc. ... Then to lunch at the famous Town Hall, lunch in the Golden Hall, very Eastern, all gold mosaic and great oriental figures. Reg and Claudia had to attend a meeting that night, so Linda took myself to see Caruso in the Kungsgatan near the modern Konzerthuset with the great Carl Milles statues. I adored Caruso and ate good Swedish chocolate in interval. Next day, The wives were all taken over the various factories where the Swedes make their lovely patterns, weaving and silver, all being fashioned by hand ... and then were given a lunch at the largest shop, the Nordeske Kompaniet. Mrs. Sach, the wife of the owner, entertained us, a Swedish girl told me that Mrs. S. used to be a famous film star ... Talked a lot to nice young Danish wife married to Swedish doctor, she told me all the gossip about Prof. Preben Plum and his exotic wife. They don't like her in Copenhagen.

A friend of Linda and Reg's from Perth with European connections, Shelley Garner, had arranged a meeting for them: Met Reg after and went to some place to meet some old Estonian men who were in touch with their friends behind the Iron Curtain, it was through Shelley Garner. They couldn't speak English and had an interpreter and wanted to know about Australia and we did our best ... I went back and changed for the grand dinner at the Stathuset. Reg and I were at the top table. I had a Lord St. John next to me ... met famous old Norwegian Dr. Kion, liked him so much. After some shopping next day, she took motor boat to Waldermasadde near Djur Garten to Prince Eugene's lovely villa on the water, beautiful garden, statues, 1 by Rodin and caught a train back to Stockholm. On 14th. she and Reg went to dinner at Fred Jacobsen's (Leo Buring's friend), lovely house on the water, Australian mother, wife couldn't speak English ... Schnapps and smorgasbord, real Swedish meal and most enjoyable.

The following day Linda Took a trip round the canals under the bridges, very lovely, sat with Dr. Galbraith and met C. and Reg after and took train to Lidingo, lovely hotel there, Foresta, over Carl Milles' villa and saw all his incredible statues. On their final day in Sweden, Fred Jacobsen took us off to Vaxholm in his big car, wife, 4 children and German nurse. At Vaxholm we left the car, took motor boat to his island house in the archipelago ... After lunch Reg, Fred and I walked round the island through pine forests, gathered bilberries ... picked all sorts of flowers and autumn leaves ... We dined with them at night in the famous old place called Die Goldener Freden, an inn since 14th. century, in an old cellar full of atmosphere. They flew to Norway on 17th. September and stayed at a funny little hotel, Radhus Hotellet, Rosencrantz Platz, Oslo ... walked round the town, down the famous Carl Johannes Gate.

On their first full day there they Made a huge breakfast, called on Gell's friend, explored the town, it is small and poor-looking after Copenhagen and Stockholm, but pretty with the Fjord in front and mountains circling it all round at the back. We then took train up to Holmenscollen, a wonderful ski jump up in the pine-clad mountains. We walked for a long way and adored it all, wonderful views of Oslo and the great Fjord ... took Cook's tour to Bigdoy over some old farmhouses, very old church etc., saw the raft 'Kon-Tiki' and the 'Fram', the ship Amundsen went to the South Pole in. Then we went to see three great Viking ships that had been found buried and preserved. Continuing their sightseeing next day, they took a motor boat over the Fjord round the islands ... after took tram up the hill to Ekeburg, lovely restaurant and view, had lunch in the garden then took tram further up the mountain and walked round through the woods. Back to Oslo and out to Vigeland Park where all the works of Vigeland are set out in beautiful park, mountains at the back, the work of nearly 40 years. The sunshine was heavenly and the statues most impressive. On their final day Linda and Reg Had a good look at the cathedral and explored old Oslo, then tram again to Frognersleren and walked through the pine forests to lookout and gazed over the great mountains beyond.

On 21st. September, after a good look over the modern Town Hall,

121

very impressive with its great gold ornamentation and huge colourful majolica reliefs, they flew back to London. Next day, Dan (Lord Ranfurly) called for us about 12 and drove us to his estate near Chesham, Bucks ... He has a farm estate of about 300 acres, a lovely old mellow brick Elizabethan house which we entered from a walled courtyard. Hermione his wife is tall, dark, attractive and vital, I liked her right away. We had a lovely old oak-beamed bedroom, mullion windows and our own bathroom ... After lunch we sat out on the terrace in autumn sunshine. Lord and Lady Gorrie came for afternoon tea, they live at Windsor Castle ... We dressed for dinner, after which Dan's mother and the Countess of Kenmare came and played Canasta. On the second day of their visit it was raining so read the Sunday papers, all full of the King's operation to be that day. We met Lady Caroline Knox, a charming and delicious little girl of 4, Dan and Hermione's only child ... had lunch in the great dining hall, once an old barn but now joined on to the house, making a great large room, it has a minstrels' gallery.

They returned by train on 21st. September to London, where We went to 2 theatres, excellent, 'The Little Hut', arranged from the French by Nancy Mitford, and 'The Love of Four Colonels' by Peter Ustinov in which he played a big part, most intriguing play. Another friend, Tubby Ionides, took us to lunch 1 day at Hatchell's in Piccadilly, wonderful fun. Champagne, grouse, lobster ... He had an Australian girl there who was running a ceramic gallery exhibiting pottery made by David and Hermia Boyd ... fascinated by the pottery and bought a bit of stuff. Another day they went to a reception at Overseas League to meet our new Governor, Sir Charles and Lady Gardener, they were charming, do hope they will like W.A.

The 28th. September found Linda and Reg in our new hired car from Godfrey Davis, we set off to spend the weekend with Dixie Chalker at Hayward's Heath ... drove to Brighton 15 miles away to view the floodlit Royal Pavilion by night, fascinating amazing oriental edifice built by the Prince Regent. We also saw Mrs. Fitzherbert's lovely old Regency House, then went along the promenade and saw the fireworks celebrating the end of the Festival. Next day they drove back to Brighton to see over the inside of the Pavilion, it is fascinating inside with all its 18th. cent. splendour. We saw the famous Whistler picture, the Prince Regent quite naked except for a blue ribbon round his tummy.

They returned to London and on 2nd. October left by car for Lympne, where we were delayed 2 1/2 hours, amused ourselves watching the planes take off and land ... the planes take 2 cars, 1 big and 1 small and 8 passengers. The cars are driven on board by the attendant and we sit up in a cabin above. The flight across takes 20 minutes. We landed at Le Touquet. After a drive through typical French country fields, intense cultivation, horses ploughing and women working hard they spent the night at Boulogne: It was quite devastated by war and very hard to find somewhere to stay. We at last found a newly built estaminet on the wharf. Nice new bedroom and bathroom. Didn't talk English but we were delighted to find our French was useful ... set off to explore the town. It was a sad distressing sight, Boulogne is very hilly and we could see the interesting old castle upon the hill, so wandered all round it and walked on the ramparts, quite romantic by night.

The next day Linda and Reg pushed on up the coast through Calais and Dunkirk, both battered to bits and rebuilding going on quite extensively, but it would be years before they could catch up. We crossed into Belgium about lunch time ... on through Ostend, more devastation and brave attempts to reconstruct. Were interested to see all the fishing boats and fish of all kinds hanging out to be dried. At Bruges they parked in the market square and had a beer to enjoy the really lovely medieval buildings so richly decorated ... Then on to Ghent where we stopped the night at a lovely old hotel, one of the earliest buildings in Ghent dating from 14th. cent. We spent about 2 hours wandering round the town, which is almost too good to be true, so full it is of ancient buildings and yet is still a thriving industrial town today. The canals were smelly but infinitely picturesque, I think the great Castle of the Counts of Flanders was one of the most impressive.

On 4th. October we drove through fields of begonias out in all the vivid colours, a wonderful sight ... to see Rubens' house, well worth it, a magnificent house with a beautiful courtyard and gardens like the Pompeian ones ... crossed the Rhine in a ferry, it was fun to see the barges going up and down. They continued into Holland, where they drove on to an ancient old town, Breda, where we had lunch in the market square. At Amsterdam they stayed at the American Hotel: Our room overlooked a beautiful canal lined with magnificent elms looking so beautifully tranquil, as has so often been painted. Reg went to work with medical friends next day, while Linda visited the Rijksmuseum and saw the famous 'Night Watch' of Rembrandt, then on to another museum exhibition of Van Gogh. I enjoyed those as so many were of Holland and the country we were now seeing, the quaint Japanese-like bridge over the canals etc. Later they both drove along the great dyke beside the Zuider Zee to Volendam, a picturesque postcard village (fishing). The people in the old Dutch clothes. It was amazing to see the baggy pants, clogs, pipes etc. but they were in the proper setting of flat landscape etc.

They travelled to Delden on 6th. October to visit their old friends the Abandanons: through Appel where Juliana has her favourite palace. Arrived at Delden for lunch, a glorious place in beautiful woods, the trees just turning, reminded me of Austria. The Bandys looked wonderful, we lunched in their room at Vita Nova and talked much of their experiences during the war. Afterwards they drove about 8 miles further on to Enschede to a beautiful new hotel where we were to stay ... Dolf, Bandy's handsome son called and took Reg over the hospital, then we went and had drinks and tea at Dolf's house, met his charming wife Jeni and their 4 children. Linda and Reg called for Bandy next day: we three took a walk in the lovely woods and saw the old Castle Trikkel, where Baroness Van Heckeren holds court

... sadly said farewell, most probably we shall not meet again.

They had to head back south, passing through Arnhem: beautiful town, saw the famous bridge where the battle was fought, also the English cemetery, all rather sad and on into Germany, where they found the officials very grim and expressionless ... nothing but devastated towns. At Cologne they pulled up at a small interesting Gasthaus and got accommodation for the night ... we had to sleep over the road in a stark barrack-like block of concrete ... we explored Cologne by night and day. It was in ruins but strangely beautiful, the cathedral standing proudly amongst all the wreckage. By day we found pulsating activity amongst the ruins, the cathedral being restored, shops in tents etc. We walked over the great bridge and viewed the mighty Rhine. They passed on through lovely scenery to Bonn, headquarters of British Zone, also very bombed ... turned up the Ahr Valley and that was a glorious drive. Narrow winding valley, terraced vines on the steep hillsides and lovely old coloured half-timbered cottages, casks of wine being pushed in primitive carts.

That evening Linda and Reg got to Adenau about 5, glorious old German town, chose a sweet hotel, Hotel der Goldener Schwein. Next day, 10th. October, they had a Simply heavenly drive down to Cochem on the Mosel, absolutely fairy tale places, castles on high pointed crags, lovely villages, terraces along the river to sit and drink the famous wine. They crossed into Luxembourg, where everything was shut so we wandered round and viewed the palace of the Grand Duchess and so back into France, through desolated inexpressibly dreary neglected sad French villages that had suffered ravages of 2 wars in a generation. Got to Rheims about 6, could see its great cathedral spires a long way off, and we watched the sun set behind them. Settled in at the Hotel Jean D'Or which is a very famous hotel.

The diary ends here; presumably they returned to London for the passage back to Australia.

13. ITALY AND MALTA

In 1953 Jenny and I were living in Malta, where I was on exchange service with the Royal Navy. My squadron was chosen to go to England to represent the Mediterranean Fleet at Queen Elizabeth II's coronation review at Spithead in June. Linda had planned a visit to Italy to see her friend Shelley Garner, who was staying there, and to Malta to visit Jenny and Andrew (then a year old) while I was away. She travelled from Perth by ship and her diary starts at the first port of call, Djakarta, on 28th. March: A lot of shipping and many sunken old hulks in the harbour. Indonesians looking like Japs on the wharf, with helmets, guns and revolvers, a few Dutch. Much frenzy and disturbance on board wondering about going ashore, however only the ones with visas were allowed ... I remained on board, very uncomfortable, the ship was filled with visitors taking up all the space and drinking and smoking all the time. We had an early lunch as the Captain entertained about 80 visitors from the shore to lunch. Pressmen and their wives, I was told.

Back at sea next day, Linda Talked to 3 young English boys who got on at Djakarta, 2 are in Cable and Wireless and 1, Levett, in Bank of Hong Kong. They are all so thin and have had a hard time. Java is impoverished under the strain of civil war etc. He said the Dutch are hated (with some individuals excepted), they are hoggish and mean. The ship "crossed the line" on 30th.: Excellent ceremony of King Neptune's court all the morning, most amusingly and well done. Fancy dress ball at night ... I was one of the judges so sat with the Captain. On arrival at Colombo she rang Mavis Montgomery who gave me a warm welcome and said she'd pick me up at the Galle Face at 12.30 and take me to lunch ... then walked up the main street, no one asked me to buy so couldn't have looked like a tourist ... Had 2 pink gins, excellent lunch ... back to the ship at 5. I was most delighted to learn that I could keep my nice cabin to myself.

The next port was Aden on 7th. April, where Linda went shopping: I bought pyjamas for Pat, 15/-, 2 lighters 5/- each, pack of naked lady cards 5/- and some white beads 5/- ... back to the ship at midnight. Had a letter from Jen saying she had to prepare for twins. At sea two days later, About lunch time Neptunia signalled to say 'man overboard' so we stopped for about 2 hours. Neptunia circled round and also lowered a lifeboat which rowed about ... Had a long talk to Mrs. Appelbaum, Russian jewess who had all her toes off, they were frostbitten in Siberia when she was 10 and was fleeing from the Bolsheviks. On 11th. April she watched us glide into Suez, saw some of the ships anchored there go off and up the Canal. The bumboats came alongside with the usual leather bags, suitcases, pouffs etc. After a lot of going on we eventually got into our tender and went over to Suez to start our day of adventure in Cairo ... It is about 90 miles to Cairo, most of it utter desert broken by arid hills, odd camels and wandering Bedouins to be seen and we passed ever so many military camps, 1 was British. We stopped halfway at roadside house, had wonderful Turkish coffee and rolls with cheese made of goat's milk. Then on our way and all of a sudden straight out of the desert we were in the amazing modern city of Heliopolis. Wonderful buildings, modern flats, villas, hotels and shops and tree lined streets. It was an eye opener, it oozed wealth and progress. It is 6 miles from Cairo and practically merges into Cairo.

They joined a tour and drove through the streets, fantastic and fascinating sights everywhere ... we went first to the Museum and were given a hurried but comprehensive tour concentrating mostly on the remains of Tutankamen's tombs. After that the party went through Old Cairo, narrow streets teeming with life, dark veiled women, men with fezes, minarets and mosques and domes breaking the vista. We climbed up a steep hill to the citadel and old walled fortress, built by Saladin ... on the top of the hill the biggest and most famous mosque of the Moslem world, the mosque of Mohammed Ali, built only in 1840. Alabaster outside and marble inside

... stood on the rampart and gazed over all Cairo, it is really mud colour just as if it were hewn out of the desert on which it stands. We could see the Nile and the desert and away in the distance the Pyramids. We drove through modern Cairo and were overwhelmed with the magnificence of the splendid modern buildings.

With a guide, they went to a mosque where are the tombs of the Mamelukes, most remarkable ornate costly affairs, on to an old Greek Coptic church, down into a crypt where the Holy Family are reputed to have taken refuge after the flight into Egypt, then to the oldest synagogue in Egypt where they had a copy of the Pentateuch over 1500 years old, written on gazelle skin with vegetable ink and bamboo for a pen. We also saw the book of Esther, which is the oldest known edition. Next they headed for the desert: all our party had camels and off we went, it was wonderful, the camel ride and the Pyramids. There seemed much more excavation than I remembered, it is going on all the time. We went into 1 underground burial place, the temple was like a miniature one of Luxor or Thebes. Their final excursion was to a place called Ding Dong Bazaar. Jewellery, fine brocades, everything of the treasures of the East was there. I bought an Indian bag and belt, red leather slippers for £1. He then took us to a scent shop, rich looking place with handmade carpets and icon-like dangling lamps, we were told to sit down and lovely Turkish coffee was brought us, which we sipped whilst all the perfume oils were displayed for us. The scent of any flower was possible. None of us really wanted any, however we all took a few grammes for £1 sterling. I adored it all and sorry we had to hurry at the end.

They drove back to Port Said to rejoin the ship: It was lovely driving through the cool night, again the strong scent of jasmine. We were stopped about every 1/4 hour, the driver said they were looking for hashish. Passing the Straits of Messina and Stromboli, the ship "arrived at Naples about 9.30, lovely sight at night with all the lights", and Linda went ashore next day and walked through the Galleria Umberto, all rather depressing as it was cold and drizzling with rain, Naples needs the sunshine. On 16th. April they passed close along the lovely Ligurian coast, La Spezia, Rapallo etc. Lovely approaching Genoa as behind the town we had a wonderful view of snow covered Alps. Arrived about 11, Shelley was on the wharf, looking very well and very excited. I was excited too, it was grand to have someone after being so much alone on the ship.

They stayed at the Hôtel des Gènes: Genoa a fascinating mixture of old and new, as are all the European cities after the war. It is frightfully noisy, almost unbearable. We got sick of the noise and clatter and took a funicular up to a high hill behind the town called Righi, wonderful view of mountains, Genoa and the sea and behind the famous Campo Santo ... went about 8.30 to the famous new restaurant Graticiello, meaning skyscraper. A superb view of Genoa by night, lovely food, enchanting music. We danced and were gay and happy. Next day Linda and Shelley took a bus along the coast towards France to a seaside resort called Pegli, went up the hills behind the town. Read and basked in the winy sunshine, then came down and sat by the sea. Returning to Genoa, they Visited the Soprano, old medieval gate, the house of Christopher Columbus. Also visited the Publica Assistenza. There are baths, showers, toilets, pedicure places etc. So many people have to use them as there are no such things in their own houses.

They caught another bus on 18th. April and had a beautiful drive but winding and climbing all the way, the road round the mountains skirting the sea. Went through the Riviera Dei Fini, where Santa Margharita, Portofino and Rapallo are ... to San Terenzo, Shelley excited to show me his former dwelling place. He lived in the famous Casa Shelley for 4 months ... on round the next bay to Laici, where we stopped for lunch, Hotel de Shelley. Modern frescoes on the wall depicting Shelley, Byron, Lawrence, Dante etc. The whole place is permeated with the influence of Shelley. They went on to Pisa, where they found masses of people surging round. We walked through the old streets of Pisa and down to the Arno. They stayed at the Anglo-American Hotel in Florence: We went to Doneys' famous restaurant of Victorian and Edwardian days on the also famous Via Tornabuoni ... then we walked round Florence and we were excited and enchanted, finding the great Duomo, the Ghiberti doors and the Campanile by Giotto, and the wonderful Piazza de Signoia, with the Loggia dei Lanzi and the statuary.

Next day Linda and Shelley, refreshed and in good spirits, walked along the Arno in the spring sunshine, looked at the Ponte Vecchio ... into the Uffizi Gallery. Hundreds of people everywhere, however we had a quick tour, saw Botticellis including well-known 'Bath of Venus' and 'Primavera', Tintorettos, Titians, Correggio, Canaletto and some famous statuary including the 'Hermaphrodite'. They went by bus for a really lovely journey climbing up the hill, passing villas, lovely gardens with wisteria, lilac and the famous cypress trees of Tuscany. Fiesole is a fascinating little place, but it was packed with people. We gazed at the Tuscan landscape, looked at the Roman ruins and Etruscan museum. On 21st. April they looked at all the beautiful shops. Then found the Church of San Lorenzo and the Medici chapel, a glorious thing lined wholly with the most beautiful marble I've ever seen and great sarcophagus of Cosimo, Lorenzo etc. Saw the Michelangelo sculpture to Lorenzo ... to the Piazza San Marco to see the world-famous statue 'David' by Michelangelo. It was so perfect and so inspired that we were knocked speechless. It was a great experience. Then to Bargello, old palace of Justice ... It was a glorious building, I like it best of all, there is a museum there with Donatello and Michelangelo statues, great Della Robbia, Cellinis, a magnificent bronze by him of Cosimo.

Later the same day they walked over the Ponte Vecchio, along the Arno, lovely view of Florence from the other bank and also the hills bathed in the soft Tuscan light ... We walked along a lovely boulevard lined with elms, chestnuts and leccia. Interesting villas and peeks of fascinating Italian gardens, great pots, wisteria everywhere, lilac, azaleas etc. On return to their hotel Linda found her friend Mrs. Gordon waiting: She was staying up at Fiesole and had just received my letter sent on from Perugia. She took us up to Fiesole where she is staying in some sort of convent place run by the Sisters of the Blue Cross, it is an old Medici villa ... Mrs. G. introduced us to various nuns, brothers etc. and we had a good simple meal ... After this Mrs. G. took us to her room and we had a good talk about her family affairs and problems, thoughts on Italy and Italians ... a remarkable woman and has translated Dante's 'Inferno' and now doing the 'Purgatorio'.

The following day she and Shelley were up early for our 2-day excursion to Rome via the Tuscan hill towns ... A beautiful Alfa Romeo called for us at 9 a.m. and we shared the guide with a nice American couple in their 50's ... along Arno through beautiful valleys, vineyards, olive groves, wheat, little ancient farm buildings, white oxen ploughing and pulling the carts ... this part of Tuscany is called the Garden of Italy. Their first stop was at the medieval walled city of San Gimignano, clinging precariously to the great hill ... It still has 12 towers left, but had about 40 at one time. The towers all had bells, which were the great means of communication. We went into the ancient old church, 1200, primitive frescoes covering the walls, sat in the square, gazed down the deep narrow streets where families have lived for centuries. After that they continued through the same enthralling landscape endeared and made familiar to us by poets and painters through the ages.

At Siena they saw beautiful buildings of stone, brick, marble etc. of incredible beauty. The Duomo was a great sight, built of black and white marble, a fashion the Crusaders brought from Byzantium, with an amazingly delicate and lovely facade in a palest pink ... Inside was more beautiful than any other Italian church we'd seen ... frescoes, the richest and freshest I've seen, by Raphael's teacher and the famous Siena marble which is a mustard yellow colour. Farther on, We stopped at Lake Trasimeno for a cup of tea, it is connected with a great battle in Hannibal's day. Very beautiful lake, the little town was called Lido Perugia. Their next stop was at Perugia, where they passed Through the great gates, past the University for Foreigners, through an incredible Etruscan arch and bits of wall built of solid blocks like the Pyramids, this was an old Etruscan city, they first discovered how to make an arch in stone with keystone etc.

Finally they reached the Brufari Palace Hotel, magnificent building high up looking over the valley and hills of Umbria for miles. It is on the famous Corso which after 5 is closed for traffic, while the Italians take their promenade. I got an enchanting room at the end corner of the building, french doors onto a balcony from where I can see all of Umbria and Tuscany, I think, as well as look down on the indescribable ancient hotch-potch of roofs. After settling in, Linda and Shelley set off to promenade on the Corso, lively as if it were a special fete day rather than a nightly occurrence. We stood in the square and gazed at the ancient building of the Podesta and all the other lovely buildings, the stone and the old bricks and tiles and just everything leave me speechless.

Next morning they woke to the chattering of birds, clanging of bells and echoes of reverberant voices shouting to each other, it was 5.30 and Perugia was wide awake. They set off for Assisi: We first came to a small town in the flat valley where there was a great new Duomo built over the original ancient chapel of St. Francis who died in 1226 ... In the days of St. Francis it was all thick wood and the little chapel was in the centre of the wood. From here we could see the town of Assisi perched high up on the side of a great hill. The approach was wonderful, a fitting preparation for the great experience to follow. The stone and the buildings were of great beauty and we saw his tomb and the frescoes by Giotto depicting his saintly life. Crossing the Apennines, they had lunch at Orvieto, "another hill town of great age and beauty", and then went on to Rome through the Pontine

Marshes. We came in by the Villa Borghese gardens, Porta Purciano, past the Hotel Flora where I stayed in 1925, down the Via Veneta ... finally got to the Pensione Waldorf, Via Abruzzi, right against the old walls, the other side of which are the Purcio Gardens.

On 25th. April, they found our way to the Piazza de Spagna at the foot of the Spanish steps, right alongside is the house where Keats died, it is now a museum but shut today. We sat on the steps with the rest of Rome and admired the view, I like it almost best of Rome. We went down the Via Lardotti, the famous shopping street, but all was closed, then we made our way into the Corso towards the P. de Venezia where the great Vittorio Emmanuele Monument is, a great white majestic edifice to celebrate the 1st. King of United Italy. In this square is the balcony from which Mussolini made his orations. Behind all this is the Coliseum, Palatine and Capitol Hills. After this they went back to the Fontana di Treve and threw in our coins ... tea and cake at Doneys' beautiful tea rooms. We stayed there for about 1 hour gazing at the fascinating inmates, all well dressed and it is obviously the fashionable thing to do.

The next day Linda and Shelley took train outside the Porta Purciano over the Tiber, then proceeded to find the Foro D'Italia, the modern Olympia founded by Mussolini. It is a long way out on the outskirts of the city, nestling under the great hills. It is very impressive, vast with lots of colossal statues of great men of Jupiter-like appearance and strength. They then visited the Vatican, where they saw St. Peter's toe being kissed, saw the 'Pieta' by Michelangelo ... over the lovely St. Angelo Bridge, that is a lovely vista of Rome. We walked along the Tiber under the plane trees, saw some lovely old houses once the haunt of artists, then up past a glorious untouched 15th. century square and found the Borghese Palazzo, we went into its beautiful courtyard and sat and admired the gardens, the wisteria creeping over the lovely old stone balustrades ... had tea at Babbingtons' Tea Rooms, we could have had muffins and scones, the tea and cakes were good and we were amused at the English atmosphere.

Their next excursion was to the house where Keats died in arms of his friend Joseph Severn, fascinating data about lives of Shelley and Keats there ... took tram to the English Cemetery, a glorious little quiet place in a cypress grove. The graves were interesting and very beautiful, saw the graves of Shelley and his friend Trelawney and out in the meadows was the grave of Keats. Afterwards Linda went into the great shop La Renascente and had fun making a few purchases in Italian. They returned to the Vatican to visit the museum and were almost stunned by the treasures we saw, however managed to concentrate on the great Michelangelo work of the Sistine Chapel and a much quicker look at the Raphael rooms ... I in most fluent Italian engaged a taxi driver to take us to Tivoli for the afternoon, 6000 lira for 4 hours and after picking up an acquaintance of Shelley's, a Dr. Gallio, off we went out to Hadrian's Villa, Villa D'Este and Tivoli, we heard nightingales singing in beautiful old gardens of the ruined villa of Hadrian, 130 A.D., the buildings covered 8 miles, theatres, baths etc. I loved the view of the ancient old hills and the cypress 600 and 700 years old ... Dr. Gallio in true Italian style held my hand and made overtures d'amore when Shelley wasn't looking, it gave me much amusement.

On her last full day in Italy, she and Shelley popped into a famous old cafe in the Via Condotti, Il Greco, quite a little museum of all the famous authors, painters, sculptors etc. who have congregated there over the last 200 years ... to dinner at a nearby Taverna, good food and wine and we were gay and happy. On 30th. April ("Last day, very sad"), she bade goodbye to Shelley and flew to Malta: Lovely view of Sicily and Mt. Etna, snow covered, and also exciting going over Malta, we got there about 5.30, Pat only there to meet me, Jen was with Andrew who was just getting over the 'flu. Soon after, I was with Jen and Andrew was just going to bed. We had a drink and talked a great deal and Jen gave me all the lovely family mail to read which was wonderful.

Next day, Andrew still not very well so passed the day more or less quietly and talked much. We had a walk along the High Street, filled with shops of all sorts, I felt as if I was in the native quarter of Aden, donkey carts, bird shops, street vendors and criers of all sorts. Jen's house is very Eastern, a great double door opens right off this street onto a marble hall off which is a small courtyard with fig, almond and orange trees. Up great stone steps to the living rooms, 4 big airy tiled floored rooms, a terrible brown closet of a kitchen, quite a nice bathroom and a terrace overlooking inland Malta. After lunch she and Jenny called on Jen's friend Marianne who lives round the corner, she and Jen are the only non-Maltese in this area. M. is German, married to an English dentist, a baby girl 8 months and a boy 3 years. M. is charming, intelligent and sensible and must have been a great help to Jen. J. and P. went to a naval party at night and I minded Andrew and cooked a chop for myself on the primus in the terrible kitchen, felt rather clever.

I had been told that I would be eligible for a week's special leave in England after the coronation review, and when I told Linny she made a typically generous decision: have decided to mind Andrew here whilst Jen goes to England with Pat ... Pat, J., A. and I had a drive round through Sliema, where all the English live, Plevna House Hotel, along the beaches, saw and went inside a wonderful domed church called Mosta, then to Rabat, ancient capital of Malta and into the old walled city of Medina, quite fascinating, had tea at a lovely little place run by an intrepid English woman, you could stay there if you liked. On 3rd. May she and Jenny went for a short drive to the Governor's residence, St. Antony. The grounds were thrown open for some sort of fete. Quite a lovely old house with beautiful bougainvillea and the gardens were quite lovely ... Went down to Pat's ship, HMS. Fierce for buffet meal and film after. Malta was beautiful at night driving round the various creeks where all sorts of warships are anchored and all lit up. They apparently all entertain on Sunday.

The following day she went into Valletta, booked a passage tentatively with Flotta Lauro on the 'Sydney' leaving July 4 ... took bus to Sliema and tried to find Mrs. Long and Mrs. Comrie where I was expected for tea (Jen had to go to the dentist). I wandered all round along the sea front by Plevna House, couldn't find them so bought some Spanish sherry and was going to take the ferry over to Valletta but it started to rain so took taxi home. On 6th. May, Pat went off on his 7 weeks' jaunt to England. Jen, Andrew and I went down to Tigne Point near Sliema and watched Pat's minesweeping flotilla sail out of Marsamxett Harbour. It was a beautiful sunny morning and it was a wonderful scene gazing over to the ramparts on which Valletta is built and seeing the British Fleet move off. There were many young wives with their children waving goodbye. Next day Linda went to the hospital to get a medical certificate from Jen's lady doctor, the first stage in the complicated process of getting a driving licence ... took Marianne and her children to a lovely little town called Balzan and went to a convent where they had the most glorious handwork. Bought an exquisite cloth and napkins, £13, and gave it to Jen. We had Cyprus oranges in St. Antony gardens.

Another day they Had an interesting drive through the 3 old cities, Senglea, Vittoriosa and Cospicua, very old, very Arabian looking, to a little seaside place called Marsa Scala where a friend of Jen's lived, Mary Learmount. She lives in a typical quaint Maltese house with all the usual inconveniences ... took Andrew for a walk in his new pusher. We sat on some rocks beside the blue sea, on the other side of the inlet was an old fort, it was all most picturesque and different. They went on 10th. May to Rabat and Medina, had a walk round both places, full of atmosphere and interesting old buildings. Rabat is outside the ancient walled capital of Medina, which is rather like the hill fortress towns of Tuscany and Umbria. We visited a Malta weaving place in Rabat and made a few purchases. Also went to an old house in Medina where they made lace and I bought some mats. We admired the ancient Casa Inguarez, the seat of the noble Inguarez family for 600 years.

Linda went to Hamrun next day for her driving licence: Mr. Avela the garage man took me along to Police Headquarters to try and get my licence ... Mr. Avela took me out and gave me some hints on what was expected ... The test was quite nerve-wracking and the P. very serious. However I got my licence and felt most grateful to Mr. Avela ... Jen and I pushed the pram to the Marsa sports club, where there was a polo match, Lord Louis Mountbatten was playing. Jenny left for England on 22nd. May: Jen excited, drove her out to Luqua airport at 9.30 a.m. to find the plane was grounded and probably not leaving till 8 p.m., very disappointing ... went into Valletta and had a nice gelato in the main Palace Square ... took Jen to the Phoenicia Hotel at 6.30 where she would get the bus to the airport. Her first day on her own went off very well. Took Andrew for a walk to the Botanical Gardens and then sat on the terraces in Floriana and watched them build a great gaudy rostrum in front of the cathedral for a festival.

We had a Maltese maid who had promised to help Linny while we were away: Mary Gafa the little maid popped in to see how I was getting on. I was glad to see her as I felt tired and sorry for myself. She took Andrew for a walk while I coped with all the washing. Marianne came round and asked me over for tea ... had a chat and pushed Andrew up to Floriana and we watched the religious procession, all the dressed up priests sitting on the rostrum, it all seems so stuffy and silly and pointless. Masses of people just staring in a rather dull way, lots of ice creams and sweet cakes being bought. It just wasn't an edifying performance, I felt and they have so many of them and here in Malta one feels the truth of the Communist statement that 'Religion is Dope for the People' and here it really is so. Afterwards she Had a good night, but A. made a mess all over his bed at 5 a.m. Took a lot of coping with. However, those are the vicissitudes of life looking after a 10-month-old baby.

For a while Linda Gave up trying to write the diary - highlights during

Jen's absence were Coronation Day, June 2, lovely day, Andrew beautifully good and was able to listen to the wireless all day. At night I went round and had a lovely meal, curry etc. with the so nice Smiths and listened to the Queen's broadcast at 9 p.m., very moving. Daily entries began again on 4th. June: A holiday, some feast day, so took Andrew, Mary, her mother and 2 little brothers for a drive, went round St. Paul's Bay which is quite interesting, then inland to the other side of the island to Ghain Tuffieh, high cliffs and rugged coastline. When I got back found a card from Eric Rice asking me to ring him and have lunch. Eric was an Overseas League acquaintance and next day I called on Eric Rice and enjoyed the experience. He stays at the British Hotel, Valletta, St. Ursula St. which is a narrow dark street, masses of washing and children. The British Hotel incredibly dingy and old-fashioned, but a heavenly view over Grand Harbour and the old cities on the other side. I climbed up 4 flights of narrow stairs and met Eric Rice and arranged to have lunch on Monday at Union Club.

The following day she took A., Mary and her sister and drove round the other side of the harbour, parked the car and wandered fascinated up and down the labyrinthine streets of Senglea, then we went on to Kalafrana, a pleasant little fishing harbour, after that we went off into the country, through the quaint town of Zabbar, through the narrowest roads and found ourselves at the sea, quite fun. Again on 7th. June, Linda Took A. for a walk in the pram in the morning and got caught up in the Marsa festa, a terrifying experience, the street a surging mass of shrieking, yelling people letting off fireworks, home made bombs, paper like confetti filled the air and it might have been a revolution, much more like it than a Saint's day. We managed to take refuge in a dark, cavernous vegetable shop till the worst had passed. Mary Gafa came round next morning and off I went to the Union Club for lunch, enjoyed it very much, it is an historical club and has many interesting and unique architectural features which I was delighted to see.

She went to Rabat with the Smiths: wandered round the Roman villa with the babies in arms, then into Medina, past the old house of Count Roger the Norman, now belonging to Golleba, and up onto the Bastion where we sat and enjoyed the view. On 11th. June the 50 years old lavatory went wrong, most distressing. At night went to cocktail party at Overseas League to celebrate Queen's birthday. I dressed up in my best black hat etc. ... Masses of people, mostly Maltese, met a nice pair called Campbell, retired Navy, live at Lija, have daughter in Kenya, very intense about Maltese problems. About 9.30 left Eric Rice and went off with 2 women, had a lovely feed at an interesting cosmopolitan little pub called The Bonheur off South St.

In the week before Jenny returned, Linda Took the Smiths for a drive, went south where the villages are fascinatingly primitive. Got lost near Qrendi, got into a maze of narrow streets and couldn't get out. No one talked English, after several adventures eventually found our way out of the maze ... Pushed A. up to the Barracca Gardens and enjoyed the view of Grand Harbour. A. made friends with a handsome Sikh off one of the Indian warships now in harbour ... Took A., Mary, her mother and cousin and went off to explore Lija, one of the most beautiful of Maltese villages. Many important people live here in fine villas and have lovely gardens. The Hon. Mabel Strickland lives in the Villa Parisio here.

The 17th. June was Very hot, went to the beach, Andrew fell asleep on the way home so couldn't meet Jen at 7, so Marianne and Bill Smith met her for me, brought her home about 1/4 to 8. Andrew fed and in bed asleep then. Jen very tired, had had a lovely time, had a wonderful talk and to bed ... Jen pleased with Andrew and me and said so which was very nice. Andrew shyly knew Jen but was so used to me and still looked to me for all the important things of his little life. Linda found that With Jen summer arrived and no longer possible to push the pram on sightseeing adventures. I forgot to say that one day I pushed the pram up the very steep Guarda

Mangia hill overlooking Pieta Creek and had a good look at Villa Guarda Mangia where Philip and Elizabeth stayed whilst in Malta ... took A. by bus to Sliema to visit Jen's friend Madeleine Comrie, she had 2 children, 7 and 5, who were sweet to A. M.C. said she wants to look after Andrew whilst Jen has the other baby. She wouldn't be a bad one, must see what Jen thinks.

On 21st. June, Mary the little maid took me to a Maltese wedding. The bride lives opposite and is surely the tallest bride I've ever seen ... M. called for me and took me to her house, spotlessly clean and neat, M.'s mother, 2 cousins, 2 sisters and 1 little brother all came, M. the only one who can speak English. We all piled into a bus to Qormi, a rich country village a few miles away. Then into a very hot hall, guests seated on either side, masses of grandmas, babies, children of all ages. Bride and groom seated on a dais under a silver horseshoe and very self-conscious. I shook hands. They passed round at intervals very sweet confections and very sweet small drinks, also neat brandy and aniseed. Then they began to dance, first bride danced, she couldn't but the groom pushed her round and they fell over, much hilarity. I took my leave at 8.

Two days later, Mary's mother and cousin who spoke a little English called for me and took me to pay my respects to the bride. I gave her a small present. Bride spoke no English, B.groom was quite nice, in the Army, spoke English and we had quite a chat, he gave me hot beer and I had wedding cake, given a large bag of sweet cakes to take home. Saw all the wedding presents. Linda notes that on 26th. June "Pat arrived home, Jen thrilled, Pat delighted with Andrew", and her final activity is recorded on 29th.: All left home at 6 and with the Smith family, drove through Qrendi to Zetenez, where we took a dhaisa and went round the coast to the Blue Grotto. It was lovely being out in the freshness of the morning, babies enjoyed it too. The Grotto was quite impressive, high cliffs, interesting formation and beautiful water all colours, blue, mauve etc. We got home about 10, very hot, Jen and Pat went for a swim and I minded Andrew. Very hot afternoon, I went off about 5 into Valletta and sat in the lower Barracca Gardens near Fort St. Elmo, it was very lovely.

She probably sailed for Australia on 4th. July, the date she had booked when she decided to look after Andrew for us.

PART FOUR

1958 TO 1964:
GRANDMOTHER

PADDLING AT THE TAJ MAHAL, 1963

Linda next travelled overseas with Reg in 1958; they left Perth on 9th. March on a Qantas flight to South Africa via Cocos Island and Mauritius. After a day's delay, they arrived by night at Cocos, where the diary starts: **Very hot and steamy, but moonlight and plenty of coconut palms. It was good to have a stretch, nice cold drink and sit out under tropic skies and listen to surf pounding on reef. Went aboard at 10.30 p.m. and settled down for sleep thinking of Mauritius in the morning.** However, they woke up to find **us going into the sunrise, we were in a world of heavenly clouds, but also we were soon told that we were going back to Cocos ... our splendid captain was flying through the night to get the cowling to the Queen Mother's grounded aeroplane and after the point of no return was ordered to go back to Cocos by the Queen's pilot because of cyclone at M. We were all crestfallen and dazed at this further misfortune and a night in the plane for nothing.**

After returning to Cocos, **we were given rooms facing the coral lagoon ... wandered round the lagoon, vegetation of coconut palms and mangoes looking attractive, bathing unattractive because of the coral ... Drank with Chief Engineer of the plane and discussed our chances of getting away, we were to be told at 8 p.m. Messages and weather reports kept arriving ... we went to bed for sleep to await the decision. Woken at 7 p.m. with the news that we were departing at 2 a.m.** On 11th. March they arrived at Plaisance Airport, Mauritius at 9.30. **A beautiful island, mountainous and lovely coast, lush growth mostly sugar. We were taken in buses about 9 miles and 1800 ft. up to Curepipe and deposited at Park Hotel, beautiful hotel with lovely black and white tiled terrace, white pillars and wrought iron. I noticed all the grey and white small French chateau type of house. The whole atmosphere very French.**

Later that day Linda and Reg met Mrs. Rose, wife of Qantas manager.

Her husband was just about dead, no sleep during the enforced stay of the Queen Mother, and what with the cyclone, the decision to turn us back with the spare part, the Queen Mère they said had been the only unconcerned one. Government House was in a complete flap. They were introduced to a Dr. André, who called for Reg to show him the hospital and took Pop and I as far as the town, very shoddy, mixture of French, Indian, Chinese, African etc. The streets were lined with people to see the Q. Mother depart, so we took up a place of vantage and presently saw her come by, dressed in orchid pink and as charming as ever. They received a message that we were to leave at 1/4 to 8. There was a terrific thunderstorm and the lights all went out and everything was a shambles ... piled into cars and back to the airport ... All officials heaved a sigh of relief that Queen Mère had gone, although as finishing touch of misadventure her dressing case was left behind in car and a message arrived to say send it to Clarence House.

Finally they arrived at Johannesburg on 12th. March, about 3 a.m., got through Customs and went to look for Bob Almond ... Bob drove us off, he said we would have a few hours' sleep and leave about 9 for Kruger Park, we should have gone the day before - his wife Ruth had already gone with friends. After resting they set off for Kruger Park - interesting drive over High Veldt, the farms and native life, then into the lower Veldt ... got there about 5 p.m., the gates close at 6.30 p.m. Arrived at the rest camp, the others were still out so we had drink. Bob drove us round, the grass is very long (summer rain), winter is dry and best for seeing - saw zebra, wildebeeste, impala, water buck with white rings round behinds, lots of birds, hornbills, guinea fowl etc. Had to come in at 6.30, met the others, Ruth, Bob's wife, Brian and Ivy Doherty who had organised the trip and Mrs. England staying with them ... they had brought all the food and drink with them and their own native cook ... We had 2 bungalows between the 7 of us, they were built for Queen's visit and very luxurious.

Next day Linda and Reg went out of camp to see the animals, not long before we saw giraffe, zebra and hornbills all together. We went to the Hippo Pool but hippos were lazy, saw herds of impala, wildebeeste and baboons. We had a picnic lunch ... great thrill, 6 young lions right by the side of the road. They had fed and were lazy, but lovely to watch. On 14th. March they were Up at 5 and Dohertys, Reg, England and I went out, it was wonderful, the country is thrilling, great mountains in the distance, interesting trees and animals, just what one would hope Africa would be like, saw the lovely proud kerdus, jackals, zebra etc. but no more giraffe ... then Bob took us to Pretoria, beautiful homes and gardens of the Diplomats etc. The Union bldgs. are uniquely beautiful, as is their high position gazing out over the open veldt. We visited the grim granite memorial to the Voortrekkers, who trekked from the Cape to the Transvaal in 1836.

The following day they were again Up early, Reg went off with Bob to city to see hospitals etc. Eva Williiams called for me and took me to her home not far away ... Almonds drove us to airport ... nothing much to see but empty open Africa till near Vic. Falls, the Zambesi in full flood, then the spray from the Falls, a quick glimpse and landed about 4 p.m. ... through Livingstone, along the swollen Zambesi where baboons were playing over the bridge over Zambesi gorge, first peep of falls very thrilling but much cloud and mist from the huge density of water. The Falls Hotel is now a great luxury hotel filled with tourists of all sorts and descriptions ... walked to the nearest end of the Falls, Devil's Cataract and were just stunned with the immensity of this great work of nature.

On their second day there, Linda and Reg went for an air flip over the falls, 20 minutes for 25/-. It really was worth it and we got the whole complete picture which is impossible on land ... we set off with raincoats and hats to do the Rain Forest. The bus took us to the Bridge and then we started on the Forest which is the other side of the Gorge to the main part of the Falls. The Gorge is very narrow, the Falls are about 1 mile wide and the flooded Zambesi crashed, thundered, swirled and bellowed over into the deep narrow gorge and the spray rose up for hundreds of feet and came down again in the form of the heaviest rain I have ever been in ... After 4 we started again and explored the Eastern Bank of the Falls, Livingstone side. There were wonderful views here and the walking was much drier than the other side.

They flew to Bulawayo on 17th. March: to a smart brand new Hotel Victoria ... to Museum. Interesting to see animals, natives and incidents relating to settlement of Rhodesia. Livingstone and his journeys, Rhodes and his dealings with Logenbula, Chief of the Matabeles. The same day they travelled on to Salisbury: Sam Straiton, friend of Bob Almond met us, nice big chatty Scotchman. Drove us to Ambassadors' Hotel ... walked round after, lovely still night. I like Salisbury. It has many many beautiful new buildings of great elegance and distinction, not just modern creations. Linda noted there a variety of interesting tropical trees, specially 1 with great orange flower called Spathodia, West African tree and lovely flowers called Gloriosa Superba, Flame Lily. Sam Straiton called for us at 10 ... told us so much, he has been in Africa since a boy and done most everything ... He took us to the tobacco market where it is all bought and sold, the auction was just over but we saw the place that makes Salisbury tick ... I can't think how a town of only 35,000 Europeans can support such bldgs. and private houses, Sam Straiton wouldn't tell me either except that for financial reasons they federated with Northern Rhodesia and Nyasaland.

From there they went to Nairobi: Nice soft-spoken American man next to me, comes from California and says that he has crossed zebras with donkeys and calls them Zonkeys, his friends make money out of them at fairs ... sends Bible to Nigeria for nothing to people who personally apply. American Bible Society said Nigerians only wanted their bibles to use as cigarette papers. Linda and Reg had come to Nairobi to visit old friends, Molly Ryan and Lady Dollie Bruntisfield. They arrived on the evening of 18th. March and went to the Norfolk Hotel: Dr. Gregory (friend of Molly

Ryan) to meet us, long letter from Molly ... message from Dollie Bruntisfield.

After a day of sightseeing with Dr. Gregory, Dollie arrived: We left Nairobi at 12, very excited. Lovely drive through Great Rift Valley, huge old volcanic mountains all round, saw some zebra, buck, ostriches and many birds ... Got to Thompson's Falls, about 160 miles, about 3.30 ... the town is small but important centre for all the farmers around and has a granary. D. lives 30 miles out into the Aberdare Mountains. Lived alone here all through the Emergency. The farm is 600 acres, pigs, cows and lovely native cattle called Zebu, white with a hump in behind their heads. The house is charming, low white stone, shingled roof, long stoep looking onto the Aberdare Mountains with a pleasant garden going down to rippling stream ... We have a separate little cottage in garden, bathroom etc. and everything to make us comfortable in a lovely rustic simplicity ... D. says she lives just the same when alone. She has a cook and houseboy, an overseer boy and various other natives all about with wives and children. Next day they went into the town, full of farmers ... watching all the various types of natives with their various methods of dress and adornment. Out to Mrs. Meiklejohn's for lunch (sister Mrs. Jameson in Perth). Her husband was murdered in front of her by Mau-Maus and she attacked and shockingly mutilated and left for dead. She bravely struggled into car and drove it to warn others and then collapsed. She is the heroine of Kenya and has the O.B.E. Queen Elizabeth specially asked to meet her. She lives in the same house with her daughter ... I thought Mrs. M. one of the most special personalities I've ever met ... her manager Mr. Wallis came in and met us. He is also very famous as during the terror he used to go disguised as a native into the Aberdares and capture many of them. Linda and Reg returned to Dollie's, where An interesting neighbour called, Annie Van der Wiele, she and her husband and 1 other man had built a 45 ft. ketch called 'Ooma' and sailed round the world. Husband's health made it necessary to sell their loved yacht in Mombasa and came to settle up here, he wanted to be a white hunter but didn't have the right personality to deal with the wealthy and spoilt American clients. She has written a book, 'With the West in My Eyes', which Dollie has given me to read.

On 22nd. March they went over to a neighbouring farm for lunch ... really glorious garden all along a river bank with everything imaginable growing. We strolled along the bank and were entranced with the beauty. Afterwards, Dollie drove us 30 miles out into the Ranching Country, grass and thorn trees, where there are large ranch holdings of 100,000 acres, grazing only. We were fascinated with the country, saw buck and lovely big strange dancing birds, some sort of cranes like our Brolgas. The herd boys from the strange primitive tribes interested us. Dollie took us to a place run by a famous white hunter called Can Hartley. He goes out and traps the animals and brings them in for Zoos and to be used in films, Kenya Film Productions is nearby and here they make many African films of wild life. He also has the famous lion whose picture is at the beginning of all the Metro Goldwyn films. There must have been about 80 giraffes, their necks rather like a waving forest, many beautiful lions and cubs etc., cheetah, lynx, mongoose, all sorts of buck ... All around were traps, old jeeps, strange natives and their kraals, white rhino, elephants and tortoises wandered round in the open, a great chimpanzee was chained to a tree.

Another day Linda and Reg tried unsuccessfully to get in touch with Molly Ryan: regretfully abandoned the idea ... came home very crestfallen as that was the last chance of getting contact with Molly so that we could arrange to get to Molo. They walked to a neighbouring farm: loved being in the bush and seeing Mt. Kenya most beautifully. We walked back along the river in thick jungle ... We came back to where Dollie's boys were cutting down the bush with their great panga knives. They use them for all the bush work and it gave us the horrors to think they used them to attack Europeans. Afterwards, Dollie took us for a lovely drive into the Aberdares ... it looks very rich country and has many trees, beautiful Podo trees and

Cedar. The Podo is the most beautiful but the Cedar is the best wood. We drove back and Dollie took us to the most famous garden in Kenya, belonging to a man called Sharp ... I called it the Kew Gardens of Kenya and wasn't far wrong. It is on a river and there are beautiful vistas of green smooth lawns interspersed with great forest trees, beautiful Podo and Cedar and all around flowers and shrubs from every part of the world all growing in the most beautiful way there, great lily ponds with peacocks about, wild ducks and many birds.

They went into Thompson's Falls again, where Linda decided to ring Molly again and was delighted to get her, she says they will come to Nairobi and spend a few days with us there, so that will be fun. They paid a return visit to the Van der Wieles: They are full of plans for their great safari in amphibious monster over the uncrossed swamp in Bechuanaland. On 28th. March Linda and Reg went off to Tree Tops ... into Thompson's Falls to take the cream, then out on the Nyeri Road all along the Aberdares ... through lovely hilly country, forest gorges, open plains, lovely cape chestnuts out in their pink flowers and lots of widow birds, mad things with long fluttering black tails like widows' weeds. They fly in a most ungainly manner, rather like a helicopter gone wrong. At Nyeri, We parked at the Outspan Hotel, the owner of which conceived the idea of Tree Tops and had it built ... Notices were up to say visitors to Tree Tops must not have a cough and must be able to keep silent, must wear soft shoes and must be agile.

They joined a party and set off about 2.30, 18 of us in 2 safari wagons ... We drove about 10 miles into forest and then sent out to walk about 1/4 mile up a steep path through the forest. The white hunter, a nice young man called Smith, led with a gun. On either side were rough ladders made of tree branches by which we could shin up a tree if necessary. Well we all climbed safely up the ladders to the house in the 3 fig trees, all given rooms which just had beds in, everywhere were parts of the trees protruding through walls and floors. Out onto the veranda where there were comfortable chairs and we gazed down on a great natural round pool, which has potassium and natural salt and a great meeting place for the wild things of the forest. On top of the bedrooms was another lookout place from where you could see all the surrounding forest and my biggest thrill of an enthralling night was about 5 o'clock, quite light, I saw two different herds of elephants emerging from separate places in the forest and filing along in slow measured fashion full of caution and awareness to the pool, extra salt had been laid out and they adore it.

They spent their time watching for animals, and From the time of arrival we never had a dull moment, the baboons were there first, leaping and swinging in all the trees, cleaning themselves, playing with their babies. Here and there were odd shy bush buck made confident by the presence of the baboons. Then a family of rather ugly old warthogs wandered out of the forest and waddled round the pool. Then a lovely family of black giant forest hog, quite little babies wandered round and then about 5 the elephants, about 40 of them at first with lots of babies and children. We watched them till dinner, they are the most careful animals and have sentries posted and we could see them changing guard. Every now and then our tree house would shake as they bumped a support. After dinner, by the light of an artificial moon one could see a brave rhino emerge, the elephants trumpeted nervously. The rhino approached cautiously, the elephants were 100 to 1. Anyway, the rhino took a bath, had several skirmishes and retreated ... then a magnificent buffalo appeared, huge head and horns, he wallowed in the mud just underneath us. There was always something to watch. At about 12 we all retired to bed because a car came up, police looking for escaped Mau Mau.

After things settled down again, Reg got up at odd times during the night, but only a solitary rhino and buffalo. We got up early and the animals had all gone and you had to pinch yourself to think it all wasn't just a dream. However, all the foot marks and great dollops of elephant dung were evidence enough that it was no dream ... a night of unique and marvellous experience. Linda and Reg said goodbye to Dollie Bruntisfield and took a bus to Nairobi to meet the Ryans, staying at the Norfolk Hotel: to the Markets and we had great fun picking over all the specimens of African art. We bought some elephant and giraffe hair bracelets and a piece of wood carving, a small head and I saw some lovely beaded stools used by the chiefs, and hope I can arrange to have some sent home. That evening they went for dinner to the Mutharga Club (very posh and exclusive) and met our dear Molly and her nice Tony ... the talk was all about the great Lanyuki wedding they had been to, a white hunter, 800 guests at the local club using all the hunters' safari tents, masses of champagne and all the hunters old and young.

They spent another day in Nairobi with the Ryans, meeting some of their friends and dining with them again, and then on 1st. April had to organise their onward flight to Rome: Molly and Tony came in to say goodbye and dear Molly took my best dress, of which the zipper burst, round to an Indian tailor and in a trice was back with a new one in. We had some refreshment together and a nice little talk, then they pushed off on their way back to Molo. Linda and Reg flew via Khartoum and Benghazi and arrived at Rome the following morning, staying at the Albergo Minerva, Via Pantheon: Fell in love with the hotel straight away and know we are going to be happy. It is in the centre of old Rome 100 yds. from the amazing Pagan relic Pantheon. It just has everything I could wish. Out of our window we look over a tangled mass of roof tops, here and there a terraced garden and over everything we can see the great bronze horses on top of the wedding cake Vittoriano.

On Good Friday, 4th. April, they set out to walk across the Tiber to San Pietro, but first went all over San Angelo ... good view of Rome right out to the sea. On to St. Peter's, went all round and gazed in awe. Next day they went to the Vatican: thousands of tourists all pushing and shoving to get into the Vatican. After a tedious process we shoved our way in and tried to absorb the breathtaking matchless treasures. The beautiful soft tapestries designed by Raphael, the 2 great pictures by him, then the sculptures, the great porphyry vase, the hall of animals (sculpture), the Egyptian rooms, the hall of the maps, then the Raphael stanzi, 6 in all, the Forum of Athens and then at last the Sistine Chapel, packed tight with milling tourists, shouting guides. We did our best to cope with it all and then the Library, old manuscript of Virgil, bell rang and we were out, dazed and anxious for refreshment. They decided to go to Tivoli: went to Via Veneto to book up with a tour, talked to an old Italian who said he'd take us for 8000 lira. We accepted, went to Tivoli and Villa D'Este, Hadrian's villa and enjoyed it very much ... Went to the Pizzeria in St. Ignatius Square, a heavenly square and a famous restaurant, photos of famous people, signatures of Clementine and Sarah Churchill I saw.

On another drive, found ourselves at the back of the Quirinal, wandered round to the front, very lovely huge marble statue of horseman ... to San Pietro, it was Easter Sunday and millions or so it seemed were streaming in all directions to see the Pope ... we parked near St. Angelo and joined the throng, couldn't get very near but saw the scene, pope on balcony etc. They went further into the mountains to Lake Mundo Migliore, a lake in perfect crater, on the other side was Castel Gandolfo, summer residence of the Pope. We drove right round the lake into the quaint little village, at the end of the square were the great entrance gates to Pope's Castle. Fascinating views through the narrow streets of lake below. We drank wine in an old taverna and got very gay and chatty. On 7th. April Linda and Reg Sadly left our adorable Albergo Minerva and the great old Pantheon, took our stuff to the great air terminal and modern railway station combined and flew by Alitalia to Paris.

En route they had a lovely sight of the Swiss Alps in full snow, the Matterhorn sticking through the clouds, also Mt. Blanc, glorious sight.

They stayed at the Hôtel de Noailles, Rue Michodière, and walked round all the old haunts, along Quai D'Orsay, over Pont Neuf to Place St. Michel, it started to snow so we had a vermouth cassis ... into Notre Dame to get out of the cold for a while, admired specially the beautiful stained glass and little rare Persian carpets. Then they drove to Vincennes to visit their friends the de Nios: We left the river to go through the Bois de Vincennes and the old castle to our rather funny little hotel. Up 2 flights of rickety stairs, quite a nice room very heated, bathroom with bidet but no loo for 2000 francs per night without breakfast. There were 2 nice big windows overlooking the castle, it was all different and we were pleased.

Later Linda and Reg met Jean and Jeannette de Nio for dinner: We set off for Paris by Metro, walked up the Boulevard St. Michel and settled for one of the big student restaurants, plenty of students, many black, but holidays at the Sorbonne at the moment. Next day they went to visit the great old Château of Vincennes. It has a great part in the history of France, has been a castle for 1000 years. It is enormous and took nearly 2 hours to see over it. Henry V died there, the Duc D'Enghein was shut up here (by Napoleon) and many other things of interest. In this war Nazi Headquarters and they blew a lot of it up, which is now being rebuilt. Afterwards they had lunch with the de Nios, Then we all 4 set off by Metro to visit the Louvre. A great many people there but most interesting. We hurried through the great religious pictures of the Italian School till we got to 'La Gioconda'. Having looked our fill we hurried on to the sculpture, saw the 'Venus de Milo' and 2 statues of Antonus, Hadrian's loved young boy friend ... Reg sat on chair consacré to Bacchus. Guide tipped him off.

On 10th. April it was Still cold and snowing ... went for a bus ride to Rogent-sur-Marne, a darling little place, a real pleasure resort in the summer ... walked along to Joinville where the Marne joins the Seine. J. showed us where she worked at the Pathé-Gaumont Laboratories, making English captions. Later Linda spent a pleasant, fascinating and strenuous few hours in the basement of Galeries Lafayette. Had bought 2 scarves, a nylon dressing gown, and was having great fun trying on frivolous French hats, onlookers enjoying it as well with remarks of 'C'est belle, c'est magnifique', a young interpreter came up and helped me. Anyway I found myself buying 2 hats, then a big bag thing to put them in so I could get a 22% discount. As I saved that I bought 2 little bottles of scent. Next day they went on a Cook's tour past the little church where Millet painted 'The Angelus', to Barbizon where Millet lived and painted, now a school of artists. It was a lovely little town full of houses where artists lived and have lived. At Fontainebleau they Enjoyed seeing over the castle, the glorious Beauvais Tapestry, the rooms Napoleon used. He abdicated here at Fontainebleau. Francis I altered it from an old Gothic castle into an elegant Renaissance bldg.

Linda and Reg said goodbye to the de Nios and on 12th. April flew to London, "thinking how nice and orderly and comfortable England was". They went on to visit her niece Wendy Walduck: Got the train to Hatfield and came out in the dear old village right opposite Hatfield House, home of the Marquis of Salisbury. Wendy met us looking young and fresh and slim and drove us to the house, which was quite lovely, Georgian I think, a beautiful square hall with 4 large white pillars, all papered in the most lovely large Wedgwood blue and white wallpaper, great lovely scrolly white wrought iron doors into the sitting room and a wonderful pink Persian rug, soft and exquisite, on the floor. Never saw anything modern I could admire so much ... Wendy and I had a walk over the farm after, 400 acres, 24 employed and about 12 cottages and a herd of pure Frisian cattle.

After staying the night they returned to London, where Linda visited her friend Kath Herd, who worked at Marshall and Snellgrove's: bought some clothes for my grandchildren and really spent all day behind the scenes and enjoyed it very much. They went to see various friends, including the Chalkers at Hayward's Heath: Ann brought her young Italian lover, Enrico, who didn't talk English. Ann talks good Italian and anyway we had great fun. Another day Linda went Round the shops deciding on a coat, which I got at Jaegers' for £52 and a summer suit at D.H. Evans for £33 ... Went to Haymarket Theatre at night, Ralph Richardson and Celia Johnston in 'Flowering Cherry'. Very excellent acting but dreary and tedious subject matter, was irritated I had chosen that. On 19th. April she Took Reg round to Regent St. and we bought £80 worth of handmade peasant Yugoslavian rugs ... went off to Tate Gallery, saw the lovely John Sargent portraits ... lots of French impressionists, Turners, Constables and then the Moderns, all very puzzling, a portrait of Helena Rubinstein by Graham Sutherland, a thing of Russell Drysdale's, a Ned Kelly thing by Sidney Nolan.

They hired a Morris Minor for a tour, stopping first at Madame Tussaud's: both enjoyed it, saw Bob Menzies, not very good, Royal family in nice modern dresses, thought poor Queen Mary came off worst. Afterwards they went on through Aylesbury to Cuddington, found Doreen Vigne in her 15th. cent. half timbered cottage, an old carter's house of the original old form ... spent the afternoon with her, had a lovely drive round, saw glorious old villages, Longharden, Little Witchenden, past Notley Abbey where Laurence and Vivien Olivier live ... spent the night at Bull Inn, Aylesbury. Linda and Reg continued through the Cotswolds: Got to Benford, called on David Phillips at Fulbrook, he was at the Lamb Inn, pushed on there, met David, had drinks, booked in for 2 nights, it was such a special inn. Going on via Marlborough, Bath and Winchester, they returned to London on 28th. April.

Next day they went back to Winchester and had lunch with Fanny May, who lives in a top flat of a beautiful old Georgian house in the cathedral close and overlooks the Cathedral. We were delighted with it and after a good lunch Fanny guided us round, saw the famous old tombstone of the Grenadier Guard, looked over the cathedral, the tomb of William Rufus is there, also the bones of the old English King Ethelbert, 600, Ethelberg etc. up to 800. Jane Austen is also buried there and the old Bishop of Winchester founded the school in 1400. We wandered through narrow streets, saw the spot where William the Conqueror had a palace, the old Buller Cross, King Alfred's statue and a wonderful old inn from 1300 called 'God be Got'. Then up to the Law Courts where King Arthur's Table hangs on the wall with all the names of the knights. All fascinating to think of, so much early English history.

They also visited Fareham, where we found Wallington Lodge (Col. D'Arch Smith) where Jen and Pat first lived in England. It was a darling old stone partly Georgian house and a beautiful garden. We pushed on up the Meon Valley to Droxford ... we enquired about Jen and eventually found her house. On 1st. May Reg worked in London and afterwards they drove to Glyndebourne: The gardens were so glorious we wandered round in a sort of dream of beauty too good to be true, the weather is so wonderful. Every now and again we could hear snatches of opera from rehearsing. We got into the auditorium and saw all the actors fully dressed for the opera 'Falstaff', very clever young producer talking to them in 4 different languages. It made me long to go to a real performance. Two days later, after visiting Brighton and Arundel, they had dinner at a typical good English Pub with an atmosphere that is unique. The gentry were drinking in the main bar and the locals, farmers etc. in the other one, the locals much more interesting.

During their last week in England Linda and Reg Took ourselves off to Leonard's Lee near Horsham, a wonderful garden belonging to Sir Gerald Loda, been a show garden for 3 generations. The trees, sloping lawns with ponds at the bottom were like Melb. Botanical Gardens, but the garden is massed with azaleas, camellias and rhododendrons. Their final night was spent at Drury Lane Theatre: My Fair Lady was wonderful, Rex Harrison quite perfect, Julie Andrews adorable and sweet voice and old Stanley Holloway also. Cecil Beaton's decor was glorious, the Ascot scene all in black and white and the ballroom scene were outstanding. We came away very happy and full of it all. On 7th. May they bid farewell to their London friends and flew to America to continue their travels. En route, We called down at Shannon in Ireland, a free port, it was like David Jones, everything for sale. Irish linen, Limerick lace, Donegal tweed, bought a cashmere sweater.

15. U.S.A. AND CANADA

Linda and Reg went to the United States to visit Linda's cousin Gwenda and her husband Dick Schanzle and to attend medical conferences. They arrived at Boston about 11, Gwenda there to meet us, all very excited, she looked smart and fascinating, talked a great deal ... she gave us a lovely drive round Harvard University and the lovely old bits of the town, the famous houses. We were fascinated, the buildings are so beautiful, almost too good to be true. She lives about 15 miles out in a beautiful suburb, all wooded and the houses peer through the trees. Next day, Dick took a holiday and we went for a drive to historic Concord and Lexington, scene of the first battle of the Revolution ... both little towns of great charm, the old Puritan white wooden churches are lovely. They flew to Washington for their first medical conference on 10th. May, staying at the Shoreham Hotel, "quite superb, heavenly garden and fountains etc., 16 dollars per night", and visiting Capitol Hill: inside Congress Library, just a dream of magnificence, great white marble pillars, mosaics and frescoes in beautiful colours. Saw bits about Washington, Jefferson, Lincoln etc.

They registered for the conference next day and had a long walk round Washington, past Australian Embassy, delighted to find it a beautiful large house in a most spacious garden, lovely trees and the most exciting show of azaleas. While Reg attended conference sessions, Linda and other wives got into buses and were taken to lovely Art Gallery, built with splendour and magnificence in the best traditions of the Old World. A quick guided tour, picking out 1 picture to discuss each phase of art. Giotto, 13th. cent. to 14th. cent., Rembrandt and Franz Hals 15th. cent. Lovely room of El Greco, then Baroque and French impressionist 'Odalisque', Monet. Lovely Constable, 'Salisbury Cathedral' and Gainsborough, 'Georgina Duchess of Devonshire', Whistler, John Singer Sargent - lastly Salvador Dali's 'Last Supper', huge impressive work painted in Spain. At a Presidential reception at a Dr. Everett Gordon's, the Powder Room took my eye, in the style of French Empire, Fleur-de-Lis and much gilt and black marble.

On 13th. May Linda went on a bus tour to Lincoln Memorial, quite wonderful, worth coming to Washington for ... wonderful bronze sculpture and view over the Potomac to Capitol. Next day she had a quick visit to White House ... loved the famous Blue Room and the graceful chandeliers ... I was introduced to Mrs. Foster Dulles, rather deadpan face and not young, dressed in beautiful silk suit and black hat. Afterwards they went by launch up the Potomac River to Mt. Vernon, were given lovely lunch boxes on board of the most heavenly fried chicken. Had a lovely wander round the gardens and dear old house, so beautifully situated on the Potomac ... were driven through the perfectly glorious old colonial Georgian town of Alexandria, full of history. At the Australian Embassy that evening she and Reg Met the Marks, Naval Attaché here, used to be Pat Burnett's captain, asked back to their house for dinner. Another day, I took myself off to George Washington's Memorial, an obelisk over 500 ft. high, very beautiful and simple and dominates all the very lovely buildings.

They travelled by bus on 17th. May to Baltimore, where Linda "left the men at the John Hopkins Hospital" and drove with Mrs. Eaton, the president's wife, to an old sea captain's mansion dating from 1793, name Ridgley and the house Hampton ... It was fun going over it, seemed so full of life and so different from the English and continental great houses. First Ridgley was a friend of Lafayette, his portrait is there, he grew rich with the Baltimore clippers. Beautiful gardens, great hemlock, spruce and cedar trees. Afterwards they all set off for Wilmington, capital of Delaware, famous for Dupont Institute ... We walked over to view Mrs. Du Pont's palazzo and magnificent gardens, a vista lined with pink flowering chestnut trees and then white, which stretched for miles down to a great stone colonnade, past fountains down to a Temple of Love. She is 74 and when she dies it will be given to the American public. Back to Institute, shown over the wards, marble floors, murals, 85 beds for children up to 16 and they do not pay.

Their next stop was Atlantic City, where they stayed at the Atlantic Sea Hotel. While Reg worked, Linda toured the sea front, 5 miles of board walk alongside the sea shore, all divided into lines of chairs with board walks along the sand. On other side were shops of all kinds ... another thing was the rolling chairs, some pushed by coloured men, others with a sort of engine to take 4 or 5 people, just to go up and down the board walk for those who didn't want to walk. Many many mink capes and coats were to be seen. From there they went to Philadelphia, huge city on the Delaware River, 3rd. biggest in U.S.A. Has 5 universities and the greatest number of medical students in the world ... Went to the Independence Hall in old State House, lovely Georgian building where independence was signed and later the Constitution was drawn up and for some time Philadelphia was the capital. We were shown lovely old Hospital, date 1735, corner stone laid by Benjamin Franklin and the old Christ Church cemetery where he and many other great men of that period are buried.

At New York they stayed at the Barbizon Plaza Hotel overlooking Central Park. After work Linda met Reg and went up Empire State Building, a truly gigantic experience. Felt I was looking down on a city on another planet. They had dinner with a friend, Joy Small, and walked through Greenwich Village, Washington Square, Eleanor Roosevelt's house, saw the men playing chess at the chess tables in the Square. After visiting Broadway, Times Square and Fifth Avenue they travelled by train to Toronto on 21st. May, staying at the Royal York Hotel. They went to Niagara Falls, but found them an "anticlimax after Victoria Falls". A visit to Montreal was more successful: liked Montreal straight away, very French and nice buildings, spacious with character.

They next returned to Boston, where the wives of conference delegates were taken to Isabella Stewart Gardner Museum, just too fabulous for words. Loved the beautiful courtyard, Venetian windows and such wonderful flowers. Treasures simply packed together ... Drove back through lovely Lexington and Cambridge, saw Longfellow's house, very large and yellow. The conference finished on 26th. May; Linda and Reg, who were now staying with the Schanzles again, went for a lovely walk in the beautiful evening air across the Boston Common to the Gold Domed State House on Beacon Hill, along the famous walnut and chestnut st., Louisberg Square, along the River Charles, back by the Park. Next day, we had a lovely drive all along the Atlantic Coast through historic town of Quincy. The drive got lovelier and lovelier ... through the glorious town of Cohasset (like Lexington with village green), lilac, wisteria, dogwood, maple all making lovely splashes of colour against the vivid green of grass and trees.

They went to Manchester to visit friends, Thomas and Judy Gardiner: to Gales Point, a large incredible old weather-worn wooden house, a massive pile of towers, windows, curves and nooks ... beautiful views of water, rocks, islands etc., looking out to the opening of the inlet and Atlantic Ocean. We felt excited and elated. From there they drove to Salem: House of the Seven Gables in Turner St., 1600 and something, dark brown wood, right on the sea front ... wandered round some of the lovely old merchant houses of bygone days, mostly in American Georgian style, very distinguished, their dignity and proportions beautiful, simple and elegant. At a party they attended with the Schanzles, Linda noted that people all drank and talked at once as always seems to happen when meeting strange Americans.

On 1st. June they flew back to New York, where Reg had arranged some work visits, and stayed in a flat by the East River: we walked through great silent eerie Downtown, Sunday evening, all was deserted. We walked down Wall St., silent as the grave, just like a great mountain canyon. While Reg worked, Linda went to the Metropolitan Art Gallery: saw Salvador Dali's 'Crucifixion', good work but different and rather theatrical, lovely Monets and French impressionists, Whistler's picture of his mother ... a lovely portrait of Consuela Vanderbilt, Duchess of Marlborough and her son Ivor by Goldoni, Italian, lovely romantic thing. Etruscan pottery, old Grecian urns, 500 B.C., brown and black, Rodin sculpture, Persian carpets, Chinese porcelain, all too much to take in. Another day they took a bus down 1st. Ave. to United Nations Bldgs., very modern, very vast, very imposing, lots of people. We went into an Assembly Room, not the main one (it was not meeting), this was on International Arbitration or something. Listened to involved speeches in English and French, interested in the seating arrangements, all alphabetical so Israel was next to Jordan. The Holy See also had a place.

On 4th. June they walked through Central Park to 8th. Ave. West to the Planetarium, masses of children waiting to go in, it was all rather fascinating, we hadn't quite known what to expect, except we saw all stars of the Northern Hemisphere, not so good for us ... we proceeded to a Bohemian type of interesting restaurant on 3rd. Ave. called 'King of the Sea', very large place, every sort of fish, Reg had stuffed flounder, I had shellfish au gratin, loved the company. Next day Linda saw a chiffon dress advertised at Russells', 36th. Ave. and 5th. St., so I gathered up steam and took bus to R., nice kind New Yorker served me, it was difficult as there were 3 lovely colours and styles all suiting me, I just couldn't decide, chose the flame one in rather a chemise style, 49.50 dollars and went off well pleased ... to Frick Museum, 39th. St. and 5th. Ave. A millionaire's house turned open for the public, lovely pictures ... enjoyed it all very much, especially walking on beautiful thick carpets.

They paid a flying visit to Canada to see friends at Toronto, the Harrises: we took ourselves to a large shopping centre, had beer in the Brass Rail Tavern, saw many Canadian lumberjack types, saw many fur stores ... we set off for their weekend home on Georgian Bay ... unloaded all the stuff into a water taxi, no roads to the house. We went 10 miles by water, lovely Canadian scenery, inlets, islands, rocks, pines and interesting houses on the headlands ... took us for a canoe ride round to see Katy, a character

165

who lives here all year round and attends to the needs of the people who come here only in summer.

Linda and Reg flew to Chicago on 10th. June and stayed at the Sheraton Hotel, bizarre, foyer like Temple of Karnak, later American Gothic and American Renaissance. The following day, "my birthday today, 55 I think", they went to the Art Gallery, where they saw lots of bright double-faced Picassos, 2 gorgeous Turners, Constable and lovely French Post-Impressionists, Monet specially lovely, 2 glorious Renoirs and a curious Salvador Dali ... wandered to the Conrad Hilton, 3000 bedrooms, said to be world's largest hotel, wandered through all the lounges, bars, stalls and shops and down to the Exhibition Hall, where we had read the funerary people were exhibiting. We were shoved off as we weren't registered, but not before we had seen an amazing sight, gorgeous coffin after gorgeous coffin lined with pink satin and other rich stuffs and also something like a dress show, presumably fine raiment to dress up the departed. They visited nearby friends, the Masons: They have several acres of woodlands and a large modern studio house right in the middle. They are both artists ... she showed us her large studio filled with dried things from the woods, she makes prints of these and does lithographs ... the results she showed us were most lovely, Japanese-like in simple beauty.

On 12th. June they flew to Minnesota, where they stayed at the "Kohler Hotel opposite the magnificent Mayo Clinic". While Reg worked at the clinic, Linda joined a conducted tour round the buildings ... It is a unique set-up, founded by the Mayo brothers, now about 350 doctors all pooling their knowledge, run by a board of governors who control the finances, all are paid salaries, as well there are over 500 fellows, doctors who come to specialise and stay from 3 to 5 years, there are special houses provided for them and their families. Last year they saw 156,000 patients ... the whole thing an amazing and unique organization. Linda had her hair permed by a nice little girl who hadn't met an Australian before and wondered how I spoke English so well. They next travelled to Denver: fantastic airport, masses of shops displaying wild west goods, Mexican and Indian products of all descriptions. Masses of people all wearing these products in some guise or other, making much to watch. Their hotel was filled with large shapeless unlovely elderly women and a few husbands of the same ilk. They were all bedecked with flowery hats, bags, jewellery etc., they were a convention of American Gold Star Mothers (mothers who lost sons in the war).

They flew on to Flagstaff, right over the Rockies, much snow in many places, about 13,000 ft. high, we flew about 2000 ft. above that and had wonderful views. On 16th. June they drove to the El Tovar Hotel at Grand Canyon, right on the rim of the Canyon and it is just enormous and defies all description ... Had a look at various Indian curio shops ... their silver work and turquoise studded jewellery is really very fine, so are their hand made rugs and in fact many things are good, but surrounded by so much rubbish and awful people buying the rubbish and decking themselves out as Red Indians, cowboys and Mexicans. They went for a bus trip along the East Rim: There is so much to see. In the Canyon rise up great eroded peaks, many having names of Oriental temples and that is how they look, they reminded me of the Borobodur Buddhist temple in Java, the Potala in Tibet and many Indian temples.

On their return trip Linda and Reg went to the Desert Watch Tower. It was nearly at the head of the Canyon where the 2 Colorado Rivers, great and little meet and we could gaze over the Painted Desert, which is comprised of many many different coloured sands. The Watch Tower was a copy of similar towers built by the Indians in their ancient days ...there were Indian paintings on the walls, faithful copies very like aboriginal paintings and then a picture made of the different coloured sands, just as they really do for their various ceremonies. Next day they walked a little way down the mule trail; "it is about 8 miles to the bottom. Takes about 5 hours". They then went by bus to the West Rim, where they could see more of the Colorado River. We went to a place called Hermit Lookout, where we could look north to Utah and Salt Lake City ... we had excellent views of the mule trail, we could see the various parties wending their tortuous way up, we waited at the top to see some of them arrive, all seemed very young but thought it wonderful but exhausting. We watched the mule man unsaddle a string of about 1 doz. mules.

They flew to Las Vegas on 18th. June, staying at the Show Boat Hotel: we passed along the famous Strip where all the luxury hotels are, Tropicana, Il Rancho Sahara, Royal Nevada, Desert Inn Sands and about 10 others. All outdoing each other in luxury and novelty ... summoned up energy and strength to go out and face Las Vegas, feeling very queer and out of our element. The first impact was the Casino of our own Show Boat, a huge room, red carpet, long heavy carved wooden bar, great brass chandeliers like the old gas ones, huge paintings all round of naked ladies and every sort of gambling imaginable ... to the city to see the bright lights, glitter gulch it is called, more so than Broadway it is said. For about 1 mile there is nothing but bars and casinos all lit with strange and different signs. The following day Linda and Reg went shopping: wandered all along the main street and went into the Golden Nugget and had cool drinks and watched their show, an orchestra of 4 girls ... did some more shopping in one of the many fantastic and amazing curio shops and then got bus back laden with parcels and quite happy ... got a taxi to the Strip, the air was still blistering, the taxi man said it was 106 and the day before 112. He was very chatty and discussed all the merits of the various shows.

On 22nd. June they went to the airport, to find our plane delayed 1 hour. Sat in the almost dark bar having odd drinks and watching the strange types that flitted by, funny man McShane spoke to us, really quite interesting but rather tight, he was drinking vodka and introduced us to 2 blonde girl friends, said they were Cherokee Indians and very fine people, they looked like blonde Jewesses. They flew to Los Angeles, staying at the Hotel Westwood Plaza. Linda was delighted with all I saw, the palms in the streets, the hills looming up through the ends of the streets and all the different gay types of architecture ... I adored Disneyland, much much better than I expected, the train ride through the Grand Canyon, Painted Desert and the boat trip down the Amazon stand out as highlights. We were there from 6 till 10.30 so saw it by day and night and both were wonderful.

Next day Reg went to work with medical friends, while Linda went shopping: there is a glorious little shopping place called Glendon, they are all Spanish type with tiles and lovely shrubs and flowers and you go into patios and inner courtyard and up wrought iron staircases and the shops' contents are as interesting as their exteriors. Later she met Reg and they went into the famous Brown Derby, haunt of the Hollywood stars, then we walked up Rodeo Ave. towards the hills. Beautiful day, beautiful street, exciting shops, then lovely houses, all so different ... We wandered on right up to Sunset Boulevard and right through the Beverley Hills Hotel, lovely grounds. On their last day in Los Angeles a doctor friend drove us to Santa Monica Beach, met Leo Carillo, dashing Spaniard, American actor of the old school, now a well-known T.V. artist and then on to 20th. Century Fox, where they were taken round and shown all the various sets ... We were taken inside where they were filming 'The Remarkable Mr. Pennyfather', Clifton Webb.

Linda and Reg flew on to San Francisco on 26th. June: as we set foot out into the streets we were happy with San Fran. Lovely fresh sunny weather, beautiful shops, interesting bldgs. and steep hills and views all round of blue water. We took the famous cable tram up Powell St. to the Nob, quite fascinating, then elevator up to the top of the Mark Hopkins Hotel, very crowded, well dressed people drinking cocktails and we could see all round, Golden Gate Bridge, Berkeley Oakland Bridge etc. That evening, Capt. Gross called for us and drove us through Chinatown to Fisherman's Wharf and gave us an expensive and enjoyable meal at Franciscan, great glass walls and windows looked right over to Alcatraz Prison which was brilliantly lit. Next day they went out with a friend from the American Medical Association who took us up the steepest hill in San Fran., Union St., then down a fascinating street called Lombard, it was lined with pink hydrangeas ... up to Telegraph Hill, glorious view of the Bay ... Then over the Golden Gate, a great thrill, it is slim and graceful and has the lovely Sausalito Hills as a background ... wound up the hill again to a large and beautiful hotel called Altamira, a huge alfresco terrace with an incomparable view over the Bay and mountains beyond and the lovely white jumble of bldgs. on the peninsula that is San Francisco, watched the lights come on and the moon come up behind the California pines.

On 28th. June, Dr. Elphick took us for a splendid drive ... to their pretty little suburb El Cerito and their house ... the architecture is so varied, such fun, it reminds me of many European cities but it is nevertheless unique. They went next day on a bus tour to Oakland and Piedmont, to the home of the giant Redwoods, we walked through the forest and gazed in joy, glorious soaring things they were, I enjoyed most how they grew in clumps together ... they have a huge base like a big Doric column and they grow as high as the canyon to get the sun. Also growing were masses of bay trees, mountain laurel, they call it also Buckeye, and alderwood. On their last day in San Francisco they walked to Fisherman's Wharf for dinner at the Franciscan, where they watched boats come and go and the lights of Alcatraz come on, then took the wonderful cable car back, great thrill going round the curves and down the steep hills ... Home to bed happy and yet sad - our last night in U.S.A. We have had a splendid time and agree that the people are kind, polite, generous.

Linda and Reg flew by Qantas to Honolulu on 1st. July and found the same beautiful flowers everywhere and people in colourful island dress, the long shapeless muu-muus adopted by all shapes and sizes of women caught my eye. They stayed at the Reef Hotel and walked along the gay Boulevard where the shops are magnificent, filled with island wares as well as beautiful sophisticated things. Everywhere tall waving coconut palms and frangipanis. Linda saw again the Royal Hawaiian Hotel at Moana; "I had stayed there 30 years ago when it was the only big hotel". On 3rd. July they Woke up and savoured the de luxe view from our de luxe room in our de luxe hotel, knowing this was the last of our de luxe adventures for many a long day. Next day they flew back to Sydney via the Gilbert and Ellice Islands and Fiji.

16. ASIA AND EUROPE

Five years after their visit to the U.S.A., Linda and Reg again set off on their travels. This time there were no conferences and sightseeing was the main object, although as usual Reg had arranged a few medical visits at places on their route. They flew by Air India to Singapore on 17th. July, 1963 and stayed at the Goodwood Park Hotel, The old part very rococo, once a German embassy, then during war Mountbatten's headquarters ... spacious and most elegant. Beautiful Chinese lacquer furniture and jade green and black Thai silk furnishings. They rang the Chinese novelist Han Suyin, given us by Henrietta Drake-Brockman. She was away in Hong Kong ... Singapore much changed since my visit in 1927 - Still the lovely old English buildings on the grand scale, but masses of new large blocks of flats and the traffic absolutely terrific, still the polyglot collection of races and creeds, gone the rickshaws, now the trishaws and men on bicycles. While Reg went to work with medical friends on 18th. July, Linda drove to Johore and saw the Great White Mosque and found Han Suyin's house and delivered the books H. D-B. had sent to her per me.

Next day they flew to Bangkok, staying at the Trocadero Hotel Plaza. They took a boat trip on the klongs, the canals which thread the city: saw the fascinating life on and by the river, all the floating markets, people selling water kept in huge great jars, selling ice cream, ice and even hot breakfasts. They seem to cook delicious food on tiny little charcoal braziers. They passed the Royal Barge House; the barges were gorgeously decorated graceful affairs 160 feet long, some made out of 1 single teak tree. They are brought out once a year in October when the river is high, 60 oarsmen in ancient dress. Next they went to the Emperor's Palace and the Temple of the Emerald Buddha. A mile of golden pagodas, flowered pagodas, great jewel and gold encrusted temples, dragons, Buddhas, gold half-bird half-woman statues, live Buddhas in their saffron robes and all enclosed by a great gallery painted with murals of ancient history and legend. I thought of Kublai Khan and the ancient capital Marco Polo discovered or perhaps the walled city of Peking.

On 22nd. July they flew to Delhi, to be "greeted by atmosphere that seemed a blast from Hades itself". From the Askoka Hotel they took a taxi into town past all the grand buildings of New Delhi designed by Sir Edwin Lutyens ... shown various sights but too hot to bother about them ... Old Delhi with much of the old walls and gates, last remains of fascinating old Moghul houses with overhanging balconies and filigreed grilles. Teeming life going on as it always had. The Great Mosque and the great Red Fort, but too hot to explore them. They took a bus to Agra: the scenes of country village life intensely interesting and all along were ruins of mosques etc., old mud villages clustered round and in fascinating ruins of past Islamic splendour, sheep, goats, cows, peacocks, water buffalo, slender Indian women carrying water in beautiful brass containers, much life round the wells as in biblical days. First stop was a sikandra, a beautiful Moorish gate leading up to the mosque where Akbar's tomb was. Akbar the first great Moghul King and responsible for so many of the lovely Moghul buildings.

Linda and Reg went on to Agra, the heart and core of India and centre of the Great Moghuls ... to Fathepol Sikri - the great ancient capital fortress of Akbar ... in spite of the heat we were enthralled with the country life and the villages and surprised to see so many trees dotted around ... Then the great crenellated walled fortress came into view, passed through the great gates and into the citadel. All very red and vast, court after court of Moghul might, pomp and splendour and oh so hot. Soon they came to Akbar's Red Fort on the River Jumna, a huge walled fortress outside but inside exquisitely lovely, a fortress was really a palace and from the delicate white carved filigree and coloured inlaid quarters of the women, had a wonderful view over landscape and the river below and about a mile up - the Taj - so we saw the Taj after all the other wonders and there it was, serene and beautiful, a perfect thing surrounded by the lovely gardens. A long walk up from the entrance gate. Inside was just as beautiful, the white marble was inlaid with cornelian, agate, turquoise and jasper and I don't know what other colour, making lovely flowers and exquisite designs and patterns. The great terrace surrounding it and the 4 beautiful minarets, harmony and poetry in stone, spiritually and physically refreshing.

On their last day in India they took a taxi to Old Delhi once more, this time we saw all the Great Mosque, largest in India ... the old Red Fort a must, full of beauty inside, all white marble, delicate filigree carved marble screens, fountains and the audience hall, most beautiful, the work of Shah Jahan of Taj fame, grandson of Akbar. Linda and Reg flew to Istanbul on 26th. July and found the skyline dotted with mosques and minarets, minarets very slender and classic after the rather garish and bizarre ones of India, over the Golden Horn to Hilton Hotel - quite a fabulous place, huge open air marble terrace overlooking the Bosphorus ... India was a deep experience but one was glad to go, it filled me with a sad despair. Here the background is of magnificent Sultans, harems, sweetmeats, soft breezes, singing birds etc. The people are so much gayer, the climate so much kinder.

During their first day they Did a trip to the Topkapi Palace, palace of Suleiman the Magnificent ... now been made into a museum after the Revolution in 1924 by Kemal Ataturk, a wonderful collection of Ming, Tang and Sung china etc. - saw all the jewels, jewelled head-dress for turbans, jewelled quivers for the arrows, amazing thrones. Best of all Peacock Throne, on peacock green enamel studded with 25,000 matchless pearls, diamonds, rubies, emeralds etc. - The last Sultan had built himself a beautiful new palace right on the B., thought this was too old- fashioned. They finished the day at a night club, where they saw a programme of Turkish dancing - very very good, a troupe from Konga where the dancing is the Whirling Dervish type.

Next day they went for a boat trip up the Bosphorus, which is 20 miles long from Sea of Marmara to Black Sea, about 1 mile wide in the widest part. We passed the New Palace of the last Sultan, all sorts of lovely villas, gardens, villages and open air restaurants. Then past the famous old fortress almost at the Black Sea entrance. They were doing Hamlet there, wonderful. Landed at a village for tea, saw the old men lined up for a hookah ... apparently a speciality there because looked into the kitchen and saw great charcoal fires and saw them winding the tobacco leaf round the stem of the hubbly bubbly - had a puff and very nice it was. They started their final day with a tour of the mosques, beginning with the Blue Mosque, in front of ancient Roman Hippodrome, filled with beautiful bluish ceramics and masses of antique colourful carpets on the floor, and finishing with Sant Sophia, a sort of Westminster Abbey of history. A Christian church built by Constantine in 600 A.D. ... all the rich Byzantine Christian mosaics are there. Then they took a boat trip to the island of Buyukada in the Sea of Marmara: shore lined with open air restaurants filled with people. Walked up to the square and found it filled with horse carriages and rather villainous drivers ... apparently no other transport but bicycles and horse carriages. I said how lovely the scented gardens, humming birds, roses and peaches all were. Reg replied 'Smells of horse piss and manure'.

On 29th. July Linda and Reg flew to Athens by Air France, staying at the Palace Hotel: People rest here in the summer from 1 till 5 and then work from 5 to 8 ... French much spoken, more than English. Later they set off by bus to Acropolis to see a thing called 'Les Sons et Lumieres'. Dined in an open air restaurant facing the Acropolis ... walked up through the pines up the limestone way to top of hill, saw all the mountains and hills round about glowing with lights, took our seats to gaze on Acropolis. Then the performance, beautifully done by French people, a gift to the glory of Greece. By clever sounds and lighting they took us back to the days of Pericles and the victory of Marathon and Salamis and building of the Pantheon. Lovely thing to do on hot summer night in Athens.

Next day they went by launch through the Saronic Gulf to Aegina: Islanders all lined up with donkeys to take people up to the Temple of Aphaia ... Lovely setting on old limestone smooth rocks under the pines, gazing at the B.C. Doric temple like a small Pantheon ... passed right close to the little homespun whitewashed village. Guide said Demosthenes committed suicide there. After a picnic lunch they continued to Hydra, Little fishing port with promenade lined with shops of local arts and crafts and street cafes and restaurants. Behind the cubist whitewashed houses with coloured shutters, mostly Reckitt's Blue, struggled up the pine-clad limestoney mountains ... Went into the little Byzantine church and monastery, cool and whitewashed, filled with icons and gold mosaics. Climbed up steps through narrow streets and got the idea of Hydra. Still think Capri the most beautiful of all islands, but this is still simpler. In Athens they dined with a doctor friend at a Plaka taverna - it is the old Greek quarter and old Turkish one also, narrow streets, whitewashed houses, overhanging balconies. Our funny little restaurant climbed up 2 flights of stairs amongst all the intimate domestic affairs, then on flat roof, vine covered pergola, tables and chairs, music and crowded with people.

On 31st. July Linda and Reg flew to Crete by Olympic Airways and visited Knossos: did the museum, saw the original jewels, tools, ornaments, jars, potteries. Neolithic, then Golden Age, Decadent period and then the Dorians conquered them ... Watched Cretan dancing, music quick, rather like Highland dancing at times except the men leapt into the air and sideways, kicked their legs together with great clicking. They flew on to Rhodes next day, stayed at the Belvedere Hotel and went to Lindos, ancient city, full of history, early mythology, Dorians, Crusaders 1309 to 1522. Suleiman the Turk took it then and the Knights went off to Malta ... First view of Lindos was an acropolis standing up on a craggy peak, sea behind and village below. Thought of ancient Carthage, said so to some woman who crossly said 'I do not know Carthage, it is ancient Greece' ... mounted donkeys to go up the steep approach, wonderful view, gathered at the bottom of steep old steps leading up to the Crusader part of the fortress, a bit like Mont St. Michel, up through the gateway and onto the top, where were the remains of Doric temple and an ancient old Byzantine church.

Next day Linda recorded: forgot to say that Helen of Troy came here for refuge and her friend was Queen here. The Queen eventually had her hanged from a tree and then they made it a holy place, calling it St. Helen of the Tree. She and Reg went on a tour of Rhodes: Fascinating little harbour where the alleged Colossus was, mixture of architecture, mosques, minarets, Italian Byzantine overlooked by the giant Crusader fortress citadel. In through a great gate, into the world of the Crusades, 1309 to 1522. To the museum, the old Hospital room, 30 beds for knights, 130 cell-like things where presumably their servants slept near them. Saw some remains of old statuary - Venus drying her hair and Clytemnestra, very beautiful. Then up the Street of Knights where all the knights of different tongues had their Auberge or Inn, ceremonial crests carved on the outside showed whether French, Spanish, English, German or Italian ... we could see that of Richard the Lion Heart. We walked up this most famous and well-preserved street of the Moyen Age to the Palace of the Grand Masters.

Before returning to Athens on 2nd. August they went for a walk: We wandered through a maze of narrow streets, all sitting in the streets or in the open doors of their cave-like houses, tailors making things sitting on the doorstep gossiping to the shoemaker next door, women feeding baby sitting in street gossiping to old woman doing some needlework. Then they took a bus to the airport, where they had an awful shove and push to get wedged into small hot plane, worst journey ever, no cooling system and packed to the utmost, 1 hour of torture. Returning to the Palace Hotel, they went by bus to the Acropolis: Reg went off on the hill to take photos ... came back having seen the cave where Socrates took hemlock ... Had a happy time wandering where we liked instead of being pushed round by a guide ... Walked down by the Theatre of Dionysius and the Odeon and into the Plaka, just as fascinating by day as at night. Came to a darling little toy square, trees, houses with shutters and balconies and even a little Byzantine church, a few tables and chairs stuck out in the street and table full of gay young French girls. So we thankfully sat down and ate and drank happily. The fat old mine host took Reg into the kitchen to see first what he should get. We had tomato and cucumber salad and delicious kebab and fried potatoes.

Another bus trip took them round the coast: at one smart resort was the yacht of Onassis, Churchill had been with him a few days ago ... Climbed up to the Temple of Poseidon. Wonderful view of all the Cyclades Islands. Their doctor friend drove them to the Piraeus, crowded with people eating out of doors. Sat right on the waterfront, all the sea craft bobbing about in front. Had lovely seafood. On their last day Linda and Reg were "both with horrid colds, so feeling sleepy and pianissimo", but nevertheless undertook a classical tour to Corinth: great Venetian fortress up on the highest hill, below ruins of lovely old Doric temple ... 600 B.C. Then many Roman remains, an Agora, statues etc. The place where St. Paul addressed the Corinthians, 52 A.D. From Corinth to Mycenae in the most mountainous, craggy, melancholy country. The acropolis on a saddle back between 2 great peaks - Great walk up to the Cyclopean Walls and the Lion Gate, all so old, strong and primitive ... we visited the supposed tomb of Agamemnon, 1 of 9 Beehive tombs excavated by Schliemann of Troy fame. I found this most interesting, the great entrance was almost Egyptian ... many things found in these tombs that have given valuable information. All this antique part of the world goes back to the legends of Ancient Greece, Hercules, Jason, Medea etc. The last stop was at Epidamus, beautiful place, lots of shady trees and pine groves etc., old Roman remains, Hippodrome and temples and this wonderful Greek theatre, 17,000 people, remarkably preserved.

They flew to London by Olympic Airways via Rome and Paris on 5th.

August and stayed at the Overseas Club. Their old orthopaedic friend Jacky Burrows and 2 young doctors took us to old Anchor Inn in Southwark, on Thames near Globe Theatre, saw old house with plaque saying Chistopher Wren lived there whilst building St. Paul's Cathedral. Katherine of Aragon also slept there after coming up Thames to marry Henry 8th.

Here there is a fortnight's break in the daily diary entries, covered by a brief summary of social doings with friends. Then on 23rd. August Linda and Reg went with her sister Ritza to Paris, staying at the Hôtel Louvois in Montmartre: At night went looking for interesting Left Bank restaurant, got lost far away from transport. I spoke to Frenchman (no English), my French became fluent. In the end he took the 3 of us all round Paris in his car looking for restaurant ... all closed. All Parisiennes shut up in August and leave it to the trippers. Next day they wandered round the Seine, its banks and isles, Notre Dame, Ile St. Louis where there are all 17th. cent. houses, with plaques of the famous people who lived there.

On 30th. August Linda and Reg flew to Vienna and found lodgings in Lobkowitz Platz. They took a bus to Kreuzenstein Castle, Lovely troubador Charlemagne castle, turrets, moats and drawbridge, old weapons of war, battering rams, catapults, then into the courtyard - great torches lit it up, old Gothic and Byzantine galleries and cloisters. Then some string music of Mozart and some great trumpet music of Beethoven, lovely and fascinating. Another bus trip took them to Kloster Neuer Berg, 13th. century, very rich ... lovely view to hills and woods ... quite near is Durerstein Castle where Richard Coeur de Lion was imprisoned. On 2nd. September they Went over the Hofnung, learnt a lot of Habsburg history, many pictures of Franz Josef, Sissy, Maria Theresa, Marie Louise, L'Aiglon etc., Marie Antoinette - popped into Kapuziner Kirche near us, all the great mammoth Baroque tombs of the Habsburgs are there ... had a happy lunch in a famous old inn, Griechensgrebel in the Fleishmarkt dating back to 1300, once an old quarter of Greek merchants, famous signatures on wall, Beethoven,

Mozart, Schubert, Stefan Zweig, Strauss, Richard Tauber etc.

The following day Linda and Reg went to Schonbrunn, loved it, wonderful guide, each room grew more splendid in rococo style, the Blue Chinese Room, the Russian Room, the Persian Room, the room where L'Aiglon died at 21 of T.B., his Death Mask ... the Coach House and State Coach, last used in 1916 when Carl was crowned King of Hungary ... we loved it, all so recently used and easily the best of all palaces to see. They also did a tour of the Vienna Woods, old Castle Lichtenstein, near where the King of Saudi Arabia has a house ... then we went to Herlengi Kreutz, visited the lovely old 1200 abbey founded by Leopold ... on to Mayerling in the beautiful woods.

They flew to Kiev on 7th. September and stayed at the Hotel Kiev: lovely buildings, lights, gardens, statues - ancient capital of Ukraine ... it seems a fine city, wide pavements and tree-lined boulevards but a scruffy atmosphere, proletarian ... shops quite pathetic. Next day they had Breakfast at 9, much confusion, sat with 2 stupid Americans who were using a dictionary and trying to order most difficult things - eventually we moved and ate what was given us. On a bus tour they found Kiev An elegant city of the past, great high tree-lined banks over the Dnieper ... saw the old palace of the Czars, now a museum and used for Soviet officials - lovely gardens, wonderful war memorial to heroes who fought the Germans. Lovely old 11th. cent. church with beautiful gold onion bulbs, frescoes inside and mosaics all restored, they care for their ancient monuments ... boat trip on the Dnieper, wide river, many bridges - people boating, fishing, swimming. At the Ukrainian Museum the exhibits were Mostly the life of the hero poet Scherchenko - a serf liberated by fellow poets and sent to exile for 10 years because he led a revolt against the Czars and landowners.

Linda and Reg travelled to Moscow on 9th. September and went to the Leningrad Hotel near the Kremlin: we were overcome when we got inside, it was like entering a huge Egyptian temple, thick gold embossed ceiling, enormous gold chandeliers and candelabra and colossal marble pillars - It was built in 1956. They were driven round the city, past the Kremlin, St. Basil's, Soviet Centre, various other monuments, Chekhov's house, now a museum - Then to the great new University ... Moscow is a large drab dreary city with wide gaping streets. At an Exhibition of Economic Development, they found out about Lumumba University, 3 years old, where Kruschev pays for the education of Africans, Congolese, Somali etc. – his influence has spread all through Africa ... We met a gentle Russian from the Urals, a botanist and scientist ... trying to find out about the underground as we wanted to get to Red Square. He spoke a little English and wanted to help. He paid for 4 of us and took us there, escorting us around G.U.M., Lenin's Tomb etc., all rather exciting.

On their last day in Moscow, they had a look into the big station crowded with people, peasant type, sleeping on benches and on the floor, talking or just waiting and with masses of bundles and bags and wordly possessions, it looked like a mass migration. I think they must move large work forces all over the great U.S.S.R. ... went through the great Kremlin gate into the interior, 3 large onion bulb cathedrals. A pleasant yellow building for the U.S.S.R. Parliament, a great bell tower and the palace of the Czars, now a museum. We trailed through seeing thrones of carved ivory and all sorts of gifts given by visiting potentates and ambassadors, dresses worn by Catherine the Great etc., Ivan the Terrible. Interesting great double throne of heavy silver. They also went to Bolshoi Theatre for Russian Opera, music by Moussorgsky ... lovely theatre ... superb scenery.

Their next visit was on 12th. September to Leningrad, where they stayed at the Hotel Europa near the Nevsky Prospekt, "their most beloved street for promenade". On a tour of the city they had lots of interesting talk with our charming and intellectual guide. The sky was overcast and very misty, it gave it all an extra charm. The River Neva, great wide river, nice style buildings all along and lots of canals and nice little bridges. Lovely square like our street all in pale yellow called Theatre Square. Winter Palace, same idea, more decorated in green and white, other buildings are in rose and white and blue and white, really most lovely. Next day they went by bus to the Summer Palace, founded also by Peter the Great and very baroque and lovely and the gardens a mass of fountains and gilt statues all restored ... lots of fountains have little tricks, a seat under a tree, if you sit on it the water shoots up, Peter was practical joker. At the Hermitage and Winter Palace they saw lots of treasures and magnificent rooms ... loved the Pavilion of Catherine the Great, also the Rembrandts ... to our theatre and saw ballet, very very good, Solveig and Peer Gynt, music of Grieg. Every seat full of diverse humanity in diverse clothes. In the Royal Box sat 4 coal black Ghanaians, 2 women in beautiful native dress.

Linda and Reg flew to Vienna on 14th. September and went by train to Kreuzenstein Castle: felt so happy to be alone and free of guides etc. ... loved seeing the ancient old interior, kitchen, bedroom, banquet hall, chapel, library, utterly fascinating in its Middle Age atmosphere. Two days later they flew to Beirut, where they stayed at the Hotel Phoenicia: found the fascinating narrow bazaars teeming with colourful humanity, bought some delicious grapes. This is the land of milk and honey, happy people ... somehow we collected a tall handsome Yugoslav in Lebanese army, officer - knew German, little English, he acted as self-appointed guide, showed us the famous mosque, once John the Baptist cathedral of the Crusaders. Their next visit was to Sidon, old Phoenician seaport, a Crusader castle from 1200 something, taken over by Saladin ... fascinating Ottoman style palace built by a Lebanese sheikh prince in the 18th. cent., now restored and used as a summer residence by the Lebanese President. Lovely courtyards, fountains, carving, gardens, and the tomb of the sheikh all perched on a commanding crag, overlooking the terraced valleys, centuries old cypresses etc. enhanced the picture.

On 19th. September they set off on a road tour with our driver guide,

Mustafa Kraqim, who soon told us he was known as King of the Desert and had just returned from Turkey, driving a French princess around the desert castles. At a place known as Dog River they saw on the rock face first of all Assyrian inscription by Nebuchadnezzar, then Rameses II, then Saladin ... on to Bibylos, fascinating old town and castle on much the same pattern as Sidon, lots of excavations going on. Found old Phoenician tombs and at least foundations of 7 different civilisations, also neolithic remains ... 3000 metres up we came to all that remains of the Cedars, about 600 altogether ... wonderful drive down to Tripoli, ancient old Levant town, old walls, bazaars, mosques ... scrambled over the old Crusader fort. They crossed the Syrian border, where they found more grazing and shepherds, pleasant people, humble little villages ... saw the great Krak des Chevaliers perched up on a mountain top. Linda and Reg spent the night at Homs, a great market town, full of Arab humanity, animals, noise and dirt. The Hotel Rajdan, the best in Homs, was quite dirty and the strangest we'd ever stayed in ... many interesting types all round us, not a European to be seen.

They returned to the Krak des Chevaliers: Lovely views of the great Krak as we approached into the mountains ... It is enormous and well preserved. We loved it, climbed right up to the top of the highest redoubt and what a view. From there they went out to Palmyra, $3^1/_2$ hour journey into the desert ... camels in great numbers, village life, strange beehive villages built of adobe, women in black, women in red with pitchers on their heads, shepherds with their flocks ... the Roman ruins are over a huge area and quite stunning ... rows of great tombs like outposts, these are 110 A.D. ... climbed right to the top and adored the view of desert mountains, palms and Roman columns, specially a lovely Arab castle perched on a crag overlooking everything. After that we went into underground tombs, 300 B.C., Phoenician I think, great stone door, dome inside with painted frescoes and slots in the wall for the bodies, some lovely carving and statues wearing Greek dress ... at sunset to the colossal tomb of Jupiter, lovely golden light, wonderful climbing over fallen Roman relics.

Linda and Reg stopped a night at the Zenobia Hotel and then drove to Damascus with Mustafa: set out to explore the town, soon collected a slim smart young Syrian who offered to show us around ... said I was like his mother ... saw the remains of the International Fair, finished yesterday. They stayed at the New Omayad Hotel and next day again looked round Damascus, first to the Great Mosque, 2500 Persian rugs on floor, tomb of John the Baptist, remains of Christian basilica inside and outside, in lovely jasmine scented garden, Saladin's tomb ... down the Street called Straight to Paul's church and Judas' house ... then to Baalbeck, colossal and magnificent.

They returned to Beirut and on 23rd. September flew to Jerusalem, where they saw excavations showing traces of 16 civilisations, River Jordan, Dead Sea scrolls cave, Qumran and then went to their hotel, the National Palace. Next day they drove to St. Stephen's Gate in the Turkish walls of old city. Left the car and walked through the narrow, picturesque streets and came into the most lovely place of the Dome of the Rock. Beautiful Islamic architecture, the best I have seen ... lovely view of Mt. of Olives and altogether a wonderful place. The Mosque of the Dome of the Rock full of history, too much to take in, but most beautiful round blue tiles outside, wonderful carved stone windows and coloured glass, looking like fine Persian carpets, rich but beautiful decoration. Afterwards they went to the Church of St. Anne St. Franciscans, Virgin Mary's birthplace, lovely old simple Crusader church, very little done to it, nearby excavations showing up porticoes etc. around the pool of Bethesda ... then to the Church of the Holy Sepulchre. It was all dark with lots of scaffolding, as they were making great restorations. There are about 6 different churches who have bits of all the venerated places. You see Golgotha where the Crucifixion took place and the rock of Mt. Calvary split by the storm that followed.

Linda and Reg continued out the lovely Damascus Gate and went to the Museum given by Rockefeller after they had found the Dead Sea Scrolls, for somewhere to house everything and also for the people to work and study all the various material that was being handed in at that time. A lovely museum and so well displayed ... lots of interesting relics of Stone Age, Bronze Age, Hellenic, Roman, Byzantine, Islamic etc. ... Most interesting to me were the big pieces of Bas Relief from Sennacherib's Palace in Nineveh, 701 B.C. They were huge and clearly depicted the Assyrians' siege of Lakash, carrying off the treasures and all the old fighting chariots. Finally they Walked to some French convent ... an elegant sister came to show us around. The thing was that in 1926 they discovered deep under it very old Roman pavement and various things to make them think they were over Pontius Pilate's house, so they built a chapel ... We made a few purchases in between times, 2 rather nice Crusader silver crosses and some little soft leather bags, then we walked right up to the Jaffa Gate ... then on to the very top to a Pilgrim Hotel called the Hotel of the Knights.

The diary ends on 25th. September with the entry "last walk round Jerusalem" and their return to Beirut, whence they flew back to Australia via Hong Kong.

17. ASIA, CANADA, U.S.A. AND MEXICO

The last overseas trip which Linda and Reg made took place in 1964, and again the occasion was attendance at orthopaedic conferences. They left Perth on 3rd. June, farewelled by the Lemann family, and went to Singapore by Air India, staying at the Cockpit Hotel. The inaugural cocktail party of their first conference was a quite exciting affair. The Europeans, about 20 and their wives were well in the minority and the other visiting doctors were Indians, Thais, Chinese, Japanese and Malay, some wives in kimonos, some in saris. Everyone got together in a very wonderful way, thanks to the untiring efforts of the host and hostess, Prof. and Mrs. Gunn, they both kept on introducing people and mixing them up. At a picnic on 7th. June it was good to see all the European, Asiatic and Indian children playing happily together, and at the farewell dinner, a 10-course Chinese banquet at the Singapore Island Club, The talk was that it had been a wonderful meeting, it was hoped that it would be the beginning of many more. They all felt the Japanese had something very special to contribute.

Linda and Reg flew by Japan Air Lines to Tokyo on 9th. June and drove to the Maranouchi Hotel. It was not like being in a city at all, but just in a labyrinthine world of freeways ... horribly expensive in the hotel. They went for a day trip to Fujiyama by train: lovely country, mainly rice fields, crops of wheat etc. ... we soon got into the mountains, lovely scenery, rich green and stony mountain torrents ... had our first peep at Fuji, shyly poking through the mists. Drove on to Lake Kawakuchi, wonderful viewing spot for Fuji, on clear days it is mirrored in the lake. At the hotel where they stopped for lunch, they walked in the gardens, lovely azaleas and maples, Perkins roses. We went down to the lake and looked back to find Fuji in full view and sunlight, the clouds had all rolled away. Fresh snow had fallen yesterday and she was very sparkling ... visited a rather beautiful shrine (Shinto), beautiful because of the wonderful old cedar and cypress trees,

2 enormous cedar ones over 1000 years old. Here is a starting point for the climbers of Fuji, pray and purify first.

After lunch, we drove halfway up the mountain, 6000 ft. up. A wonderful new road, opened on April 1 ready for the Olympic travellers ... Again the sun came out and from then on we had wonderful views of Fuji ... we were able to see the whole of her sloping up from the flats right up to the top of her snow line, a lovely sight.

On return to their hotel, Linda "had a letter from Jolyon, so ended a good birthday for me". She and Reg visited the Imperial Hotel on their last day, 12th. June: built by Lloyd Wright over 40 years ago. They call it a Symphony in Stone and it all looked very ancient and unlike anything I've ever seen. It was built of small lovely mellow bricks and decorated with ancient looking stone with lots of holes in it. It was even more fascinating inside than out. They walked back past the Imperial Palace, lovely gardens and the palace moat, swans floating in it, every now and again a pretty bridge over the moat and interesting old watch towers on the great palace wall. Later that day they travelled by Canadian Pacific Airways to Vancouver. Linda and Reg stayed at the Vancouver Hotel: We wandered round the town, seemed so little different from 40 years ago, quite country town-like and the traffic very moderate, lots of nice woollen shops and antique shops all with an English flavour ... took the bus to Stanley Park, 1000 acres on the estuary, across which are snow-capped mountains covered in clouds and the beautiful Lion suspension bridge spanning the estuary, ships filled with timber, great soaring fir trees, cedar trees and hemlock trees, rhododendrons etc. Next day they registered for the conference and spent five days busily engaged in organised activities which are rather cursorily reported in the diary, including official receptions, shopping trips and drives to the mountains. On 19th. June they flew to Seattle.

There they stopped at the Benjamin Franklin Hotel and explored the Fair: spent about 3 hours wandering round. It is dominated by a huge space needle over 600 ft. high and very attractive shape, also a lovely white lacy pavilion. The following day they went for a steamer trip in Puget Sound, lovely Red Indian country, fir trees, islands and water, rather cold but drinks flowed all the time and everybody got very cheerful ... After two hours we entered Agate Sound, very narrow and beautiful and lots of holiday houses amongst the great trees. Got off at a lovely log cabin place, gardens, trees and fresh air and lots more to drink. Then food, clam soup, excellent salmon and splendid whole potatoes. On 21st. June Linda and Reg flew to Portland: saw the lovely high volcanic snow-topped mountains, Mt. Rainier, 15,000 ft., then St. Helen's, rather like Fuji.

They were met by a Dr. Jones and taken for a drive through the city: beyond poking up through the mist were the 4 giant snow mountains, ethereal, magically beautiful. They stayed with the Jones, and while Reg went to work, Linda strolled round the garden, saw many different things, hazelnut trees, elderberries and the Gurka tree - I was interested in this as they were the trees that grew on the streets of Tokyo. Moving on to San Francisco on 23rd. June, they stayed at the Hilton Hotel during a two-day meeting and had a look over the fantastic Fremont Hotel, old style decor, enormous Baroque columns, gold everywhere. Their round of conferences ended with three days in Los Angeles. While Reg and the other doctors worked - "all think the work being done here terrifically interesting" - Linda went on several tours and organised a Mexican trip.

On 28th. June they flew to Mexico City, where they stayed at the Hôtel Genève Calle Lendres and found lots of lovely shops with fascinating things. So colourful and gay and great artistry, silver, leather, baskets, gay toys and papier maché with lacquer plates, trays, dishes and fabrics etc. Next day they did a tour of the city: to main square, all the buildings around its great vast emptiness were built by Spanish in 1529 or near that. The enormous cathedral, very Baroque and the Emperor Cortez' palace, now the President's Palace ... the most wonderful and enormous murals of Diego

Rivera, now dead. They depict all the history of Mexico ... colourful, exciting and unique as only Mexican art can be. After another day of sightseeing which included the Alameda Gardens, Musée des Belles Artes and the handcraft museum, Linda uncharacteristically found it "all too much, the eye grows weary, the brain refuses to function".

She and Reg hired a car on 1st. July and drove to Puebla, into the country, wide open spaces, corn and cactus and pepper trees, then as we climbed higher through pine forests, got to about 8000 ft. ... had a peep of Ixxacahuetl, snow covered and of Popocatepetl, 18,000 ft. high, lovely rich country all in the bowl of volcanoes ... then on to Cholula, the town of 365 churches, went to the oldest, 1529, so old and rough-hewn and simple, 7 round naves. At Puebla they saw an enormous cathedral, ugly outside but staggeringly ornate and fresh inside ... we went into the side streets and saw them making by hand lovely pottery like in Talavera in Spain, leather work, carving the onyx, quite marvellous what they do and have done through the ages ... then up further to an old fortress where the Mexicans beat off the French, and a wonderful view of the whole valley surrounded by mountains, churches dotted the landscape in all directions. Loved the ceramic domes and cupolas of bright yellow, turquoise and green, Popocatepetl and Ixxacahuetl lost in clouds.

Next day they again went for a drive, to Teotihuacan, where they have excavated the ruined city of the Toltecs and the Aztecs ... Drove through shambles of home-made factories and all sorts of a messy hotch potch of poor people living in some way. We even saw great disused train carriages used as dwelling places, hate to think of the drainage system. Masses of cactus in all shapes and sizes, donkeys and great activity in the fields. First stop a village, many stalls in the streets with their gay goods for sale, very tempted but restrained ourselves. We saw a great cactus from which they drain the juice to make the spirit pulque - they are cultivated here for that and the cactus is called Maguey. It takes 10 years and then just before it blooms they take the centre out and the juice runs out ... Then it is put into wooden casks and ferments ... they get the fibre from which they make so many of their textiles, they even use the spike as a needle and they tear off some sort of tissue thing which can be used for paper.

When Linda and Reg reached Teotihuacan they found First of all a good museum to help you understand it all - This place apparently built by the Toltec Indians some time B.C., the Aztecs came in and took it over. We climbed up the 244 steep stairs of the Pyramid of the Sun. Up these steps went the Aztec victims who at the top got their hearts plucked out alive as a sacrifice to one of their gods ... saw the Pyramid of Quexacotl, the God of the Plumed Serpent and all the great grotesque god carvings. Later that day they flew to Merida, capital of Yucatan, an old Spanish colonial town with a fascinating main square, cathedral and Gov.'s palace and old mansion of Señor de Montego ... then down a narrow street to our funny little Spanish type Hotel Colon.

On 3rd. July they drove with a guide through the steaming jungle to the Maya ruins of Chichen-Itza ... He said in the days of the Mayas 400 years ago all from Merida to Chichen were beautiful cities. Now the jungle has taken over ... We passed through several Indian villages, beautifully clean and neat, all the same type of adobe and wattle and daub huts with palm roofs, quite small but they sleep in hammocks they make out of the cactus fibre, many of them are direct descendents from the marvellous Mayas, the women wear a long white dress embroidered round the neck and sleeves. At Chichen they saw arcaded buildings around the square but all simple and painted in bright blues and yellows ... Can't do justice to the ruins we saw, so rich and beautiful are the carvings ... gay beautiful birds, brown and turquoise with long tails divided into 2 called clockbirds ... Serpents everywhere, sacred symbol of life. Remains of the richly painted plaster and wonderful carvings everywhere, all built of limestone, some B.C. and some as late as 1100 A.D. and then the Spaniards came. Now all detailed knowledge is lost, no one can understand their hieroglyphics.

In another area they visited they saw a truly wonderful sight, a perfect pyramid in the middle with temple at the top, 4 flights of steep stairs, 91, leading up and the sides of the pyramid richly carved. It was perfectly preserved. In the temple was "a large red stone jaguar with huge eyes of jade". Another building was the King's Palace: again wonderful carvings, dragons' heads and great tails, rain gods, warriors coming out of serpents' mouths ... we went along the sacred way to La Cenote, a great natural hole in the limestone filled with crystal running water. Next day they drove to Uxmal, which was intensely interesting and of fairly late period, they think, because in such good condition ... an enormous Governor's palace up on a series of impressive terraces. On their return, Linda and Reg walked round Merida: had a good look at all different types of houses, I like the early Spanish the best, all the houses are right flush with the street, big doors and long windows covered with iron grilles of all styles. Inside are the patios and peeps of pleasant tiles and gardens.

They returned to Mexico City on 5th. July, to be greeted by a minor earthquake the next day. On a guided tour they visited the splendiferous and extravagant new Hotel Maria Isabel just near the Independence statue on the Reforma. On a drive through the mountains they saw Taxco perched high up on a peak, the Cathedral Maria Presca towering over it all. There are rich silver mines all around here, the people have mined the silver for centuries and also made the most beautiful silver ware ... the cathedral very pink stone and old and lovely outside, inside full of the rich riotous carvings of gold. At Cuernavaca they stopped for the night at the Hotel Posada las Jacarandas, a fine old hacienda set in a great garden with huge shady trees, birds singing and wonderful air of peace.

Next day Linda and Reg walked round the town: wonderful old ancient palace of Cortez, built 1529 ... wonderful murals by Diego Rivera line the walls of the balcony ... watched life go by in the square - old crones, children with great baskets of bread on their heads, women with their babies completely smothered in their rebozos, men selling sarapes, musicians and so on. On 10th. July they were picked up by friends, the Crofts, who had been in Mexico for 20 years and had them to lunch: we ate off marvellous impeccable silver plate and drank out of richly designed silver goblets. Edna said she collected them early in her married life as silver then was cheaper than English bone china and more lasting - not now of course. Afterwards the Crofts drove them to Tepoztlan, "right into the jagged, turreted, castle-shaped mountains, old Aztec town". They returned to their Mexico City hotel the following day.

They went for a day tour to Xochimilcho, the famous floating gardens, people of Mexico glide up and down the canals in flower bedecked boats and there is music and fun, and also to see the Ballet Folklorico: It was really wonderful, beautiful colour, clothes, music and dancing from all the various parts of colourful Mexico ... to the Zocolo to see it lighted by night ... a fascinating sight, specially the Palace of Cortez and the great Cathedral. By day all rather grim and sombre, at night all the architectural features show up magnificently. Linda and Reg moved on to Texas on 13th. July: U.S.A. customs very amused with all the tourists and their Mexican purchases, huge guitars, enormous hats, great paper toys. They stayed at the "famous Gunter Hotel" in San Antonio and found a church dedicated to some heroes of 1821 ... once Texas belonged to Mexico, but broke away and became independent, later on joined with U.S.A. Later the same day they flew to Corpus Christi, where they had arranged to visit the 80,000 acre King Ranch at Kingsville, specialising in quarter horses and Santa Gertrudis cattle, with which Haden's brother Martin Lemann was associated in Australia: people have 7 properties in Aus., one of which is Brunette Downs in N.T. ... land dotted with oil drills, pumps, wells, pipes etc.

They went next to New Orleans, staying at the Monteleone Hotel in the French Quarter. On a coach tour on 15th. July they saw canals to take away the torrential rain, 63 inches per year ... went along the St. Charles Avenue, many wonderful old plantation houses still there and crepe myrtles in blossom growing everywhere gave a good touch ... it is all full of history ... The French settled first, got tired and gave it to Spanish, called Louisiana after Louis XIV. The Spanish had it for about 40 years and then sold it to America, great property with the sugar plantations all along the Mississippi. Next day Linda and Reg set out with guide book to find all the places of interest that we still haven't found. You never get tired of the fascinating, unique atmosphere ... we tried some Creole pralines, seemed a speciality here, very good but very sweet. Creole comes from the Spanish 'to create', crear, distorted to creolledo, 'little baby', created thing, then the French made it into creole and now stands for any person born out in these parts of pure stock, either French, Spanish, German etc.

Later they went into the Phillip Steegman house ... belonged to the Miltonberger family, they were iron makers and so their houses were elaborately decorated as advertisement, one daughter married Duc de Richelieu and one descendant married a Prince of Monaco ... Opposite is the oldest house in the quarter, 1726, most of that period were destroyed by fire. It is a very plain house, used by a slave owner and seller, right near the docks of course and we could see a Mississippi river boat's masts peeping out over the sheds at the end of the street. They ended the evening walking along Bourbon Street, full of dives with the difference that they let you have a peep of what was going on inside. Mostly scantily clad females gyrating in sexy attitudes ... 1 had a black shimmy which she kept lifting up, another one quite enormous bosoms, never seen such large ones exposed to public gaze. We finished up in Paddy's, famous bar ... women beefing out Dixieland, blues and jazz, even heard 'Tie Me Kangaroo Down, Sport'.

On 17th. July Linda and Reg took a boat trip through the Bayou country, swamplands typical of all these states. Some parts were very beautiful and others very dreary. The French Canadian Indians live here by trapping mink, marmot etc., a hard strange life. After they returned to their hotel they walked down Charles Street to see Frances Parkinson Keyes' house, a fine dignified house opposite a lovely old convent. We were glad to have seen it as she is somehow New Orleans to me. The same day they flew to Miami to stay with friends, Dorothy and Elwin Neale, who took them to Palm Beach: The whole place seems white and spotless, full of canal-like waterways, palm trees, boats, motels, hotels ad infinitum ... Drove right along Atlantic Ocean, not very beautiful, grey sand, grey shallow sea, but great rich Spanish type Palazzo houses all shut up, winter is the season. Down one of the most famous and rich shopping areas in the world, North Avenue, so elegant shops, fascinating architecture, mostly all closed until the winter, winter sunshine is the commodity they sell here.

They visited Key West with the Neales on 21st. July: a series of islands joined up by great long bridges and causeways, it is 7 miles long ... full of old world atmosphere, rather like an island of the Caribbean, which of course it really is, old stone walls, palm trees, colonial type houses with balconies all round ... The most beautiful house is now a museum, where Ernest Hemingway lived for 40 years. The house dates from 1789 or something and has a lovely garden. Next day Linda and Reg went over a lovely 18th. cent. house called Audobon House because Audobon, celebrated botanist, stayed there for long time whilst observing and drawing all the numerous birds in these parts.

The diary ends on 23rd. July with an entry about shopping and packing; presumably they flew back to Australia shortly after.

PART FIVE

1965 TO 1974:
GREAT-GRANDMOTHER

<small>In a hard hat for a mine visit, 1972</small>

In 1965 Linda and Reg made the first of six trips together through outback Australia; the others followed at regular intervals over the next nine years. On 20th. June they left Perth Airport with three friends, Mabel and Lance Barrett and Flora Bunning, and flew to Wittenoom via Meekatharra in a vintage D.C.3. There they were met by their tour guides, Graham and Brigid Robertson, in their Toyota bus and taken 30 miles out to the camp ... we saw dawn with its pink clouds, lots of birds singing and a beautiful spot, great iron red cliffs all round, tawny spinifex, ghost gums, graceful tall river gums and paperbarks. With five others in the party, they set off for tour of the Gorges, first to Dale Gorge, quite wonderful, fascinating formation and colour of rocks - formations look almost man-made, emerald green water at the bottom, the Fortescue Falls cascading down. Afterwards they made a hair-raising rough trip to Red Gorge ... Here we were at the junction of 4 gorges, absolutely precipitous cliffs of jagged ochre, rock shapes and colours of amazing, awe-inspiring patterns, pools of green water below.

On return to their camp, they had a wonderful shower rigged up with a pump from a fresh spring ... we made our beds all together out in the open. Next morning Linda woke about 1/4 to 6 with first light ... Then came the big pack-up, a major task, all the stretchers to be dismantled and shower, lav. and mess tent. They drove to the mining town of Wittenoom, with "lovely views of the Hamersley Ranges", and had a beer at the pub: Graham said Wittenoom was an unhappy place, didn't make money and everything went back to the monopolistic company. At Mulga Downs Station they had a picnic lunch in the dry river bed and saw "2 emus, 4 kangaroos, lots and lots of Sturt's Pea." They had been following underground Fortescue River, then at vantage point it came to surface, gazed down on beautiful sheen of water, palm tree lined. Their crossing however was impassable, and while Graham detoured with the bus, they "took out necessary packages and forded the stream in bathers" before camping for the evening.

During the night, previous to the rain I had a major call of nature, so with torch wandered some way off into the tangle of paperbarks and reeds etc. Operation over, I faced to go home. All was pitch black, no moon, no stars, I wandered in what I thought was the direction to find a creek full of reeds, so back I went. I was lost. Then I called softly 'Reg - Reg Hall', then louder 'Reg Hall, I'm lost'. Lance thought it was a strange bird, eventually heard 'I'm lost', told Reg and he shone the torch and I made my way back. At about 1.30 a.m. it started to rain; it stopped near morning and we emerged from our half sodden bed clothes and struggled into our rather filthy ones of yesterday.

After striking camp, the party got onto the main Wittenoom-Roebourne road, really quite good and along the Spinifex Tableland, then round a bend and we gazed into another world, dramatically. We were on Mt. Herbert but didn't know till we came to this great Breakway, looking down into an enormous water-like space with all sorts of shapes and colours forming the walls all round. We came down to Python Pool, most adorable place, a lovely deep clear pool at the bottom of steep 2 or 3 hundred ft. high walls of red ironstone, vivid green trees hanging on here and there. Bits of Sturt's Pea out and we could see many interesting sorts of shrubs and flowers. They drove on to the township of Pyramid, through Pyramid Station, after which it is called and one of the oldest stations and so on to Roebourne, full of history and story, a lovely collection of stone houses beautifully built, Bun says her father did them in 1885.

Further along the coast at Cossack, we walked along the beach to the pathetic cemetery, young men, children and babes all there. Lovely old Customs House and various other ruins tell of the hopes of the past. On 23rd. June the group reached Port Hedland, a sort of boom town now, being the port for Mt. Goldsworthy Iron Ore ... had a thoroughly happy,

restful day, thought Hedland had a lot of atmosphere. Next day they were
Up at 4 a.m. to do the 400-odd miles to Broome over the horror stretch of
the Pardoo Sands ... found driving in the early morning very pleasant,
scenery changing and soon came to a wet part near De Grey Station, saw
brolgas and white cockatoos and lots of cattle good and bad, sometimes a
glimpse of the sea on our left. After passing Eighty Mile Beach they stopped
at Nita Downs Station for lunch: a real oasis, gorgeous garden, mangos,
frangipani, bougainvillea, everything interesting round a lovely low shady
comfortable house. Later the bus broke down with radiator trouble and
had to be towed into Broome after dark by a truck.

Broome had a fascinating atmosphere of tropical gardens ... lovely trees
all round, poincianas, baobabs etc. ... set off to do the town, we loved it,
full of Elizabeth Durack, there was the little tin church she had painted,
the wide streets of the old town and all the blacks with their coloured
cotton dresses. After lunch Linda and Reg walked to Lighthouse Point,
incredible red coloured rocks of every wind formation imaginable, of all
reds here was the reddest, I thought. They visited a friend, Sam Males:
tropical house, all open and spacious, an enormous verandah all round
and furnished with beautiful cane furniture, carved objets d'art from the
Orient. His description of life in the Kimberleys "seemed to make life in
suburban Perth very pussy". Their party spent the evening in the Roebuck
Arms: saw all the polyglot population of Broome enjoying themselves
dancing, dart playing, drinking.

On 26th. June they headed for Derby: stopped at Langley Crossing over
the Fitzroy, quite a bit of water in the river, pelicans and cranes about ...
soon after the old bottle trees or Baobabs became part of the landscape
and kept us very interested, so varied, grotesque and fascinating they were
... historic old baobab about 1000 years old, hollow inside and once used
as the town jail. After a drink and a Chinese meal they set out along the
old Fitzroy Crossing Road to Windjana Gorge ... came onto the homestead

of Kimberley Downs Station, wonderful position in a valley surrounded by great hills ... came on a huge lovely billabong covered with ducks, cranes, pelicans, bird life everywhere, galahs, budgies etc., went on our tortuous exciting way, hoping to find a waterhole to camp, but at last we made Windjana Gorge, of all the wild west movie scenes this was it, cattle lowing, donkeys braying, all drinking and churning up the ground round the water hole in the gap of the wonder-making Napier Ranges, wonderful because they run like a fence for miles and miles east and west, very jagged and serrated at the top, rather like a palisade.

Next morning they went from their camp through the gap to the water, which is full of crocodiles, have to be very quiet ... I saw only 1 but a beauty, long snout and great bulging eyes. They are protected for some reason and so eating all the good barramundi. On the road again they drove past the stone ruins of the old Lilymoola Police Station, police stationed there in the old days when there was a gold rush at Hall's Creek and things were booming ... went to join the main Derby-Fitzroy Crossing Road, skirted the interesting Ookar Range, not high but fascinating shapes and colours and the most lovely baobabs, they seemed in complete possession here. A blowout caused them a five-hour delay and they reached their campsite at Giekie Gorge after dark.

Linda found the camp site by day quite magical, with all the creepers growing over everything, wild passion fruit ... up the Gorge. Fossil Downs is on the other side from our camp and their boat was moored there. The Gorge is all that is said of it and worth coming up here for it alone. A great broad stream of water, the Fitzroy. Huge overhanging cliffs of all shapes and colours, we glided in under them the better to feel the strange effect of them, one cave was filled with bats ... It is full of sharks, crocs and barramundi, so no swimming. They landed on the Fossil Downs side, an entrancing spot, I christened it Arcadia, it was so dream like ... the cliffs in the water were dream like, great flights of herons and white cockatoos screeched up and down.

On 28th. June they left Giekie Gorge and drove to Fossil Downs Station: we met stockmen, cattle trains, stockyards, a line of attractive houses and buildings formed a row leading up to the homestead, 2 storey with green roof, trees filled with cockatoos. Everything was there that one could imagine of a great cattle station. After being shown round they drove on 200 miles to Hall's Creek, where they arrived "absolutely filthy" to spend the night in a caravan park. Next day they went to Old Hall's Creek, typical mining country ... the ruins were quite interesting, large jail and police station built of mud bricks, 4 large wells all filled up, the rush was about 1865. At Alice Downs Station they saw the most spectacular scenery, hills and ranges blue in the distance, red in the foreground ... we are all happy and love the open air life and the camp sites off the beaten track.

The following day they crossed the Ord River and reached Kununurra, where they drank beer in the hotel garden and talked to locals who all loved it here, just something got them, they said. About 700 people live permanently in the town. They camped at the Ord Dam caravan park and Woke up at dawn to the screeching of hundreds and hundreds of birds ... saw many kingfishers and bower birds disporting themselves. On a guided tour of the Ord River Scheme they "saw fine sugar cane and rice, all experimentally grown" and went for a flight 30 miles up the river to where the new big dam site is to be ... went off with Greg McQuine in his beautiful little blue speed boat, up the Ord for about 20 miles.

They broke camp on 4th. July and drove to Timber Creek on the beautiful Victoria River ... great ranges with strange ridges that looked like ramparts on the Great Wall of China ... we arrived at Timber Creek store hot and thirsty, to find 2 unkempt men telling us that they were out of everything except tyres. The place looked too dejected for words, filthy old refrigerators, an old sewing machine and typewriter. One man had been there for 3 weeks and no stores, supposed to come out from Katherine. Camping at the waterhole, they saw lots of birds in the morning, bronze finches with red tails, galahs, black parrots, mask and blackheart finches were drinking at the dripping tap in front of Timber Creek store. Heading on to Katherine, they found the "road was awful and the dust excruciating", but it was worth it when they got to their next camp at Katherine Gorge to see a gorgeous view of lovely water, pandanus and other lovely trees including the beautiful golden Grevillea, somewhat like the Queensland silky oak.

Next day the group set off about 9 a.m. to do a lovely boat trip, quite the best Gorge of all, great towering red cliffs, lovely trees and pure rippling deep water, we went past a huge cliff rock that was Jedda's Rock. Saw very interesting native paintings, men, kangaroos, wild duck, tortoises, in fact everything that entered their lives ... went for a most delicious swim, so tropical and lovely, cascading water over smooth stones. After a picnic lunch they walked to the top of the Gorge with the aid of ropes before returning to their campsite for another night. On 7th. July they returned to Katherine and took the Stuart Highway to Adelaide River, where Linda found the pub still run by Mrs. Myrtle Fawcett, who has run it for about 30 years - Buffalo horns, crocodile jaws and other things of interest in the bar. That evening they had their "last night under the stars" at the camp at Berry Springs.

In the morning after packing up, Linda had a swim in the lovely pool, I even had a swing on the rope – quite the most perfect swimming place one could wish for. Then they drove to Darwin: the outskirts have spread enormously ... recognised some of the old landmarks, Victoria Hotel etc., noted the fine new modern Post Office, Darwin Hotel looked nice, spacious and tropical, specially noted the polished concrete floors in lovely shade of mustard yellow. Went into Rigby's Bar, had snack lunch, fascinated by all the types of young men, some really Tarzan types. After a drive round the town they retired to the Don Hotel for dinner and the night. Next day, after a stroll, they found the others drinking in our room. Poor old Graham was telling his domestic troubles. His glamourous little wife Brigid can't take the arduous life and has been dissolved into tears every night. So has decided to send her back to his mother on the plane with us and carry on for the 5 more trips alone. We all felt something was wrong and B. was not pulling her weight. That night they all had dinner at the Fanny Bay Hotel and "had a very happy night in lovely surroundings". On 10th. July they flew back to Perth.

Two years later in 1967 Linda and Reg again travelled north, returning to some of their previous haunts. This time they went by bus up the west coast, leaving Perth on 4th. August and reaching Carnarvon that night, where they slept on the bus. Next day they arrived at the port of Dampier: lovely harbour, blue sea, all sorts of construction everywhere, aluminium houses all air conditioned, rather like construction camps at the Snowy River scheme, except red dust rather than snow. They found Port Hedland "bigger and busier than ever" and stayed at Boondarrie Station there. They walked to the Turner River, huge dry river bed lined with pretty white gums, bronze and green kingfishers and lots of red-beaked waxbills. Back in Port Hedland the ship Iron Knight was unloading steel plates for the railway. Sat at the Pier Hotel and saw the great variety of customers, packed with beer drinkers.

On 7th. August they drove to Marble Bar: It was race day, the town was en fete, never seen so many real aboriginals collected together. The Ironclad Hotel was doing a roaring trade, we fought our way in, had a beer and lots of badinage, it was the best slice of real outback local colour I think I've seen. Had a look at the really splendid old stone buildings on the hill, now Police Station, Administrative quarters and Native Welfare. They went on to Jasper Bar, terribly exciting, gorgeous coloured stone all in layers of different colours, pink, red, black etc. Tried to chip off some with my hammer, only succeeded in getting one piece, for the rest we all picked up other peoples' chipping, back to the bus with our treasures. The party visited Hill Crest Station, beautifully situated against the long ironstone spinifex-covered ranges ... now a cattle station run by a Mr. and Mrs. Lang. Picturesque old white homestead, huge cement verandah, established old garden, picturesque outbuildings in the compound, horses, galahs, cockatoos, no natives and they dined in the garden, where Dorothy Maymott played a squeeze box, she and the music were not the height of romance.

Linda and Reg revisited Wittenoom: drove along the Hamersley Ranges, past the entrance to Mulga Downs Station (Lang Hancock) ... took a drive up the Wittenoom Gorge to the asbestos mine (closed) ... around the town, all deserted and sad houses and gardens empty and neglected, however still the store, post office, hospital, police and the nice-looking hotel. They met a Dr. Oxer from the Tourist Association, who showed them round and said another party had found some aboriginal carvings chipped out of the rocks, very good and rather rude, they said, and apparently unknown to anyone before. After dinner Dr. Oxer showed us some of his films of this country, which he loves and has explored most of the Gorges himself in the cause of getting them more opened up to the public. They also went again to Dale's Gorge and "had a lovely climb round Circular Pool at the northern end".

On a drive through Rio Tinto Gorge to Mt. Tom Price on 10th. August they broke a spring on a rough road, and had to wait for a new one to be flown from Perth: in the meantime all our luggage is piled up on the side of the road, the bus is jacked up and all the travellers strewn round the stony landscape, making the best of the sorry plight we find ourselves in. Had meal round campfire, sat round it for a while, some slept in bus ... others slept on ground ... the dew was heavy, we slept fitfully, could squeeze the dew out of the blankets in the morning. Next day at 1.30 p.m. springs arrived, they had come up by plane from Wittenoom with a mechanic who brought them out, Doug and he worked like Trojans and at 4 we were able to get on our way and do the 13 miles to Tom Price. Wonderful to see the great red mountain of almost pure iron being attacked by the most powerful and expensive machinery that scooped 25 yards of stuff and 12 tons of iron ore. We saw the crusher and the stockpiles of 8000 tons of ore, a train load for Dampier takes 1 hour to load. It was all most awe-inspiring, big men and big nature.

The group headed for Coolyawanah Station to camp for the night, A very scenic and dramatic drive through the open cut made for the railway, winding round and round ... night fell, we grew sleepy and hungry and thought the traveller's lot a hard one, at last came to the gate, 15 miles to the homestead, thinking we'd never get there. Next morning, 12th. August, they saw over 100 kangaroos all feeding and frolicking in the freshness of the morning dew. Large and small, red and grey, singly and in groups of 6-8, but all a delight to watch and kept us very interested and happy. At Mt. Herbert on the way back to Port Hedland, they stopped to admire the amazing view of the plains with all the strange little hills and ranges rearing up here and there in their odd shapes ... A short hurried stop at Python Pool, which is a spectacular beauty spot, lovely vegetation there including Sturt's Pea out in its full beauty. Their bus made the airport at 20 to 2, plane leaving at 10 to 2, a wonderful effort on Doug's part, the rest of the passengers not so happy at having to be rushed in such a way, and Linda and Reg flew home to Perth.

In the wet winter of 1968 Linda and Reg had arranged a trip by safari wagon from Adelaide through the centre of Australia. Leaving Perth on 28th. June, they drove to Kalgoorlie and **went out to Parkeston to put car on the train, a fantastic scene, about 30 great haulage trucks waiting to get on as Nullarbor was practically impassable.** They had breakfast on the train crossing the Nullarbor on 30th. June: **Nullarbor was as green as Ireland, the whole countryside soaked with rain.** Waiting to collect the car at Port Pirie, they **wandered round the cold, wet streets and found a funny old pub, the Federal. The proprietress warm and somewhat full, made us welcome.** The 2nd. July was "wet. Horrid drive to Adelaide, got there about 10", and they stayed three nights with their friends the Martins waiting to meet their tour guide.

They went to the Tourist Bureau on 6th. July and **met Jeff Findlay, our safari leader and our 2 fellow passengers, Barbara Huxley, young American girl and Ernest Laing, a bright-eyed eager South Australian man about 60, I should say and both seemed intelligent and pleasant. At Hawker, Jeff took us to his office and showed us the great map, explaining that it was impossible to cross the Cooper at Birdsville and the Diamantina at Innamincka, so couldn't do the round trip, could only go up to Birdsville and back or Strzelecki trail and back, so all voted to go up Strzelecki trail, so that we could see where Burke and Wills perished.** Next day, off we **went through an old friend, the Moralana Gorge - this time it was green and sparkly and the former dried creek beds were all running strongly. Quite arduous driving through the creeks, the scenery was superb.** Passing through the Flinders Ranges they came to Beltana, **old mining town near Wilpena ... Old stone cutter at Beltana and we bought some of his hand made jewellery.**

At sunset they arrived at Lyndhurst: **It is an old wood and corrugated**

/

iron pub over 100 years old and is at the start of the Strzelecki trail to Innamincka, 281 miles away the signpost said. We felt we were really in the outback. Our host, Mr. Dunn, has been here all his life and his father ran the pub before him. On their way to Marree on 8th. July they met a truck that had been bogged for 1 week, the owner a store keeper from Oodnadatta had somehow flown back and paid truck from Lyndhurst 10 dollars a day and what beer he liked. The truck was full of beer. He gave us a beer, then the road grader came along and several other cars pulled up, all had beers and lots of talk in the lovely sunshine. Their next stop was at Farina, a ghost town now but once a big camel transport place. Lots of ruins and things of interest and then Marree, big railway centre, saw a memorial to Maddigan, who crossed the Simpson Desert in 1939.

The party visited Muloorina Station near Lake Eyre: As we neared the station more interesting vegetation, lovely wild orange trees, graceful and pretty yellow small berries, wild grape, wild prune, all things that cling to the sand. We came upon a huge gushing artesian bore, 20 million galls. per day gushing out. Mr. Eliot Price is an ingenious engineer, can't read or write but he takes the bore water into the old dry Frome River bed. As we got near the homestead we passed through a great belt of coolibah trees and a series of lovely lakes on which were ducks, formed from the gushing bore water. We got to the homestead about 5 to find shearing in progress, fascinating to watch. Children were playing round the great bales, lovely solid comfortable houses, sunset over Lake Eyre and a full moon, a wonderful exciting atmosphere. They stayed the night, and after dinner the school master showed us a B.P. film in the bright little school room and all the shearers came too, they all seemed such nice young chaps. The film was marvellous, all about when the Malcolm Campbell people came and stayed and had their trials on Lake Eyre, a wonderful film and wonderful to be on the spot where the film was taken. Going on to Lake Eyre, they were the first car through since all the rains ... We had to weave and wind to find passable tracks, took ages to get there. First sight of Lake Eyre rather exciting, however filled with water and no salt. They retraced their steps to Marree: Jeff says it is going to rain and no good taking us out farther as we would or could get marooned for days or weeks if it did. On 10th. July the party decided to press on to Birdsville: lots of bad patches and lots of good straight runs and made fairly good time ... Along this part of the track were stone cairns at long intervals, built by the Milner Bros. in 1850s, went up there from Port Lincoln before the track existed. One was killed by the blacks and the other went insane. At Etadunna Station they met old Mrs. Oldfield and her son and many grandchildren. Took us into the house, huge enormous verandah all round, walls 2 feet thick, built by a German, she said. It was all spacious and furnished in a rich, comfortable way. Interesting to see station life on the Birdsville Track ... Went 14 miles through treacherous 'Bay of Biscay' soil to Kalalapinni Lutheran Mission, old ruins made of straw bricks right on the Cooper, in fact we were driving in the Cooper Bed about 20 miles wide here.

The Land Rover got bogged on the way back, so they made camp while getting it out: Fairly warm and comfortable, but pretty cold getting dressed in the morning. They returned to Etadunna, then on our way up the Birdsville ... came to dear old ruins of 2nd. Mulka homestead built by Scobie family up on a hillock under a coolibah, lovely grave of Edith Scobie, 14 years, died 1892. Ruins of old stone store ... few miles further on came the third and existing Mulka homestead, a typical scene of blacks breaking in wild horses, talked to young Scotch manager's wife, who said she loved the summer, 120 degrees in her kitchen, but got up early and did all her work. In the winter she muffled up and got lazy. At the Ooroowilanie Sandhills they passed a road off to left to Cowarie H.S. right out near the Simpson Desert ... Terrible country, tracks all over the place to avoid the water, the main road was just like the Birdsville River, where the water had dried off it left a quagmire of thick sand and silt.

Later they drove **through a great gate with diamond and 1/2 moon sign, brand of Clifton Hills Station cattle** ... past the homestead where the road forks, dry weather road through Goyder's Lagoon, 96 miles to Birdsville, fork right 126 miles outside track for flood conditions. Jeff said the Page family who all perished of thirst a few years ago missed the Goyder's Lagoon signpost and took the seldom used outside track. We took the outside track and what a horror it was, right through Sturt's Stony Desert which had large sheets of water all over it, still looked grim and menacing. As it was getting dark they came to a huge running creek which looked impassable - so we made camp on a bare gibber plain - with a cold wind blowing. We made the best of it, found some wood to make a fire, had hot soup and stew and wine and brandy in our coffee, then crawled into our sleeping bags half clothed.

On the morning of 10th. July, they woke **freezing cold** ... all shivering, then we had to make the terrible creek crossing, poor Jeff had to take off his boots and wade in the cold water, eventually got through ... weaving round the water courses, slow progress, little more than 10 miles per hour ... every now and again lovely stretches of flowers. Later the little party got into the sand ridge country and the going got a little better, when we camped for lunch had about 52 miles to go. Jeff wandered off and found 3 beautiful native stone phallic symbols, said it was an old ground ... We had to find our tracks amongst the many, only an experienced person could have ever found the way. They crossed over the Queensland border, then to the Diamantina, we could see the wireless masts of Birdsville about 1 mile the other side. But the causeway over the Diamantina was awash with the fast flowing river, a formidable sight ... There was an old iron boat so Ernest and Jeff rowed across. Ernest minded the boat while Jeff walked into Birdsville, we stayed in the Land Rover.

After a while, Jeff arrived with the Police and a nice high vehicle and came boldly across the rushing water, gathered us up leaving our Land

Rover on the south side. So we all went excitedly into Birdsville and made for the historic pub. Drank beer at 75 cents per bottle and talked to Jack Gaffney of Alton Downs Station, a black stockman from Clifton Hills and a house painter, all great fun ... Good dinner and sit around lovely fire. On 13th. July there was a freezing cold wind ... round Birdsville - the old cemetery full of touching graves ... We collected in the bar and had a last drink with the pub keeper, Len Gaffney and then the Police took us over the Diamantina, we sadly set out to make our same way back to Hawker, as the Cooper was impassable to get to Innamincka.

They called at Etadunna Station next day for a christening party and joined the remnants of the party ... they had been eating, drinking, sleeping and dancing for 2 or 3 days. The group reached Marree the following morning: turned off at Copley to enter the Flinders Ranges. Had lunch at a lovely Hans Heysen creek, lovely country all the way. They stopped at Arkaroola, an old station ... They are going to develop big tourist place there, have spent vast sums on making roads, now starting a caravan park, then motel. The manager, Don Hamlyn, was bursting with enthusiasm for the wild magnificent scenery ... he took us some good few miles on the winding track into the canyons to show us special beauty spots - too dark and rushed to fully appreciate but still was something to see. Next day, en route to Hawker, they visited Chambers Gorge: lovely scenery all day, passed through some more old station homesteads and came to lovely, picturesque Blinman, old copper mining place ... we were scruffy and cold, had camped out the last 3 nights, sleeping in our clothes.

Linda and Reg had arranged to remain with Jeff for another excursion, and at Hawker on 16th. July met our 2 fellow passengers for the next trip, Diana Whiteman and Helen Hellinson, who were English nurses and have been in Australia since 1960 and are on the staff of the Prince Henry Hospital, Melbourne. They met in Canada, travelled widely together. They went again to Marree and then skirted round the southern end of Lake Eyre to visit

Stuart Creek Station: It is 12,000 square miles and the largest in Australia, owned by Kidmans ... We saw a most wonderful sight, a dam sinker's train, about 6 great things linked onto a huge tractor, one was a 2-storey caravan in which his wife and 3 daughters, 7, 9 and 11 lived, others were machinery trucks etc. He was a marvellous man (Walls), said he had a house on the Gold Coast and spent 3 months there and 9 months on the job.

After this they continued on their way, but the going was really awful, the same or worse than the Birdsville Track ... We struck the fast-flowing Margaret River again and countless other hazards. Jeff pointed out mounds of boiling mud springs on our left, but the ground was too wet to go and see better. They got bogged and were pulled out by a mission vehicle: After that we came on a really horrible bit ... a huge swampy area between 2 sand ridges, we had to walk about 1 1/2 miles whilst Jeff writhed and weaved and shuddered over the side of the sandhills. By the time they reached William Creek, we had taken 10 hours to do 183 miles ... William Creek Hotel is all green corrugated iron like the Queensland ones, a real period piece. Next morning, 19th. July, they watched at a railway crossing while "the Ghan passed through laden with cars and trucks."

Their first stop was at Anna Creek Station, a Kidman station, a very old established one, cattle of course, old stone buildings and a nice comfortable modern house with trees and lawns, it is near a creek. Mr. and Mrs. Nunn gave us a wonderful spread for morning tea, they have 9 children ... saw them making rope out of cattle hide, visited the Black camp, full bloods, Artabunna tribe, had genuine spears and woomeras. At Mt. Dutton they visited a musterers' camp ... Jeff knew them all and we had a good chat. Lots of people up here trap rabbits and seem to do well out of it. They spent the night at Alandale Station at Oodnadatta, and next morning got bogged again: as good luck would have it again our Bush Mission friends turned up and towed us out backwards, then both found a wide detour, we followed on together as the going was slow and precarious, had lunch and a pleasant chat together, then on our way - had to stop many times and fill up the bad patches with stone, specially after Arckaringa Creek, we took 3 hours to do 33 miles.

Along the way they Met an old road grader who showed us his lovely comfortable caravan house and fascinating collection of stones and also frig. stocked with beer. He took us up to show a queer view of queer country such as I've never seen ... funny chalky mountain range, had split open and spilt all their much coloured stones down the gorge. Again I've never seen country like it, we climbed up on top and gazed our fill. They camped by a creek bed for the night, and next morning arrived at Evelyn Downs Station: out to see the Painted Desert, again these strange, chalk-like hills, mauves, greys, oranges ... they are battling as they have sheep and the dingoes get them, the galahs eat the new grass and eagles eat the lambs. That night they made camp at Hawk's Nest Well on the main Alice Springs-Coober Pedy Road.

On 22nd. July the party turned off to the Everard Ranges: we passed Everard Park Station, the most efficient and well-kept one, also prosperous, that we had seen ... wonderful orange ranges and their fascinating formation, set off by the lush green covering the earth, the desert is truly blooming like the proverbial rose, after the worst 10 years' drought in living memory. In the evening they camped "under a great red rock", and next day "woke up with thick frost on all our canvas bags". At Ernabella Mission they "came out on main Ayers Rock tourist road", and they arrived at Ayers Rock about 9 p.m. to see "lights everywhere". They stayed the night at the Uluru Hotel and enjoyed the luxury of showers and a washing machine.

The following day they went out to view the rock, stopping every 5 minutes to take photos, watched the climbers who now have a handrail, then climbed a little way up ourselves. Then out to the Olgas, looking glorious in soft purple hues. The bush is just as lovely and again the poplars line the road. They drove round the Olgas in convoy with two men in a

Volkswagen, happy and enthralled with each new view of them. **Then going into the Valley of Winds got bogged terribly ... it proved a long job, the 2 young men shovelling out wet oozy mud, standing in it up to their knees ... eventually after brutal hard work on Jeff and the boys' part the 2 cars were freed.** Afterwards they went back to watch the sun set on Ayers Rock: **It was a great sight, it changed from pale mauve to a luminous glowing flame and then back to dull brown.**

After another visit to the Rock, the party drove to Alice Springs, where Linda noted "It is really a city now". Next day she and Reg took an Ansett tour to Trephine Gorge: **Saw the most perfect ghost gum of all time, then went on into the Gorge, lovely red rock cliffs and beautiful river trees.** They returned to the Alice after a day's sightseeing and after dinner walked along Todd Street, "full of lights and people, all shops open". On 27th. July Jeff drove them all **to the old Telegraph Station, which has been restored somewhat, pleasant garden, some of the native trees are named, able to identify currajong tree, witchetty grub bush and wild fuchsia ... We loved wandering round the dear old place on the Todd, the butcher birds were warbling, the morning was sparkling fresh and no-one but ourselves to enjoy it.** Afterwards they returned to Alice Springs and later set off towards Kulgera, camping at the Palmer River.

Next day they visited Kulgera Station: **Had a drink with the road grader, who came from Bridgetown. He was a mammoth with deep blue eyes and thick titian hair. I called him 'The Viking'. His name was Brooks and we took his photo.** They went on to Finke, a railway centre on the Ghan ... **lots of blacks sitting about and the main street just pure sand ... Set off from Finke along back track only used by the desert stations** and at New Crown Station met Mrs. Smith, who told them she had the Simpson Desert "at my front door". They visited Abminga Camp on the property and joined the musterers for lunch ... **Talked to the young Smith son, very happy for the good season, nearly gave up in the drought, had spent £35,000 on** windmills, bought cattle in the Territory for £35 per head, and will sell them in Adelaide for £60 per head.

They continued towards Oodnadatta: After we left Abminga the road got incredibly rough and stony, crossing many deep creeks, some still with water. Towards evening they came to Dalhousie Springs, "about 8 miles of lovely warm mineral springs on the fringe of the desert", and camped there for the night. Next morning they Set out excitedly to go into the desert ... didn't really see the great sandy desert, still fairly soggy going as about 13 inches of rain fell earlier in this rainiest season for 50 years. Jeff decided not to risk a wet crossing, so we walked on for a mile or two and got the desert feeling. I gathered a desert posy, purple, yellow and blue daisies of a kind Jeff hadn't seen before, rather like small soft Scotch thistles. He took us to see some other springs where the Afghans had planted date palms and looking just like a desert oasis. In the early days of the old Telegraph Line there were repeater stations about every 60 miles and quite a lot of people on each station, so this region had many more people than today.

They reconnoitred the next part of their route: explored 3 bad creeks to save time in the morning, as our route to Oodnadatta, only 102 miles, had not been used for many years ... We all felt a bit sad that it was our last night in the outback, but full of excitement for tomorrow's drive into Terra Incognita. Setting off on 31st. July they found that the whole country was a series of ancient crumbling breakaway plateaus ... Jeff was about 1 hour getting out of this place ... made the railway line at Pedirka, where there had been a tornado some months ago, bits of wreckage were strewn in all directions. They came to Macumba Station, near the junction of the Hamilton River which we had to cross, it was enormous, we got out and waded. Finally the party arrived at Oodnadatta, where Linda and Reg had a nice final talk with Jeff, he is a nice man and a fine bushman, knows his job thoroughly, efficient and reliable, it has been a wonderful experience to be with him.

They travelled from Oodnadatta to Adelaide to collect their car and return to Perth.

20. Alice Springs and Gove

The later trips which Linda and Reg made in their sixties were shorter, though still energetic. In 1970 they went on a 3-week safari tour to the Alice Springs area. They left Perth on 12th. August in A large, comfortable bus, 17 all told - 7 of whom were from our walking club, and spent the first night at Kalgoorlie. Next day they had a look round Boulder, past North Kalgoorlie and Great Boulder gold mines, now combined and treating nickel as well as gold ... A look at the tree where Paddy Hannan found gold in 1893. On the road to Leonora, after 100 miles, sinister noise about 3 p.m., no oil in differential, broken crown wheel. All out in the mulga, beautiful cool sunshine, erected our smart little tents, blew up our mattresses and prepared for night in the bush.

The following day the tour leader, John Arnold and his wife Anne returned after driving back to Perth overnight for spare parts and a mechanic. While repairs were being effected, Anne drove Linda and four others on to Gwalia, the scene of Linda's evacuation in 1942: Gwalia was a scene of isolation and desolation as if a tornado had whizzed through, the Hotel, mine manager's house and mine were the only recognizable landmarks to me ... We fossicked round the ruins of the old 'Hacienda', the blackboard from the S.P. shop, the opening where the huge stove was and the 2 pepper trees, the rest rubble. At the Leonora Hotel she met old friends, one of whom gave us a piece of the famous Weebo stone found out on Money's station. Some people in the town want to quarry it for building, others say it is sacred to the Wonga tribe, then others come into the row for various reasons, no-one knows the truth. After dinner the repaired bus arrived with the rest of the party and they went on to the Laverton Hotel for the night to "a wonderful welcome from Mrs. Guthrie".

On 15th. August they came to a narrow winding sandy track, undulating country, met up with desert poplars and the old corkwood tree. They had lunch at Warburton Mission, full of anti notices to passers-by ... the natives collected round waggling boomerangs, Audrey fed them all with sweets. At Windburn Rocks in the Warburton Ranges they camped for the night: rather like Devil's Marbles, wild honeysuckle, wild fig growing in the crevices. Giles' name chipped out of rock, 1873, furthest west he got. John Forrest's name, 1874, on his way east. Remains of wild turkey natives had just plucked and cooked. The next day they travelled through the Cavenagh and Blackstone Ranges to join the Gun Barrel Highway near Giles' weather station, where they turned off on a bush track to camp on a "freezing cold night".

Continuing towards the Olgas on a "very rough track surrounded by impressive ranges", they came to Beadell's plaque and dug up his visitor's book, which we all signed ... On through wonderful country, mostly desert oaks and the lovely pink ranges all around, they came to the Docker River Mission: all the buildings were of aluminium (white ant proof). They look after the desert natives, Pintubis and Pitjantjatjara. Met the young school teacher and the ganger, who rounds up the children for school. At Hall River they walked up there a bit to the cave where Lasseter was for 53 days being fed by the natives, who then turned against him, his body was found 50 miles to the east. There is a white stone cairn to mark it ... We made camp at sundown about 50 miles from the Olgas.

That night it was "very cold and ice formed inside the tents". They revisited the Olgas and Ayers Rock on 18th. August, staying at a motel. En route to Alice Springs they "stopped to see the meteorite craters on Henbury Station". On arrival in town they found the "main street pulsating with progress" and "new buildings everywhere". After a night at the El Kira Lodge, their next stop was at Glen Helen, a lovely place in a gorge with water in it. Once an old homestead ... use it as a tourist lodge. The homestead has an unhappy history of various whites being murdered by hostile blacks. Further on they came to Ormiston Gorge, the commencement of the mighty Finke River ... Got there about 6 and the great walls of the Gorge were still glowing red with the sun and there was water and great white river gums, quite the best we had seen.

The party camped there for the night and "Had a sing-song and a chat ... Reg recited Banjo Patterson". Next morning Linda Had a walk before breakfast, never have I seen such marvellous coloured rocks, pinks, greys, reds, greens ... it was truly wondrous, great towering cliffs of brilliant orange, interesting trees and the beautiful ghost gums specially attractive here ... In the bed of the gorge huge tumbled up multicoloured rocks. They returned to Alice Springs that evening and on 23rd. August visited King's Canyon, where they saw rocky escarpments that went in great half-circle bastions. The growth was lush and varied, lots of yellow cassia in full bloom and a great variety of trees, desert mallee and all the other well-known ones and lots we didn't know. After camping for the night, they climbed next morning to the top of the canyon: Once on top we were in a world of wonder, miles and miles of the most marvellous rock formations, unlike anything I had seen, they were a series of domes in layers ... They call it 'the lost city'.

The group returned once more to Ayers Rock and the Olgas for a day's sightseeing and then retraced their steps to the Western Australian border. At Warburton Mission Linda "bought a good nulla nulla for $1" and saw the most dreadful collection of skinny mixed breed dogs I'd ever seen. That night they stopped to camp in the dark and got out to find a horrible wind blowing and great claps of thunder, then big drops of rain, it was most menacing. We hesitated about putting up the tents and sat in the bus to await developments. The storm subsided and they duly set up camp. On 29th. August, at Lake Throssell, we came upon 4 wild camels trotting along our road, looked like Mum and Dad and 2 children. They wouldn't get off the road to go into the prickly spinifex, and quite some time before we persuaded them to take to the bush.

At Cosmo Newberry Mission they climbed over some more rocky waterholes and had a huge view to far horizons of monotonous grey mulga.

Laverton consisted of just 2 wide streets and the solid old hotel, brave attempts at tree planting ... Laverton now has 75 whites and 350 blacks, but keeps ticking because of all the interest by companies looking for minerals. The hotel lady, Mrs. Larkin, said they had 21 staying there, all mineral people. On the road to Kookynie they had another breakdown, this time the suspension, and all felt thankful that we weren't out in the real never never. Kookynie itself was a ghost mining town and a real old outback pub ... Odd geologists and prospectors keep it going, I think ... once a population of 7000. On 30th. August they reached Coolgardie, where they saw a wonderful exhibition of the old mining days in the beautiful courthouse, and the diary ends that evening with their arrival at Southern Cross, east of Perth.

Linda and Reg's next recorded trip was a 10-day tour to Gove on the Gulf of Carpentaria in 1972. They left Perth on 14th July with a group of four others from the Employers' Federation and flew to Mount Newman, where they went for a drive round the housing and shopping, most impressed, only started in May 1969, now houses and lawns and trees. Lovely big swimming pool and a splendid club with all sporting things and a dance floor. The party flew on to Mount Tom Price and were driven to the mine: about 3500 people, a great sports club, a community centre where the Ballet comes yearly and was fully booked this year. At Wittenoom Gorge they went to a fascinating settlement owned by Lang Hancock, who has an exploration camp there. Hamersley and Western Mining also have exploration groups around the town. These groups and a certain amount of tourism keep the town just alive. It is so beautifully situated, but ever since the C.S.R. gave up the asbestos mine the houses have stood empty and forlorn and slowly decaying.

That evening they had dinner at the Wittenoom Hotel: A large party of Hale School boys occupied a large table. They were drinking wine and smoking cigars. I couldn't resist asking them why they were on holidays at this time. They said they were Geological, Geography and Biological students on a special study tour. On 15th. July the group flew to Goldsworthy: It is the earliest iron ore project, mostly American capital, smaller than Hamersley or Mt. Newman, but so much nearer Port Hedland ... Very impressed with the mining part, so beautifully done that it really was quite beautiful. The town part is much smaller, but lovely established trees and looking a veritable oasis. Lots of the lovely acacia trees and also a cork bark tree, very picturesque. At Shay Gap near Goldsworthy, In the new township air conditioning is to be piped to every house, so windows can't be opened. Also rain mist is to moisten the whole town between 1 and 3 a.m. and somehow or other a rain forest is to be created. Each home is so placed that it makes a tunnel of shade right along from house to house.

From there the party flew to Fitzroy Crossing and then drove to Geikie Gorge, declared a National Park and the road is much improved, 9000 tourists came last year and so they have 2 boat trips a day ... It was a shock to get to the Gorge and see it full of people, campers and ladies' and gents' lavatories etc. However the boat trip was lovely and the Gorge as fascinating as ever. They returned to the Fitzroy Crossing Hotel: open air bar full of natives and tough whites, lots of atmosphere, really the rugged north ... walk round the place, gazing over the great Fitzroy lined with its coolibah trees. Their next stop was at the Ord Dam, most impressive, blue water and rugged red rock, lots of roads but big nature predominated over the man-made additions.

Next they flew to Groote Eylandt in the Gulf of Carpentaria, where they were met by a company hostess and driven to the guest house, looking over turquoise water through multi-coloured bougainvilleas ... Gemco is the name of the company which mines manganese here ... attractive settlement, houses all built of steel, high school, club, swimming pool and all the usual amenities that are provided by the big mining companies.

The same day they flew on to Gove, a bauxite mine called Nabalco, mainly a Swiss firm ... most impressive, about 3000 people, large solid rather sombre grey buildings, but the Walkabout Motel is delightful, whitewashed brick and brown woodwork, Mexican style ... lovely room with balcony overlooking the garden and the sea. On 18th. July the party visited a Methodist Mission at the Goulburn Islands: vegetable and fruit growing, bananas, peanuts, tomatoes, melons etc. There are about 600 natives and about 4 European families ... Five natives joined us for lunch, they were the head elder and the council. All very handsome and dignified, no drink on the island and they have milk each day, so very healthy looking ... It was all a most interesting experience. The island gets no tourists and is quite unspoilt.

They flew back to Darwin, "huge now", and at Kununurra met the writer Mary Millar (Durack), here to gather information to write a sequel to 'Kings in Grass Castles', she is interviewing all the old aboriginals who worked for her father ... it all takes much time and she feels she has a big task ahead, but must do it as she has all her father's diaries and is the only one to do it. The group drove to a camp on the Mitchell Plateau, consisting of tents amongst a beautiful setting of different trees, almost like a small nursery ... The company is called Amax, an American company and they are drilling for bauxite ... They built a track down to the Gulf 25 miles away and now all their supplies come from Darwin by barge. They lunched there with the staff, all either interested in botany, birds or native painting. Anyway it was all a very special experience, all these interesting young men living happily together in one of the most remote and inaccessible spots in all Australia.

Linda found that their next stop, Broome, looked exactly the same, and Roebourne, where they spent the night of 20th. July, was also "unchanged". After that came Pannewonicka, mainly American and is the new venture in the Pilbara, mainly low grade ore, which is pelletized before being shipped away. At Dampier they drove all round the great mechanical wonders ... thought it the best of all. The final stop was at Exmouth Gulf, where they saw Norcape Lodge, funny old rambling place, once just a fisherman's camp. The diary ends here and they presumably flew to Perth on 23rd. July. Linda was now 69 and had had a colostomy, necessitated by cancer. She was to record only one more trip.

21. FROM WEST TO EAST AUSTRALIA

Linda and Reg's last recorded tour together in 1974 took them right across Australia from west to east; again they put their car on the train to Port Augusta, where they collected it on 4th. July. They visited their earlier tour guide Jeff and his wife Fran at Hawker, where they were running a motel with "endless worries and troubles". From there they drove to Broken Hill, Reg's birthplace, where they visited the painter Pro Hart's gallery: he has the biggest private art collection in Australia ... had a drink at the old pub, where a famous character called Jobson has painted murals of life in the mines etc. Went out to Silverton, inspected the old gaol which now has a good little museum, dear old duck running it who was steeped in the history of the old days. I liked best old pictures of Charles Roop, who pegged the first claim, pictures of his mansion in Adelaide, his wife bedecked in furs and jewels.

On 8th. July they arrived at Bourke, where the country looked good, mulga, coolibah etc. Lots of birds in water lying around. Found Bourke interesting, fine old buildings amidst much ugliness, but historical atmosphere. They drove on to Cunnamulla, where they asked for directions to their friend Pat Tully's Texham Station. En route they had an interesting drive, the country is lovely and the old mulga trees look so healthy and handsome after all the great rains, 53 inches instead of 11. At Eulo, When we stopped for a drink we were joined by a nice old character and had a good chat. He came from Budapest years ago, went off looking for gold, found opals and eventually learnt to cut them and that was his job now, had done well and was building a small hotel.

They called at the hotel at Toompine: They had been marooned by the floods for 8 weeks ... Whilst there 3 men and lots of big dogs came in, 1 Austrian, 1 Jugoslav and the other I don't know. They were opal mining about 25 miles out and brought in some extremely good specimens, very large, in hunks of ironstone. At Quilpie they joined a bitumen road to Windorah: It is the new beef road to bring the cattle in from as far west as Birdsville, 278 miles further than Windorah ... missed the Texham turn-off owing to long grass on side of the road and the notice had fallen down. In spite of this we arrived at the homestead at 6 p.m., they were getting concerned and this is what we had hoped to avoid. We were greeted by Genevieve and Pat and handsome son Brian and daughter Anne-Marie.

Linda and Reg stayed the night and learnt that Genevieve and Pat have no help at all, labour too hard to get and too expensive ... it is a large house surrounded by lovely trees, once a lovely garden with orange and other fruit trees, however the recent floods had ruined the garden, it came right up to the house and they were marooned for 6 weeks and fortunately had an old army amphibian duck to go and get things. The house is right on Kyabra Creek, which flows into the Cooper, it is part of the channel country. The creek is wide and beautiful, lovely trees and abundant bird life, ibis, white herons, moorhen and many pelicans. Pat took them to visit friends at Mayfield with a wonderful collection of native artifacts, real museum stuff, they had collected them over many years from the Cooper. They also saw the old Galway Downs homestead, "the original house of Michael and Jenny Durack, Michael was Mary's father".

On 11th. July they went with Pat to visit Thylungra Station, the original site of old Patsy Durack's home ... now owned by a big English company, Australian Estates, chairman Sir Dennis Larson, ex-Lord Mayor of London and very rich. It is a show place. He also showed them Ray Station, his brother's property: original old Durack track ... to see the old family graves, very impressive, tall white columns, Sarah Durack and Pat Tully are buried there, they are Pat's grandparents ... they say they can't get away for a holiday. I called them 'Captives in Grass Castles' instead of 'Kings in Grass Castles'. No doubt although they still make money life is a battle and less and less people are wanting to take it on.

Next day Linda and Reg said goodbye to the Tullys and drove via Quilpie to Charleville, a good, flourishing town on the Warrego River, which flows into the Darling, and stayed a night there at the Victoria Motel. On 13th. July they reached Mitchell, called after Major Mitchell, explorer who passed through there about 1840 ... it is called the Hereford capital, abattoirs and a splendid racecourse and remains of old winery, but best of all the lovely old Baobab trees lining the streets. Their next stop was at Carnarvon National Park, where they stayed two nights: consists of log cabins with bunks, central ablution block and dining room. They walked to Mickey's Gorge: Great white cliffs towered up on either side and the bush was marvellous, tall cabbage palms and ancient macrozamia palms, white spotted gums and tree ferns. On their second day they visited Art Gallery Cave, with famous native paintings ... mostly hands, boomerangs, fish nets and phallic symbols.

Reaching Fairbairn Dam on 16th. July, they Dined at a most posh restaurant in the Emerald Star Hotel, unexpectedly sophisticated, beautiful and beautifully served, dining room crowded with interesting characters, mostly big he-men. Next day they were at Rubyvale, interesting township ... Popped over to a mine and talked to an old chap standing under a shady tree directing the water sluicing through the stuff, sand etc. goes off and the sapphires are left on the tray. He didn't think there would be much. Clermont was an old-fashioned town of typical old wooden Queensland houses and funny old pubs, Blair Athol coal mine, steaming coal for Japan, enough for 20 years more. They spent the night at Mackay, in "the land of sugar cane, tropical palms, mangoes etc."

After that Linda and Reg went on via Bowen to Townsville, where they stayed with friends and played golf. They visited a sanctuary in a great swamp, saw hundreds of brolgas, egrets, cranes and birds of all sorts, lovely coloured rainbow birds and several white cockatoos. The diary entries for the next four days record their doings at a medical conference they attended at James Cook University, mostly golf, sightseeing and dinners. On 27th.

July they took a ferry trip to Magnetic Island and saw the marine gardens, beautifully done with all the live fish and coral in sea water tanks. Coral and fish of every conceivable colour and formation. Two days later they flew to Dunk Island in the Whitsunday Passage: attractive, comfortable bungalows well concealed amongst the palms ... the boat people who organize the tour have taken over 7000 'Crown of Thorns' starfish off the reef and the coral is all growing again.

They returned to Townsville on 1st. August and spent three more days with friends sightseeing in the area. They admired the old Pacific Hotel at Eimeo and returned there for a night to ask our host and hostess in for a drink - Beatty, both old Queensland identities and told us much of the early history of the area. The old hotel was taken over by the Americans during the war. Linda and Reg stopped at Rockhampton and drove for a 70 mile round trip along the coast to Yeppoon and several other beaches. The Japanese are wanting to spend millions of dollars to make an up-to-date tourist resort, still being considered ... Lovely monument to Captain Cook called 'The Singing Ship' in concrete and steel, the steel pipes sang as the breeze from the sea blew over the great Fitzroy River and the fine city of Rockhampton. We were here years ago, when we took a trip to Heron Island.

On 7th. August they visited Mount Morgan: the whole view was of the great mine, it is, we are told, largest open cut in the world ... had a drink in the dear old 1889 Queensland wood and tar pub, with the most marvellous view of all the mine workings. At Bundaberg they saw the biggest bulk loading sugar set-up I could ever imagine, very busy with sugar trucks. We went on top of a hill called Mt. Hammock, not very high but the only height all round, remains of old volcano and hence the rich soil which produces so much sugar. On the road again they discovered a little place called Bargara: most attractive seaside resort ... we thought it a good place to retire to. That evening they arrived at Buderim, where they booked in for three nights at a hotel called Dormie House, "right on the links". Here they played golf with "kangaroos about the bushland course" and visited friends, the Campbells, at nearby Maroochydore.

After a round of golf on 10th. August, Linda and Reg lunched in our room and fed the birds, a great collection, 2 beautiful parrots sat up in the tree, whilst butchers, maggie and kookaburra and 2 bower birds with yellow eyes and beaks gathered about us. The butchers even came into the room for breakfast crumbs. Next day they went to Caloundra: as well as lovely coast you could see over to the best view of the strange old Glasshouse Mountains I had yet seen. They drove to Brisbane on 12th. August and stayed at the Albert Park Motel. There they visited friends, the Walkers and Lotzes, and the university, on a magnificent site and the main bldgs. made of a beautiful local sandstone. They dined the next evening at Government House with Sir Colin and Lady Hannah, whose private secretary, David Robertson, had been married to Haden Lemann's elder sister.

They walked round the city on 15th. August admiring old buildings: the one we liked best was the McDonald Hamilton bldg. right on the wharf, they call it Indian colonial style which describes it well. On the tower are marked the levels of the 3 great floods, 1890, 1893, 1974, 1893 was quite the highest. Next day they again toured the town and went into the old National Hotel, gets a mention in our book, 'Pubs of Australia'. The famous barman Warren who has black lacquered fingernails, mascara and heavy make-up wasn't there, comes in at 5 in the main bar. Toowoomba was their next stop and they found it a beautiful city, well-named 'Garden City', lovely trees, parks, houses and old gardens, many built round the ridge of the tableland overlooking to Brisbane, Mt. Glorious, Cunningham's Gap etc.

Linda and Reg were now heading south along the New England Highway in fine spring weather. At Girraween National Park they passed a lovely patch where tall wattles livened up the countryside with their glorious golden beauty and near Glen Innes they detoured to visit their friends the

Wollens: lovely drive, we got deeper and deeper into the mountains, their house was on a hilltop with hills all round and gazing into a mysterious collection of wild blue mountains. Travelling from Singleton to Richmond on 21st. August the country was very mountainous, lovely valleys following beautiful streams, Darkey Creek was one and the Colo another. Fertile valleys, narrow gorges, winding mountain roads, most lovely.

After a "drive round historic old Richmond" they continued on to Bowral to visit their daughters' in-laws, the Lemanns and the Williams, then both living there. They stayed at the Golf View Motel, where they had both families to dinner, "very happy and successful". This last diary ends on 23rd. August with the entry: **Got to Burnetts at 2.30, Jen, Pat, Ben and Mark all there to meet us.** After this visit Linda and Reg returned once more to Perth, where she died four years later of cancer at the age of 76. Photographs record that they made other short trips during this period, but diaries were either not kept or not preserved. It seems fitting to close her story with a short extract from my own memoirs: **Linny had been a wonderful mother-in-law and friend to me. Her end was peaceful and remarkable, as she nominated the day of her going and talked happily with her family to the end. The next day Reg, Jenny and Sonia held a wake, a memorable affair attended by her many friends. The tributes to her from all over the world soon began to pour in.**